SHOPPING, SE
& MR SELFRIDGE

LINDY WOODHEAD worked in journalism, film and fashion publicity
(the latter for Browns of South Molton Street) before establishing
her own public relations agency – WPR – in 1974. Joined by her
husband Colin as business partner in 1976, they have been pioneering
exponents of specialist development of building prestige brand reputation for many years. WPR's international fashion, fine jewellery and
retail clients have included Ferragamo, Cerruti 1881, Wolford, Karl
Lagerfeld, Louis Vuitton, Krizia, Rossetti, Yves St Laurent, Brioni,
Hermes and Garrard & Co. In the late 1980s, Lindy also took up an
external appointment as the first woman on the board of directors at
Harvey Nichols.

In 2000, aged 50, Lindy retired to develop her writing career. Her
first book, *War Paint*, was published in 2003 and is the subject of an
internationally networked American television documentary.

Currently working on her next book, she also writes consumer-
related and lifestyle features for various publications. Lindy and her
husband have two sons and divide their time between south-west
London and south-west France.

ALSO BY LINDY WOODHEAD
War Paint: Helena Rubinstein and Elizabeth Arden –
Their Lives, Their Times, Their Rivalry

SHOPPING, SEDUCTION & MR SELFRIDGE

LINDY WOODHEAD

P

PROFILE BOOKS

This revised edition published in Great Britain in 2012 by
Profile Books Ltd
3a Exmouth House
Pine Street
Exmouth Market
London EC1R 0JH
www.profilebooks.com

Copyright © Lindy Woodhead, 2007, 2008, 2012

1 3 5 7 9 10 8 6 4 2

Typeset in Goudy Old Style by MacGuru Ltd
info@macguru.org.uk

Printed and bound in Great Britain by
CPI Group (UK) Ltd, Croydon CR0 4YY

A CIP catalogue record for this book is available from the British Library.

ISBN 978 1 78125 058 7
eISBN 978 1 84765 964 4

For Colin, Ollie and Max

Praise for *Shopping, Seduction and Mr Selfridge*

'Gripping and excellently researched' *Literary Review*

'More of a social history than a biography, the book is brilliantly researched and the author draws the reader into the fascinating world of the early-twentieth century with skill. The life of Harry Selfridge is described with humour, sensitivity and sympathy ... a hugely enjoyable read. I found myself enthralled with the world of Harry Selfridge, nearly falling in love with him myself.' *Sunday Independent*, Ireland

'In this lively and compelling biography, Lindy Woodhead follows the glory years of a charismatic big spender, whose ill-advised expansion would eventually be his downfall. Her pacy narrative takes in his glamorous women, his social set, the sexing up of shopping, and seismic shifts in society.' *Director*

'This dissection of the allure, power and modern-day presence of department stores, via the history of the man behind Selfridges, is a witty and erudite look at the UK's shopping evolution.' *Easy Living*

'A fascinating look at the life of a man who started a retail revolution' *Birmingham Mail*

'Not only a biography of the man who invented the glamour of the department store and was probably responsible for our national shopping addiction, but also a fascinating look at the cultural and social background of the early-twentieth century.' *Evening Standard*

'Lindy Woodhead shows in this lively and entertaining account it was Selfridge's love of theatre that informed both his personal and his professional life ... (she) adds enormously to this fascinating history by the breadth of her research and by her thorough knowledge of the retail context.' *Sunday Telegraph*

'The story of Harry Gordon Selfridge (or HGS as he drew with his fingers if he found dust on a store showcase) is the tale of a remarkable individual ... Lindy Woodhead relates this morality tale with vigour and glorious enthusiasm. She brings to vivid life the cracking open of the social carapace of aristocracy and the frenetic hedonism of the Jazz Age. The social revolution in retailing is described with passion and verve. And even the background of Chicago under construction has an energy that sends the book racing along – she rounds out the character of "Mr Selfridge" by calling him a "jigsaw puzzle" with an essential gambler's soul.' Suzy Menkes, *International Herald Tribune*

'Lindy Woodhead returns to the glittering Edwardian era and the roaring Twenties with a biography of one of the pioneers of modern retailing. The book is brilliantly researched and the author draws the reader into the fascinating world of the early 20th century with great skill. The life of Harry Selfridge is described with humour, sensitivity and sympathy.' Susanne O'Leary, *Irish Sunday Independent*

Woman was what the shops were fighting over when they competed, it was woman whom they ensnared with the constant trap of their bargains, after stunning her with their displays. They had aroused new desires in her flesh, they were a huge temptation to which she must fatally succumb, first of all by giving in to the purchases of a good housewife, then seduced by vanity and finally consumed.

Emile Zola, *Au Bonheur des Dames* (1881)

When I die I want it said of me, 'He dignified and ennobled commerce.'

Harry Gordon Selfridge (1856–1947)

CONTENTS

ILLUSTRATIONS

INTRODUCTION

~

CONSUMING PASSIONS

The rise of the department store – or what in Paris were more gracefully called *les grands magasins* – in the second half of the nineteenth century was a phenomenon that encompassed fashion, advertising, entertainment, emergent new technology, architecture and, above all, seduction. These forces evolved to merge into businesses that Emile Zola astutely called 'the great cathedrals of shopping', and vast fortunes were made by the men who owned them as they tapped into the female passion for shopping. But arguably no one man grasped the concept of consumption as sensual entertainment better than the maverick American retailer, Harry Gordon Selfridge, who opened his eponymous store on London's Oxford Street in 1909.

In building the West End's first fully fledged department store, he quite literally changed everything about the way Londoners shopped. His visionary, larger-than-life Edwardian building perfectly reflected the character of its founder – the only modest thing about him being his height. It was Harry Gordon Selfridge who positioned the perfume and cosmetics department immediately inside the main entrance, a move that changed the layout – and turnover – of the sales floor for ever more. Selfridge created window-dressing as an art form, pioneered in-store promotions and fashion shows, and offered customer service and facilities previously unheard of in Britain. Above all, he gave his customers fun. At a time when there was no radio or television, when cinema was in its infancy, Selfridge's in Oxford Street offered customers entertainment as fascinating as that at a science museum, with as much glamour as on any music-hall stage. In giving his customers a unique 'day out', Harry Selfridge proudly boasted that after Westminster Abbey and the Tower of London, his store was 'the third biggest tourist attraction in town'. The public could buy much of what they needed at Selfridge's, and much that they never knew they wanted until they were seduced by the tantalizing displays.

Harry Selfridge perfected the art of publicity, spending more money on advertising than any retailer of his era. A consummate showman, he himself became a celebrity at a time when there were few identifiable, exciting personalities that the public could see at close quarters. When he arrived at work, there was invariably a cluster of customers waiting to meet and greet the 'famous Mr Selfridge'. His ritualistic 'morning tour' of the store, where his staff of thousands lined up anxiously by their counters in eager anticipation of a personal nod of approval from their boss, was the curtain-raiser to the daily show at Selfridge's – the only difference being that for his audience, entrance was free.

There was no shortage of shops or stores in London and many other wealthy provincial cities in Britain when – after twenty-five years working at the celebrated store Marshall Field & Co. in Chicago – Selfridge masterminded his grand plan to open in the imperial capital. The industrial transformation that had occurred in Britain had created a new spending population who were proud to show off their wealth by acquiring consumer goods, and retailers scrambled to cope with an almost insatiable demand. The new rich had large houses to equip, a prodigious number of children – not to mention an army of servants – to dress, and their own position in society to promote. Happily for retailers, conspicuous consumption, always so crucial in defining wealth and status, had found itself a much larger market.

That fashion became big business was because of big dresses. In the 1850s, when both the young Queen Victoria and the French style icon, the Empress Eugénie, both enthusiastically embraced the new caged crinoline, clothes billowed to unprecedented proportions. Women of substance were dressed from head to toe in as much as forty yards of fabric. As well as a muslin shift and cotton or silk underwear – not to mention the ubiquitous corset – the ensemble had hoops underneath, and at least three if not four petticoats, in layers varying from flannel through muslin to white, starched cotton. Add to this a lace fichu, bead-trimmed cape, fur or embroidered muff, hat, gloves, parasol, stockings, button boots and reticule – and consider that the entire paraphernalia was usually changed once a day and often again in the evening – and one can begin to comprehend the costs, not to mention profits, in supplying it all. As if this bonanza wasn't enough for retailers who stocked all of the above and ran vast workrooms making the finished gowns, there was the ritual of mourning the dead. This meant the whole thing all over again – but this time in black. Many a Victorian linen-draper's fortune was made merely by operating a successful 'mourning department', and one of the first diversifications into 'added-value customer services' was to offer funeral facilities – right down to supplying dyed black ostrich feathers for the horses that pulled the hearse.

As dress-reformers railed against 'the tyranny of women's fashion', the redoubtable feminist Elizabeth Cady Stanton used dress as a topic of debate: 'Men say we are frail. But I'd like to see a man who can bear what we do, laced up in steel-ribbed corsets, with hoops, heavy skirts, trains, panniers, chignons and dozens of hairpins sticking in our scalps – cooped up in the house year after year. How would men like that?'

The answer is that the men – or at least those who owned stores and factories – liked it very much. Fortunes were made in the textile trade – in cotton, wool, linen and silk, growing it, weaving it, dyeing it, and selling it. Associated businesses making all manner of goods from dye, needles and pins, ribbons and sewing thread to bleach and starch boomed. And as distribution systems improved, merchandise could be moved further and further from its point of production to its point of sale, meaning stores could offer a wider selection of goods than ever before.

The nineteenth-century passion for fashion wasn't the only factor in the rise of the great department stores. Just as the growth of credit had led to an explosion of shops in the seventeenth century, so the ability to buy in bulk – also on credit – benefited the new breed of retailers. The prosperous middle classes may have wanted quality, but above all, their Victorian ethics demanded value for money. Economies of buying in bulk enabled larger retailers to reduce their prices far below those of smaller, specialist shops. These independent shopkeepers – who had for decades catered to the upper echelons of society – were restricted by their credit systems. The richer the customer, the longer he or she took to pay. It wasn't unusual for accounts to be settled annually, and many speciality shops went bankrupt as a result. The emergent stores, however, were mainly cash businesses, with perhaps a monthly charge account offered to more select personal customers. Such stores developed awesome buying power – particularly as many of them operated a wholesale division servicing sales outposts in the Empire or throughout rural America – and they didn't hesitate to use it as a weapon against their suppliers, who were obliged not just to provide goods against a ninety-day payment policy, but often also to store merchandise for phased delivery.

The great stores acted as a catalyst for change in women's lives. For the first time women were able to 'cross the line', venturing out in public to buy goods for themselves, to experience shopping and be observed doing it without in any way jeopardizing their reputations. Not all stores were the size of cathedrals, but certainly fashionable women in London, Manchester and Newcastle, and further afield in Paris, New York, Philadelphia and Chicago, were spending a lot more time shopping than going to church. Small wonder when the stores were light, bright, warm and enticing. Neither did these stores cater exclusively for the carriage trade. The department store was the anchor in a rapidly expanding egalitarian, urban society, drawing its customer base from a mix of old and new money, and able to offer not just fixed prices but also sale bargains. For many people these stores were infinitely more glamorous and comfortable than their own homes. In 1880s Chicago, Harry Selfridge had pioneered the policy of browsing, making Marshall Field's an ideal location for those who were 'just looking', and opened a 'Bargain Basement' for those on a budget. He had also introduced a restaurant, a reading-room, a crèche and a ladies' rest-room complete with nurse, and so could justifiably claim to have helped emancipate women: 'I came along just at the time when women wanted to step out on their own. They came to the store and realized some of their dreams.'

He made his own dreams come true in turn-of-the-century London where, at the time he arrived, compared to the giant American department stores and *grands magasins* of Paris, many of London's 'stores' were just rather large shops. In the days before lifts and escalators, and in part due to onerous building restrictions, retail space was restricted to the ground, first and possibly second floors, with stock rooms below and workrooms above. Stores like Swan & Edgar, Dickens & Jones and Debenham & Freebody had in-house catering for their staff who ate breakfast, lunch and dinner on site. More often than not, staff lived in a store-tied hostel or in a grim and cold dormitory tucked away on the upper floor. Young people who had eschewed residential domestic service for jobs in retailing soon realized they had merely swapped the servants' hall for the staff canteen. Working hours were gruelling. When West End shopkeepers gave evidence before the Parliamentary Select Committee on Shop Hours in 1886, it transpired that average working hours were from 8.15 a.m. to 7.30 p.m. six days a week, with half an hour off for lunch and fifteen minutes for tea. If romance flourished on the shop floor, it was because workers had little time or opportunity to meet elsewhere.

Most leading drapery stores had, for the main part, evolved from a background in haberdashery, often expanding their floor space by buying sites to the left and right, knocking them through into a rabbit-warren of levels rather than rebuilding from scratch. From the main street entrance, customers entered a showroom space literally stuffed full with everything from garter elastic and dress pins to embroidery silks and bootlaces. The amount of time spent by a sales assistant in selling a shilling's worth of such goods – haberdashery being the training ground for all apprentices – was totally disproportionate to the return. The mindset of the day, however, was that ladies who bought their buttons would move further on in – or up to the first floor – to buy silks, satins, laces and lingerie.

Selfridge himself had already seen London's retailers and those of Manchester, Berlin, Vienna and Paris when he first toured Europe in 1888. Though admiring the William Morris fabrics in Liberty's and impressed by Whiteley's in Bayswater, in general he found the rest of the city's shops and stores disappointing. He particularly disliked floorwalkers. 'Is Sir intending to buy something?' asked one super-cilious man. 'No, I'm just looking,' replied Selfridge, at which the floorwalker dropped his pseudo-smart voice and snarled, 'Then 'op it mate!' Selfridge never forgot the incident and refused to hire 'walkers' when he opened in Oxford Street two decades later. Instead he employed knowledgeable, well-informed sales assistants who loved where they worked and who idolized their boss, whom they called 'the Chief'.

The time Selfridge spent time studying Au Bon Marché in Paris was crucial to his development as a retailing revolutionary. When he first saw the store in 1888, the final phase of rebuilding and expansion, orchestrated by the architect Louis-Charles Boileau and the brilliant engineer Gustave Eiffel, had been completed. What had started as a minor *magasin de nouveauté* opened by the Videau brothers on the fashionable rue de Bac in 1825, had grown to a massive enterprise under the direction of their ex-employee Aristide Boucicaut. Au Bon Marché was a masterpiece, and it set the standard for fine shopping throughout Europe. Monsieur Boucicaut was a great innovator, imposing fixed pricing, annual sales, an 'exchange' or 'money back' guarantee and *entre libre* (no obligation to buy) as well as running the first French retailing establishment to sell a huge variety of merchandise ranging from homewares, toys and perfume to sports equipment and children's clothes. Indeed, the bourgeois, taciturn Aristide Boucicaut, ably assisted by his thrifty wife Marguerite, took the Paris emporium to such majestic heights that it became the inspiration for Emile Zola's seminal novel *Au Bonheur des Dames*, a book so popular with business historians that it has tended to give the impression that innovation in retailing was the exclusive preserve of the French.

Across the Atlantic, however, another retailing pioneer was making his mark in establishing one of the world's first true department stores. In New York, an Irish immigrant called Alexander Turney Stewart established a sumptuous store so famous it had no name over the door but was simply known as 'The Marble Palace'. Among Stewart's many master-strokes in seducing shoppers was his decision to hire only the best-looking and most charming male sales assistants. He also introduced the first in-store fashion shows and live music, fitted the first plate-glass windows in America, and imported the country's first full-length mirrors, having spotted them first at Au Bon Marché. By the time the American Civil War ended in 1865, he had taken luxury shopping in New York to such heights that simply going to Stewart's was described by the press as 'being notoriously fatal to the female nerves'. *Harper's* considered this growing shopping mania 'a disease peculiar to women', even claiming it to be 'a species of insanity'. In the case of the assassinated President Lincoln's wife Mary, they were right. Poor Mary never got over the shock of her husband's death. Her already extravagant shopping habits became so bad that she ran up a bill of $48,000 (nearly a million dollars today) at Alexander Stewart's whereupon her family had her declared insane, insisting they weren't responsible for her debts.

Whatever the dangers of shopping, both Stewart and Boucicaut were men with an innate understanding of the powers of salesmanship, marketing, service and quality. It was their legacy, along with the enduring influence of Marshall Field, that inspired Harry Gordon Selfridge.

London's established retailers, although anxious to cultivate women customers, had some serious anomalies. Whiteley's was one of the rare retailers offering any sort of in-store catering, having opened a 'refreshment room' in 1872. However, when Mr Whiteley applied for a liquor licence – thinking that ladies who lunched might enjoy a glass of wine – Paddington's magistrates rejected his application in the 'interests of morality', saying that 'ladies, or females dressed to represent them, might make licensed premises a place of assignation'.

Even drinking tea or lemonade, however, necessitated a ladies' room, but there was no such provision for London's lady shoppers. Nor could respectable Victorian women be seen using one of the rare public conveniences. The only solution was to visit a hotel for afternoon tea.

Steeped in tradition, the city's retailers were alarmed by the idea of change. It was, however, long overdue. When Andrew Carnegie, the Scottish-American philanthropist millionaire, visited London in 1900 he was appalled. 'Just look at the jumble in the store windows – so much stuff you cannot take it in,' he said. 'When you go into a shop they treat you most indifferently. You are scowled at if you ask for goods out of the ordinary, and you are made to feel uncomfortable if you do not buy. These shop people drive away more customers than they attract. What London needs is a good shaking up.'

Nothing excited Harry Gordon Selfridge more than the idea of 'shaking up London', and the spirit of the age was on his side. The concept of selling to 'all classes of trade' was totally alien to existing British retailers. Stores were up-market or they were middle-market – and occasionally they catered to the better end of the lower market – but they never, ever did all three. Selfridge would change all that, just as he changed the traditional merchandise mix. When the trade press reported that he was going to sell everything from photographic equipment to glass and gloves, his drapery competitors derided such diversification, Marshall & Snelgrove stiffly announcing that 'We know what we are and mean to stick to it.'

Thanks to his commercial success, Selfridge enjoyed the lavish lifestyle of an impresario, having a penchant for large houses, fast women and regrettably slow horses. His greatest addiction other than work was gambling, which in one form or another dominated his life, from the risk he took in sinking all his money into a site arguably at 'the wrong end' of Oxford Street, to the hours he spent in casinos where he and one of his famous mistresses, the baccarat-addicted Jenny Dolly, won – and lost – hundreds of thousands of pounds. No one knows exactly how much Selfridge squandered over the three decades he lived in London, but it's reliably estimated at well over £3 million, or nearly £65 million today. The money vanished in a haze of extravagance, frittered away on jewels and furs for his mistresses, a fully crewed yacht that slept twenty, the maintenance of his three daughters' well-born but largely unemployed husbands and on his insatiable thirst for gambling.

None of these pastimes mattered when Selfridge and his store were making money. Indeed, his glamorous reputation added to the attraction of shopping there. Yet for a businessman involved in dealing with millions of pounds, Selfridge was curiously naïve, and his complex personal and social life and tumultuous business expansion ultimately brought about his downfall. In the late 1920s, advice from one of London's most flawed financiers trigged acquisitions of staggering proportions. Company revenues were drained and Selfridge was woefully unprepared when the Great Depression took hold. By the late 1930s, his personal lifestyle had left him deeply in debt to the store – and to the taxman.

In 1939, at the age of 83, thirty years after building Selfridge's, revolutionizing London's retailing and arguably creating what for years to come would be known as the greatest shopping street in the world, Harry Selfridge was ousted from what he had always thought of as 'his' store. The most celebrated retailer of his era, who had lived like a lord in Lansdowne House, was reduced to penury, dying in a small flat in Putney.

His legacy isn't just his gloriously iconic building in Oxford Street

– although the towering columns of Selfridges are an awesome monument for any man – it is that he modernized British retailing, bringing to it his belief in 'the power of experience'. A man light years ahead of his time, a true accelerator of change, he deserves to be remembered as the man who put fun on to the shop floor and sex appeal into shopping.

1

~

THE FORTUNES OF WAR

'Fashion is the mirror of history. It reflects political,
social and economic changes, rather than mere whimsy.'
Louis XIV

In 1860, as America braced itself for civil war, businessmen began to stockpile goods. No one knew better than the store owners what would happen when fabric became scarce. It wasn't silks and satins that worried them, it was cotton – and they fretted more about the lack of it than the picking of it. In April 1861, when war was declared and President Lincoln issued his Proclamation of Blockade, speculation in cotton became rife, and panicking Northern mill owners were only too glad to forge associations with men who promised to continue the smooth flow of supplies from South to North.

When Union forces captured New Orleans in 1862, trade through the Mississippi Valley became particularly brisk. Cotton was also moved out via Memphis and Vicksburg, all of which kept the mills working – so much so that during the first two years of the war manufacturers still made a healthy profit. By 1863, however, supplies were dwindling and there was a shortage of men to run the machines. American spinning mills went on half-time production. As cotton goods became increasingly scarce, those who had filled a warehouse or two could name their price.

In New York, President Lincoln's friend Alexander Stewart, the acknowledged 'merchant prince' of the day, made enormous sums of money, having astutely cornered the market in domestic linen as well as cotton. Given that Mary Lincoln, a woman who clearly sought security through her possessions and for whom shopping was an addiction, spent thousands of dollars at Stewart's Marble Palace – on one memorable visit she ordered eighty-four pairs of coloured kid gloves – it is not surprising that Mr Stewart was also rewarded with lucrative contracts to supply clothing to the Union army. Indeed, the war seemed to have no effect on the shopping habits of New York's rich. The media criticized their 'hedonistic approach during the daily slaughter wrought by the war', but the pursuit of fashion carried on regardless.

Chicago too enjoyed a profitable war. The small town that had emerged out of the swampy Fort Dearborn just three decades earlier – and where some could still remember Chief Black Hawk and his warriors swooping in to attack – was now the hub of America's biggest railroad network and the collecting point for food to supply both the East and the army. Awash with opportunity and swimming in cash, sprawling, still muddy, 'rough and ready' Chicago became a boom town. As the farm boys joined the army, production of Cyrus McCormick's reaping machines increased – as did his fortune. He wasn't alone. Whether it was pork, which Philip Armour bought at $18 a barrel and sold for $40, or luxury Pullman Cars developed by the railwayman George Pullman, Chicago tycoons were making millions of dollars – and their wives were helping them spend it.

The destination of choice for Chicago's shoppers was Potter Palmer's store on Lake Street. Palmer, who went on to become a property developer of immense skill, had started his career in Chicago in 1839 as a small-time dry-goods retailer. There was nothing small about his ambitions, however, nor his ability to judge women's desire to shop. He sold goods at fixed and fair prices, let his ladies take clothes home to try on, and left copies of *Godey's Ladies Book* (the fashion magazine of the time) in the store for browsing. Better yet, he read it himself. His maxim was 'You've got to think big', and by the time war came, he had done so, stocking up on cotton goods, filling vast warehouses with everything from petticoats and pantalettes to sheets and tea towels, and advertising his stock with a 'money-back guarantee' – a revolutionary idea at the time.

Among the men who enlisted all over the North in 1861 was Robert Oliver Selfridge. At the age of 38 he left his home in Ripon, a hamlet in Wisconsin 170 miles north of Chicago, where he ran a general store, to go to war. Reputed to be a sober, hard-working man and described as 'a stalwart of local activity', he was also Master of the Ripon Freemasons' Lodge. Robert Selfridge and his wife Lois had three young sons – Charles Johnston, Robert Oliver Jr and Henry Gordon (known as Harry). Though there has always been uncertainty in the Selfridge family over precise dates of birth, it seems likely that Harry was born on 11 January 1856. He was just 5 when his father went to war – and never returned.

Not that Major Selfridge died in battle. He was honourably discharged in 1865, whereupon he simply vanished. No one ever knew why. Perhaps, having witnessed the carnage, he had a nervous breakdown. Perhaps he simply wanted to be free of responsibilities. Whatever the case, he left his wife to bring up her family on her own, on the meagre earnings of a teacher. Harry later described Lois as 'brave, upstanding and with indomitable courage'. She was indeed brave, and she needed to be. Not long after the war her eldest son Charles died, and then her middle son Robert. She was now left alone with young Harry.

Moving with her son to Jackson, Michigan, Lois found work as a primary school teacher, earning around $30 a month. Making ends meet was a constant struggle, so she supplemented her salary by painting Valentine and other novelty cards. Still with no word from her husband, she was left to assume that he was 'missing, presumed dead'. Only years later did she learn that he had been killed in a railway accident in Minnesota in 1873 and that she was – finally – a widow. Harry was shielded from the truth, growing up believing that his father had been 'killed in battle', a story he would often repeat to the media. It would be years before he discovered the truth.

Hardly surprisingly, all the love Lois had left to give was centred on her young son. The two of them found genuine pleasure in each other's company and became such great friends that they continued to live together until the day she died. When things got bleak, they played a game called 'Suppose', which involved imaginary plots about success through endeavour. 'Suppose' they could afford a cottage with a bay window? Even 'suppose' they were able to live in a castle with lots of servants? Though a pious woman who attended church regularly and abhorred alcohol, Lois was always happy to go to a new play or concert and was an avid reader, a pleasure she imbued in her son.

Mrs Selfridge continued her career as a teacher, becoming the headmistress of Jackson High School, where the education of the town's young was entrusted to her capable care. The most important thing she taught Harry was never to fear failure. She was fond of saying, 'Why should you worry about failing? There's always something else to try and you can excel in that instead.' She taught Harry to be gracious. She taught him impeccable manners. Finally, she taught him the importance of appearance. She would check his fingernails in the morning and again before supper – not that he needed much checking. From an early age Harry was fastidious, and he loved nothing better than wearing a clean shirt to school and polishing his boots until they gleamed.

When Harry wasn't dreaming about castles or maintaining his modest wardrobe, he had his head in a book, devouring stories by James Fenimore Cooper and Nathaniel Hawthorne, along with his favourite, *Struggles and Triumphs*, the well-thumbed autobiography of the great circus showman Phineas T. Barnum. The rags-to-riches story of Barnum inspired Harry to dream of a future far away from Jackson. In many respects the two were very similar. Barnum had a rare gift for publicity. His spectacular museum in New York drew the public in their thousands and he became rich by entertaining them. Like Barnum, Selfridge had the ability to suspend disbelief. His tricks – entertaining people in a great store that was, in a way, just like a circus tent – created such confidence among his friends, family and financial backers that for years they refused to accept that his extravagant, destructive side was gradually eroding his ability to run his business empire.

All that lay ahead. At the age of 10, Harry started to earn cash in the time-honoured way, by delivering newspapers. Next he took over a bread round, and finally he took a holiday job at Leonard Field's dry-goods store where he stocked shelves and carried parcels for $1.50 a week – cash he promptly handed over to his mother. When he was 13, he and a school friend, Peter Loomis, produced a boy's monthly magazine called *Will o' the Wisp*. Harry threw himself into the magazine, hustling for advertising from local tradesmen and promising them a 'guaranteed circulation from all the boys at school'. Years later, Loomis recalled that 'Harry sold space to a local dentist who owed us 75 cents. When he didn't pay up, Harry got him to extract a troublesome tooth for free to square the debt.' His experience of publishing *Wisp* not only gave Harry a life-long passion for the business of publicity and promotion, it also introduced him to the power of the press – something he never forgot and which he played to his advantage throughout his career.

Loomis's father ran a small bank in Jackson, and when Harry left school at 14, he got a job there as a junior book-keeper, earning $20 a month. A tough taskmaster called Mr Potter taught him to write a neat ledger, as Harry later recalled in a letter to Loomis: 'He didn't exactly inspire or encourage, but he did rub things in so hard that you could never forget them.' Jotting down figures became an engrained habit, and Harry's lists make fascinating reading. In just one of his silver-clasped, cream vellum private ledgers dated 1921, he noted in an immaculate hand that on 3 June he lost £1,198 playing poker and gave 'the Hon. Angela Manners £5.5/-' (presumably a charity donation), while in July – somewhat mysteriously for a man who owned his own department store – he spent £476 17s. 6d. at the Irish Linen Company in the Burlington Arcade.

It has been said that at around this time Harry studied for the entrance examinations to the Naval Academy in Annapolis,

Maryland, but failed his physical test because he was too short. Harry was always sensitive about his height – he was a shade under 5 foot 8 inches and wore lifts in his custom-made boots to give him an extra half inch – but that fact alone wouldn't have prevented him joining the Navy, for they required only that candidates 'be not less than 5 feet'. It is more likely that he would have failed because of his eyesight. He was notoriously short-sighted, and as a consequence wore glasses for all reading and writing, initially a metal-rimmed pince-nez and later thin gold frames. He had the most brilliant, clear blue eyes and would fix people with a beguiling stare that could be disconcerting to those who didn't realize that he could hardly see them otherwise.

Harry soon left the bank and moved to Gilbert, Ransom & Knapp, a local furniture factory, where he became a book-keeper. Unfortunately, the business was already waning and went into liquidation a few months later. Being unemployed wasn't an option, so he took work at a dollar a day in an insurance business in Big Rapids, a small town several hundred miles away.

Whatever influences inspired Harry Selfridge in his quest to create a seductive shopping experience, he certainly didn't find them in Big Rapids. He was never a fan of country pursuits, and fishing and fur-trapping were pretty much all Big Rapids offered by way of recreation in those days. Neither did he drink much. What Harry enjoyed was playing cards – especially poker – and Big Rapids was almost certainly where he honed his game. At one point, boredom is rumoured to have prompted him to study law – via a correspondence course – but he subsequently admitted that it was a 'complete disaster'. In one thing, however, he remained constant. In the office he was always impeccably dressed. Years later, when Selfridge had become famous and the American press serialized his life story, an old acquaintance from Big Rapids recalled that Harry has always looked 'as if he had just come out of a bandbox'.

Harry Selfridge returned to Jackson late in 1876 with $500 he had 'saved from his earnings', although given his predilection for poker it was more likely to have been the winnings from a few lucky hands at cards. He then drifted from one dreary job to another, culminating in eighteen months at a local grocery store. By the time he was 22, he was desperate to move on. But how – and to where? Salvation came through his ex-employer, Leonard Field, who was persuaded to write a letter of introduction to Marshall Field in Chicago. Marshall was the senior partner in Field, Leiter & Co., one of the biggest and most successful stores in the city. Young Harry would ultimately help make it one of the most famous in America.

Selfridge used to say that his interview with Mr Field lasted a matter of minutes and that the man was 'so cold it made him shiver'. Terms were discussed, with Harry claiming he agreed a weekly wage of $10 as a stock boy in the wholesale department basement – but the pay at the very bottom of the ladder he determined to climb was certainly less than that.

Variously described as 'dignified and quiet', and so taciturn he was nicknamed 'silent Marsh', Field had little time for anything other than work. How a man so devoid of personality could have been so successful in the business of sales, where the ability to communicate and motivate is crucial, is a mystery. Field cared little for what he called 'frivolous methods', running his business the way he lived his life. Dry, humourless and puritanical, albeit always courteous, he was the antithesis of Harry Selfridge. They complemented one another, but although Selfridge worked for Field for over twenty-five years, they were never friends.

To call Marshall Field merely 'successful' is an understatement. By 1900, his recorded annual income was $40 million a year (nearly $800 million today) and when he died in 1906, he left an estate worth $118 million (over $2 billion today). A large part of his fortune came from real estate and his early investment in railroad stocks. He was also an original and significant investor in the Pullman Company, backing George Pullman's imaginative concept of luxurious comfort while travelling by train. Given that the journey from Chicago to New York alone took twenty hours, it is small wonder that Pullman's deluxe dining-car, called 'The Delmonico' after New York's swell restaurant, was so successful. Only the rich could travel in his cars, while the really rich bought and customized their own private Pullman carriages – the private jets of their day – fitting marble bathtubs, over-stuffed velvet sofas, piped organ music and, the height of one-upmanship, taking along an English butler to ensure the service was smooth.

The nucleus of Field's wealth, however, came from shopping. The towering department store on State Street was a Mecca for Chicago residents, but as with all the early nineteenth-century 'great store' successes, it was the wholesale department that laid the foundations of the Field fortune, supplying people in small townships all over the Midwest with whatever they needed, from dress fabric to carpets, petticoats to parasols.

Marshall Field was a farmer's son who grew up in Conway, Massachusetts, where the whole family had to help on the land. As neither he nor his elder brother Joseph had any feel for farming, both took what was virtually the only route out of rural life – working as salesmen in a dry-goods store. Marshall's first job was in Pittsfield, Massachusetts, but in 1856 he headed west to join his brother Joseph in Chicago – though it's doubtful whether the neat and tidy, church-going young man of 21 realized what was going to hit him when he got there. Reminders that Chicago was a frontier town were everywhere in the sprawling mass of timber buildings that stretched along the shore of Lake Michigan. Mud was the main topic of conversation – it was so deep that it oozed over the boardwalks, clogged wagon wheels and ruined ladies' clothes. Not that there were too many ladies in Chicago. Local men searching for a bride would 'go East' and, having found a suitable partner, return to Chicago, placing a notice in the local newspapers with the address of the new marital home. Enterprising local dressmakers would often be among their first callers. Having examined the bride's trousseau, the dressmaker would then go from door to door presenting her compliments – along with her newly discovered knowledge of the 'latest fashions from the East'.

For those prepared to take risks, business opportunities were spectacular. William Butler Ogden – who became Chicago's first Mayor – bought a tract of land in 1844 for $8,000, selling it six years later for $3 million. Mr Ogden was nothing if not enterprising. When financing for the Illinois and Michigan Canal dried up he ensured bonds were issued to raise the necessary cash. Always a step ahead, in the same year the canal was opened, he built Chicago's first railroad.

In 1856, Marshall Field had no money with which to buy land or open a store. Instead he took a job at the wholesaler's Farwell, Cooley & Wadsworth, one of the many firms busy shipping dry goods out via Chicago's burgeoning railroads to where the tracks ended in emergent new townships – where women were desperate for everything from cottons and calico to sewing threads and buttons. Field went 'on the road', meeting local merchants, sizing up the business potential and diligently doing his duty by Mr Cooley, whose efficient book-keeper, Levi Z. Leiter, was also busy in the back office, entering their profits in the ledgers. When Potter Palmer, arguably Chicago's most successful merchant, gave up wholesaling to concentrate entirely on his retail division, the polite Mr Field picked up most of his clients – at the same time keenly observing the progress of Mr Palmer's impressive new store on Lake Street.

Chicago's ladies were determined shoppers. In the pre-war financial slump they bought at discount, so much so that *Harper's* caustically advised husbands to 'observe your wife shopping if you would know her. She may be sweet in the parlor, but she is like a ghoul at the counter.' In fact there was very little else for women to do in Chicago other than shop. There were no beauty parlours, no restaurants – or certainly none where women could eat – and only one theatre. Servants took care of the housework and the kitchen. The only thing that ladies could do outside their home – other than attend activities organized by their local church – was to shop for clothes and household materials. Feminists have long raged about the consumer culture, but the early women's champion Elizabeth Cady Stanton was quite clear on the subject. While she deplored the excesses of wealthy women 'who only lived for fashion', she also implored women to seek independence through masterminding the family budget: 'go out and buy' she would shout from the platform at conventions and meetings, urging women to seize the initiative in equipping their household and clothing themselves – whether or not they were paying the bills.

Marshall Field was a man with a searing ambition to make money. All his life he judged opportunity strictly by prospective returns – and when the elderly Mr Wadsworth retired, the chance of buying into a partnership was irresistible. When the Civil War began, Mr Farwell, the sole remaining original founder, welcomed Marshall Field as a full partner. Three years later, in another management shuffle, the business was taken over completely by Field and Levi Leiter, who became partners. Somehow – despite working an average sixteen-hour day – Marshall Field found the time to meet and marry Nannie Scott, and their son, also named Marshall, was born in 1868. By this time, the Field fortunes were firmly established.

Retail historians today praise Marshall Field as one of the trade's 'founding fathers', but arguably his quantum leap to success came from buying other people's businesses rather than founding his own – and the business that really propelled him forward was that belonging to Potter Palmer. Ten years after he had opened his store, Palmer was making $10 million a year. He was wealthy, but not healthy. In 1865, worn out and worried by gloomy advice from his doctors, Palmer sold the majority equity in his business to Field and Leiter for $750,000 and moved to Paris, leaving the two men with a platform rivals could only dream about.

Palmer was soon back in Chicago enthusing over Baron Hauss-mann's spectacular rebuilding programme in Paris where wide, elegant boulevards had replaced narrow streets, and the installation of a modern sewage system and transport had finally made Paris 'shopper friendly'.

He knew that if Chicago was to have a world-class shopping district, then its stores needed a better environment. Getting out his cheque book he bought up buildings on State Street, parallel to the lake shore, until his holdings were a mile long. Lobbying the city council to widen the lane into a boulevard, at a stroke he single-handedly reoriented the centre of Chicago from Lake Street – which ran by a foul-smelling river – to State Street, which he virtually owned. He demolished the run of 'shack' shops and saloons along it to build commercial properties, and subsequently leased his prime six-storey corner site to Field & Leiter for $50,000 a year.

Potter Palmer married in 1870. As a wedding gift to his young bride Bertha Honoré, he built a hotel and named it the Palmer House. Eight storeys high, with 225 rooms fitted out with Italian marble and French chandeliers, it was Chicago's most sumptuous building. The hotel never took a paying guest. In 1871, fire swept through the city. An area of three and a half square miles was ravaged, 300 people died and 90,000 were made homeless – nearly a third of the city's population. Among the buildings destroyed were Palmer's hotel and Field & Leiter's new store. Luckily, Marshall Field and Levi Leiter were well-insured. Having recouped most of their losses, they moved to a temporary site, from which they did a roaring trade in Chicago's post-fire renaissance.

It took well over a year to clear the debris left by the great fire. Businesses had to 'make do and mend', and many men set up offices in their own homes as Chicago picked itself up and started a massive rebuilding programme. Field and Leiter bought a property on Market Street where they established their wholesaling headquarters while considering their future. At the same time, Potter Palmer was planning his new 'dream' hotel. To raise the money, he sold a parcel of land on State Street for $350,000 to the calculating men who ran the Singer Sewing Company and who were busy using the phenomenal profits from selling their patented sewing machine to diversify into property.

As a result of Isaac Singer's machine and Ellen Demorest's invention of the first paper patterns, many American housewives were becoming competent dressmakers. Observing this trend with unease, the legion of professional dressmakers upped the stakes by affecting fancy French names and even learning a word or two of the language, which never failed to impress their customers. For the newly affluent woman, however, all this home-centred activity was dull. Fashion, etiquette and beauty manuals and magazines were now pouring from the printing presses, establishing new trends at almost breakneck speed. Women wanted to go out and buy for themselves, a fact that had not escaped the property division of the Singer Company who spent over $750,000 on an elegant white marble-fronted building on the corner of State Street and Washington. In fact it was so elegant, the great Alexander Stewart himself was rumoured to want it for a Chicago outpost of his New York store. He didn't get it: instead it was leased to Field & Leiter who moved in during the autumn of 1873 just as the New York stock market crashed and a deep recession struck America. It was not an auspicious start.

~

GIVING THE LADIES
WHAT THEY WANT

'Judge not a man by his clothes, but by his wife's clothes.'
Sir Thomas Dewar

Fashion designers and marketers live in hope that a trend will develop credibility and become a bestseller. Then of course they crave a new one, because in reality, fashion succeeds as a business precisely because its obsolescence is inevitable. For true devotees, the cycle lasts a mere six months and the launch of a new look necessitates all sorts of changes. But even today, it is rare for one's entire wardrobe to become dated overnight. Not so when the cumbersome crinoline and matronly bonnet were consigned to history.

By the early 1870s no truly style-conscious woman in society would have been seen dead in hoops – she had to change her wardrobe from top to toe as a totally new look swept into fashion. To the delight of the drapery retailers, its replacement, a revival of the eighteenth-century *polonaise* – best described as a masterful combination of cinch and pouf – also required substantial amounts of material. Women poured themselves into a tight-fitting, short-waisted bodice with even tighter sleeves, worn above drawn-back, bunched skirts puffed at the rear into an elaborate bustle. The whole outfit, often overwhelmed with a profusion of ruches, ribbons and fringes, flew in the face of the emergent dress reform movement, which despaired at the complexity of women's wardrobes.

In the second half of the nineteenth century, the supreme master dictating trends was Charles Frederick Worth. Born in Lincolnshire, Worth spent some time on the shop floor at Swan & Edgar's in Piccadilly and several years working for leading silk merchants in both London and Paris. He opened his own salon on the rue de la Paix in 1858 and found fame by dressing Princess Pauline von Metternich and the Empress Eugénie. Monsieur Worth was sufficiently egotistical to think of himself as all-powerful – fashion titans usually do – but he wasn't the first celebrated royal designer. That honour goes to Rose Bertin, dressmaker and milliner to the ill-fated Marie Antoinette. Rose Bertin's celebrated skills were surpassed only by the astonishing bills she presented to the Queen. But even though she sent model dolls wearing miniature versions of her gowns to princesses at other royal courts in Europe, her reputation was restricted to just a few hundred people. Thanks to the growing influence of magazines in America, Worth was the first designer to become internationally famous.

He was the designer of choice for the wives of the super-rich – his were the original 'red carpet' gowns, created for women who made an entrance and whose husbands' bank balances could stand the cost. His favourite clients were American since they tended to order several gowns at once and never queried the design or the price. Worth used to say 'My transatlantic friends are always welcome – they have the figures, the francs and the faith.' The thrifty French grandees on the other hand – such as the Comtesse Greffuhle, one of Proust's models for the Duchesse de Guermantes in A *la recherche du temps perdu* – ordered individually and, worse, would have their dressmaker make 'alterations' so that the gown could be worn for longer.

Worth revolutionized the business of fashion by presenting his collection on live models in Paris to a slavishly devoted audience, which included most of the 'Wall Street wives'. Travelling to Europe – particularly to Paris – was an annual event for the American rich, enabling them to stock up on art and antiques and visit Worth's salon. Unfortunately for Worth, the Franco-Prussian War put paid to their travels. Worse still, his most famous client, the Empress Eugénie, went into exile in England, his sumptuous salon was requisitioned as a hospital, and the bitter siege of Paris left people more worried about food than fashion. News filtered out that Parisians were eating their horses, cats and dogs, and *Le Figaro* reported that the chefs at the Paris Jockey Club showed culinary initiative in making 'quite a good salami from rats'.

In the uneasy aftermath of the war, Worth reopened. Ably assisted by his son, Jean-Philippe, before long his business reached such dizzy heights that he had over 1,200 staff on his payroll. His master-stroke was to follow the money by taking his collection to New York and Rhode Island. There, as 'the king of fashion', his appearances resembled a state visit as society scrambled to have him as guest of honour at their cocktail receptions and dinners. Orders were then placed to be made up in Paris and shipped back to America.

There wasn't a name from the Gilded Age that Worth didn't dress, and a wardrobe by Worth became the sine qua non for rich American girls who were keen to acquire a titled British husband. Worth's lifestyle mirrored that of his clients, and his beautifully dressed wife and two elegant sons became part of the Worth publicity machine which whirred so effectively that J. P. Morgan himself considered Worth a friend and is said to have cried when he died.

Having virtually invented the crinoline, Worth was equally pleased to get rid of it, as once more he changed the way women dressed. Drapers owed Monsieur Worth a debt beyond price. As each fashion plate of his latest gown was published, women would rush to buy material and commission a similar model. At Field & Leiter alone in the mid-1870s, there were 300 girls sewing in the top-floor workrooms, all busy making gowns for the wives of Chicago's rich, while copies of Worth's newly styled and lavishly trimmed jaunty hats flew out of the millinery department.

Despite the back bustles, which involved purchasing a collapsible framed contraption called a 'dress improver', women were finally discovering the delights of lighter lingerie, as ultra-heavy boned and back-laced corsets were replaced by less cumbersome underpinnings.

Corsets were still boned, but the most popular, unaccountably named 'The Widow Machree', was a curve-inducing, front-fastening model with kid-covered hooks and eyes. For the main part, women's dresses were still buttoned up – at least during the day – but the décolleté evening gowns that were now emerging required new uplifting underwear. For those embarrassed about their meagre embonpoint, help was at hand from the Elastic Bosom Company which, having patented their padding, proudly announced that 'in case of shipwreck it would be impossible for the wearer to drown'. In an astute move at a time when virtually all sales staff were male, Marshall Field employed women to work in the store's burgeoning lingerie department, which meant that ladies could be accurately measured and fitted without embarrassment: particularly important as over-tight corsets could cause anything from fainting fits to uterine and spinal disorders.

Field's brother Joseph had by this time been dispatched to England where he set up a company outpost in Manchester, the idea being that he would source new products, imports having cachet among the store's wealthier clientele. Joseph was a dull, miserly man, given to wearing his overcoat in the unheated office and entirely lacking in the glamour associated with fashion, so it isn't surprising that his purchases had a mixed reception. He did, however, send back all sorts of specialist textiles including Nottingham lace and Paisley shawls. Field & Leiter sold lace tablecloths that cost $1,000 a time, when the average weekly wage was $10, but they had plenty of customers who could afford them and who were not at all perturbed by the prohibitive import duties that added so much to the price.

Recession hadn't halted the relentless progress of the rich in Chicago any more than it had held back the 'Robber Barons' of New York. Chicago manufactured, packed and shipped the thing that mattered most – foodstuffs – across America and over the ocean to Europe. By the end of the 1870s, the city was deafened by the sound of building as offices, warehouses and transport terminals sprang up alongside the shanty towns that housed the rising flood of immigrants from Europe. The building boom was financed by the new élite, who were also busy building themselves palatial new homes, their principal requirements being that the result should be impressively large, have the requisite ballroom, and not be anywhere near the city's riff-raff – Chicago was infamous for its brothels and booze. The city's rich colonized their own safe havens, settling in Calumet Avenue, Prairie Avenue or a little further south in 'Millionaire's Row' on Michigan Avenue.

Field himself moved his family (young Marshall II now had a baby sister called Ethel) to Prairie Avenue, commissioning the celebrated architect Richard Morris Hunt to build him a merchant's mansion. Unusually for a Chicago commission, Field asked Hunt to 'keep it simple'. Hunt, more used to clients such as the Vanderbilts (for whom he designed 'The Breakers', their faux-Italian Renaissance palace in Newport, at a cost of $11 million), was unable to exercise his imagination. Unlike the ostentatious Pullman home, or Cyrus McCormick's vast and awesomely unattractive house nearby, Hunt's three-storey dwelling for Field was a model of restraint. It was also the first house in Chicago to be wired for electricity, which shone brightly on the yellow silk-covered walls. Even so, the house was always described as being bleak and cold. It wasn't a happy home.

Mrs Marshall Field could have become one of Chicago's leading hostesses, but she seems never to have had the inclination. A gentle soul married to a man with absolutely no sense of fun, she was prone to chronic migraines and spent an increasing amount of time recuperating in the South of France, more than happy to leave Chicago's social set to compete for the exalted role of leader. That honour went to Bertha Honoré Palmer, who became the undisputed 'Queen of Chicago' just as *the* Mrs Astor was the 'Queen of New York'.

Young Bertha (who had been just 21 when she married 44-year-old Potter) had youth, good looks, quantities of money courtesy of her indulgent husband, and a sister married to President Ulysses S. Grant's son Frederick, which gave her a cachet that money couldn't buy.

Bertha adored jewels – her favourites being diamonds and pearls – and she soon had a prodigious quantity of them, seemingly often wearing them all at once. Potter enjoyed this visible display of excess as much as Bertha did, being prone to remarking fondly, 'There she stands, with half a million on her back.' Actually, it was more like half a million round her neck and another half million on her head: one of Bertha's famous 'dog collars' was set with 2,268 pearls, while her favourite tiara contained 30 diamonds each as big as a quail's egg.

Given that she was pin-thin and petite, Mrs Palmer stood up very well to the rigours of running Chicago society, which she controlled with a rod of iron. At grand functions such as the entrance march to her annual Charity Ball, Mrs Palmer was flanked by the ladies who acted as her deputies and who ran the various 'sub-divisions' of the city. The Palmers themselves ruled the North-side from their awesome turreted castle where, in a show of extreme control, there were no exterior doorknobs – guests had to wait until a servant opened the door – and where the privileged few could ride to the upper floors in the first elevators installed in a private home in Chicago.

Mrs Palmer had a great fondness for Worth gowns and for Paris, where she maintained a home, just as she did in London where the Palmers held court in Carlton House Terrace. Perhaps it was just as well they had three large houses, for they owned an awful lot of art. Always at the cutting edge of fashion, Mrs Palmer was an early patron of the Impressionists. In one single year she famously bought twenty-five Monets, and she loved her Renoir *Acrobats at the Cirque Fernando* so much that it travelled with her wherever she went.

By 1877, Bertha had only to step over to Field & Leiter to buy a new gown by Worth, the store's Paris agent having bought twelve models for Chicago's first private orders from the great man. But before they could be delivered, the store went up in smoke. People mourned its loss as they would have done the death of a relative, and the *Chicago Tribune* produced a fine obituary: 'The destruction of St Peter's in Rome could hardly have aroused a deeper interest than the destruction of this splendid dry goods establishment … this was the place of worship for thousands of our female fellow-citizens. It was the only shrine at which they paid their devotions.'

Yet another temporary site was hastily found and while Field and Leiter anxiously debated their future, the Singer Company started to clear the rubble and rebuild. Confident that it was the best site in town, Field himself suggested not only moving back in but also buying the building. Levi Leiter was reluctant. He didn't understand the new retail business; he was a traditional wholesaling man. Wholesale, he argued, was less complex to run and made much more money – in 1872 retail sales stood at $3.1 million against wholesaling at $14 million. Field disagreed. The cachet of running a prime retail site was what kept the wholesale customers loyal – one was inseparable from the other. Eventually the partners offered $500,000 to Singer, who immediately rejected it. It was $700,000 'take it or leave it'. Field was in New York on a business trip when Singer contacted Leiter for his final offer. Brusque and stubborn to the end, Leiter wouldn't budge, losing the prime site to the ambitious Scottish duo, Sam Carson and John Pirie, who leased it at $70,000 a year. Field was furious and rushed back from New York to salvage the mess. He won – as he always did – but it cost him Singer's original purchase price of $700,000 plus an extra $100,000 to buy Carson Pirie Scott out of their lease. He didn't forgive Levi Leiter and he didn't forget.

Field & Leiter moved into their new, spacious six-storey building in November 1879 where 500 assistants on the floor served Chicago's best customers. Field used to say it was 'everyone's store', and everyone came, from the celebrated actress Lillie Langtry – famous for her sexual exploits in England – to Carrie Watson, who knew a thing or two about sex herself, given that she ran Chicago's most exclusive brothel. In keeping with the style of her 'house' – a three-storey mansion with more than twenty bedrooms plus a bowling alley and billiard room in the basement for those waiting to be served – Carrie's girls were beautifully dressed. They 'received' in ball gowns, fluttered their fans in the most charming way and peeled off layers of exquisite underwear, all of which made Carrie Watson one of Field & Leiter's most valued customers.

There was no such excitement in the basement of Field's Market

Street wholesale building where young Harry Selfridge had just started his new job. Such thrills as he got were from reading the newspapers – which he devoured daily – or from visits to the theatre where he watched stars such as Lillie Langtry while nurturing dreams of his future. He didn't have long to wait. Within the year, his boss, the immaculately dressed and fastidious John Shedd, sent Selfridge 'on the road' selling lace. Shedd, who would stay with Marshall Field throughout his career, ultimately becoming President on Field's death in 1906, had joined the business as an enthusiastic wholesaling junior in 1871. He was organized, methodical and a gifted salesman who loved beautiful things. When Selfridge joined, Mr Shedd was running the lace department, one of the most profitable in the division. Shedd and Selfridge would become the two men who between them revolutionized the firm.

The Field & Leiter 'linemen', as they were known, were legendary. They were given a budget to 'entertain' alongside their suitcase of samples and swatches, and if they surpassed their target of $100,000 each year they received a bonus. No one knows if Selfridge hit the target, but we do know he hated the job. After three years he had had enough. Harry Selfridge – always urbane – knew he was an urban man and wanted to live in Chicago. Requesting a transfer to work in retail, he moved over to the State Street store in 1883.

It has always been said that Harry Selfridge worked on the shop floor, but his son Gordon claimed he never did: 'My father did not start in retail as a clerk. He was in unofficial charge of the advertising department.' Perhaps that is why Field – while acknowledging that Selfridge was articulate and in tune with the media – never thought of him as a true merchant. That accolade was reserved for Mr Shedd, already on the path to becoming 'heir apparent'. Selfridge was the store's 'ideas man' and if those ideas made money, that was all well and good. Selfridge took his role as copy-writer seriously. His copy seems dated now but for the time it was enormously refreshing. Field ads didn't lie; they were always honest, perhaps a touch self-important – but above all, they were reassuring about quality, value, respect and commitment to service. As Chicago boomed, the message went out to the public that Field & Leiter was a comforting place to be.

For all Field's lack of charisma, he was polite, calm and dignified, exuding a quiet confidence. He prided himself on caring for the customer and drilled his staff never to hustle or harass. Walking through the store one day he found an assistant quibbling with a customer over a return. 'Give the lady what she wants,' Field remarked. He was equally calm when ousting Leiter, his partner of fourteen years, who exited the business with a cheque for nearly $3 million, leaving Harry Selfridge to write ads that announced the store would henceforth be called 'Marshall Field & Co.'.

Levi Leiter took to his forced retirement rather well, moving his wife and family to Washington and setting up home in a Dupont Circle mansion, where he nurtured his property portfolio while his wife nurtured marital ambitions for her three young daughters. Despite their handsome dowries, not even Mrs Leiter could have predicted the glittering future of her eldest daughter Mary, who married George Curzon in 1895. When her husband subsequently took up his appointment as Viceroy of India, Lady Curzon, as Vicereine, occupied the most important position ever held by an American in the British Empire.

Back in Chicago, Harry Selfridge would prove Levi Leiter wrong. The future lay not in wholesaling but in retailing. The real consumer revolution had begun.

~

THE CUSTOMER IS ALWAYS RIGHT

'Remember always that the recollection of quality remains
long after the price is forgotten.'
Harry Gordon Selfridge

Harry Selfridge had a deep-rooted belief in the power of advertising. To him, it was the engine that drove the retail machine, and his faith in it never wavered. Through good times and bad, the Selfridge policy was to spread the word through the media.

His first aim was to get people through the doors. 'Getting them in' became his mantra. Once they were inside he believed in giving them comfort, courteous service and, above all, entertainment as an enticement to buy. If, having reeled them in like fish on a line, he lost some, he reckoned he could always catch them another time.

Harry was brash, bold, impulsive and imaginative, qualities which did not go down well with Marshall Field's incumbent retail general manager, J. M. Fleming, to whom Harry was appointed as personal assistant in 1885. Harry's brief from Marshall Field was to propose – and subsequently implement – new ideas. Mr Fleming was of the old school, formal in manner, traditional in outlook, bowing to every ritual and rule that had 'built the business'. Harry thought him stubborn and old-fashioned.

A year or so earlier, Harry Selfridge had been to New York – a trip apparently taken at his own expense by way of a working holiday and one which had a profound effect on him. He noted the uniformed greeters at Lord & Taylor, saw the crowds hunting for bargains at

Macy's and admired the fashionable clothes at the Bloomingdale Brothers' East Side Bazaar. All had benefited in one way or another from the influence of Alexander Stewart (though his own business had, after his death in 1876, subsequently collapsed). Convinced he could make his own mark on Marshall Field, Harry looked at what was already there and set about improving it.

He had a good base on which to build. Field himself had embraced the era's new technology, removing the old-fashioned gas lamps and wiring the six-storey store for electricity in 1882. He had even installed telephone lines, albeit only five for the whole building. The store also had a fine reputation in the community. Field's promoted their 'fair price' policy, always claiming they offered good value.

Realistically, very few consumers had the faintest idea how much goods were worth. For most, the acquisition of non-essential goods was such a new adventure that if they had the money, they willingly paid the price. In many instances – particularly for luxury items – the store buyers were encouraged to set prices at what they thought the market could afford to pay. Prices were intended to cover all costs and they included an additional 6 per cent paid to the wholesale division – from whom the retail store sourced most of its goods – and a charge levied by Mr Field against the rental value of the space each department occupied. When all these costs were covered, departmental heads then had sales targets to meet, above which they made a bonus.

The store was also becoming much more service-orientated. Free local deliveries had already been introduced, as had a 'storing' point where parcels were kept while customers browsed in other departments. There were still only two elevators, but each was as comfortable as a private Pullman car, with plush bench seats, carved panelling and ornate mirrors. Otherwise customers used the impressive sweeping staircase which was twenty-three feet wide and easily accommodated the 'back-bustle and train' dresses then in fashion. Staff called customers 'Madam' or 'Sir'. They weren't allowed to hustle for sales, eat, spit, swear or chew tobacco on the shop floor. In reality, they enjoyed the status their jobs conferred as much as customers enjoyed the status of shopping there. But the refined atmosphere was too rarefied to suit Selfridge who, at 29, was young enough to crave change, and astute enough to know it was waiting to happen.

His first target was lighting. Despite the large central skylight and new electric lighting, the store, replete with vast amounts of mahogany panelling, was gloomy, so he quadrupled the number of hanging globes. Then, maximizing the wonder of electricity, uniquely for Chicago (and very possibly any other retail store in the world), he lit the windows when the store was closed at night, bringing evening 'window shopping' to the city. Considering communication crucial, he increased the number of telephone lines, installing a central switchboard operated by female telephonists, with extensions into each major department.

Next he turned his attention to the fixtures. Shopping, he reasoned, should be both a visual and a tactile experience, one best enjoyed in a moment of private self-indulgence and enjoyment and not requiring a sales clerk to unlock a cabinet. So he put central displays in the aisles, folding stock on tables so women could touch and feel a cashmere shawl or a pair of fine kid gloves that they were thinking of buying. He lowered the old-fashioned wall units and ripped out the steep shelves, installing instead back fixtures that staff could reach without ladders. He also reduced the height of the counters, bringing them down to customer-friendly levels, with deep drawers for storage underneath to save staff wasting time making trips to the stock room.

Field may not have appreciated the significance of these moves, but Chicago's acclaimed architect Daniel Burnham certainly did. Burnham – best known today for his iconic Flat Iron building in New York – was the man who helped shape late nineteenth-century Chicago. He also became Selfridge's hero. Harry – whose greatest hobby was collecting architectural drawings – called him 'Uncle Dan', and it was he who later helped visualize the Oxford Street store. Just after Burnham's firm had completed a massive new development for Marshall Field & Co. in 1908 (a dream job that largely created the building that exists today), he wrote to Selfridge in London with news of their solution to the shop-fitting: 'the fixture question, which I am sure has been solved in this, as in no other store in the world, owes much to your early efforts'.

There was no stopping the man staff called 'mile-a-minute Harry'. He printed souvenir booklets for the 1884 Presidential Conventions held in the city and invited all the delegates to visit the store, reminding them that their shopping would be delivered to their hotels. When the city began to pay school teachers by cheque, he set up a special in-store bank to cash them – ignoring criticism from the media that he was enticing teachers to 'spend more freely in the store as they had cash in their purses'.

Ever the publicist, he also more than quadrupled the store's newspaper advertising budget and booked Chicago's first ever full-page advertisements. The advertisements always had a story – aggressive advertising never interested Harry Selfridge. He preferred to use persuasion, and the text of the advertisements was peppered with his quaint, quirky and deeply felt moral opinions. Nor would he use lurid headlines or false offers on prices. A typical trick of the day was to advertise delivery of 'a special line at exceptional prices'. When customers arrived, they invariably found that what they wanted had mysteriously sold out but that there was something similar at a higher price. Harry Selfridge never endorsed such trickery. He never promised more than the store could provide and he focused on 'service with a smile'.

Shoppers responded to what they felt was sincerity, feeling they were part of the equation in making a choice about their purchases. In truth, women are instinctively shrewd shoppers, but in choosing Field's they were acknowledging that they found subtlety more seductive than bullying. Selfridge told the staff to treat customers 'as guests when they come and when they go, whether or not they buy. Get the confidence of the public and you will have no difficulty in getting their patronage.' He was right.

His message to both the public and the staff was that there was contentment, even fun, to be found in shopping (and working) at Marshall Field. His critics sneered at him, laughing about his 'little notices' pinned on the wall in the canteen which set 'daily targets':

'To do the right thing at the right time in the right way'
'To do some things better than they were ever done before'
'To know both sides of the question'
'To be courteous; to be a good example; to anticipate requirements'
'To be satisfied with nothing short of perfection'

In reality, his methods where hugely motivational, and this at a time when – particularly in England – store staff were more likely to read a notice outlining cash fines levied for being late on the floor or for being seen by the floor-walker to miss a sale.

Selfridge himself was never a bully, but he was a disciplinarian. He liked to think of himself as a great general marshalling his troops: he once famously said at a staff meeting that he endorsed the idea of uniforms and 'wouldn't mind wearing one himself'. He drilled the staff constantly about the need to be polite and clean (nails, shirt collars and shoes were randomly checked), and if he found a dusty surface when touring the store, he would simply scrawl HGS on it – a sure signal for staff to get out the dusters. He never raised his voice and he never reprimanded anyone in public. He didn't crack jokes and he never, ever gossiped. But he had an aura. Just being around him was heady stuff. Homer Buckley, who worked in the shipping department at Field's, still remembered the impact Selfridge made on him over sixty years later: 'he would drop in at your desk, sometimes all of a sudden, sit there and talk ten minutes, ask about this and that, never talk down to you – the result was you'd be thrilled for a week. I would literally walk on air after he'd done this at my desk. I never met a man capable of putting such inspiration into his employees.'

In 1885, having already instigated the first twice-yearly mark-down sales, Harry implemented a real coup in convincing Marshall Field to open the lower ground floor as the store's 'bargain basement'.

Shoppers today are so used to discounts that it is hard to imagine what an impact it had. Chicago's wealthy were regular customers, but by now the city's population had grown to 700,000 and Selfridge longed to give ordinary people what the rich enjoyed. He didn't just target those on low incomes making a special purchase – perhaps lace for a Confirmation dress, or ribbons to trim a hat to wear at a wedding – he also believed that customers from the young, professional classes, making their way on $15 or $20 a week, would soon be able to 'move upstairs'. The bargain basement was much more than a vehicle to shift slow-moving retail stock, although of course it helped to clear the shelves, creating an aura of exclusivity around the store's core merchandise. Promoted as offering 'even better value' – Selfridge abhorred the word 'cheap' – the bargain basement rapidly became a destination for thrifty shoppers who could buy special lines that were subsequently introduced to complement the full-priced merchandise on the upper floors. The new floor was so successful that by 1900, it had a sales turnover of $3 million and had inspired a raft of competitors to copy the idea.

Originally, when presenting his case for the bargain basement, Selfridge had argued the cause of aspirational immigrants, who had an acute sense of 'Sunday Best'. This was a step too far for Field, who had a deep mistrust of immigrants and shuddered at the idea of them shopping in his store. To Field and his cronies, mass immigration, especially from Germany, meant the spreading of socialism, with its inevitable demands for workers' rights, reduced hours and higher pay. Though Field treated his own staff well, he abhorred the idea of unions. Staff who showed signs of militancy were dismissed immediately.

By the mid-1880s, there were well over a thousand staff at Field's. They worked a minimum nine-hour day, six days a week, ate well in the staff canteen and received a 6 per cent discount on their own purchases – not that many of them could afford to shop there. Field's paid less than average: a starting salesman received a weekly wage of $8, the elevator boys $4 and the cash boys $2. But a job at Marshall Field's had cachet, and the store staff considered themselves infinitely superior to the city's factory, sweatshop and railroad workers. When Chicago's railwaymen had rioted during the great railroad strike in 1877, Field staff were mobilized and issued with rifles to use against the threatening 'rabble' if they had to.

A decade later, when McCormick's workers walked out and mob violence swept the city, Chicago's burgeoning – and sometimes brutal – police force didn't need assistance from amateurs. Field himself watched the growing influence of the unions with unease. He reluctantly allowed his delivery men to join an emergent new transport union – the embryonic group that would evolve into the mighty Teamsters – but he nurtured a deep-rooted dislike of what he called 'lawless strikers', so much so that union leaders who came to shop in the store were asked to 'take their business elsewhere'. His protégé Harry Selfridge likewise mistrusted – and avoided – unions throughout his career.

Chicago's rich generally showed a blissful disregard for the poverty of their workers and continued their pursuit of extravagance. They ensured their details were recorded in the *Bon Ton Directory* whose pages listed 'the Most Prominent and Fashionable Ladies Residing in Chicago'. Among them was Mrs Perry Smith, wife of the Chicago & North Western Railway vice-president, who delighted in showing guests visiting her new mansion the butler's pantry, which was equipped with three taps – one for hot water, one for cold, and one for iced champagne. Such material excesses rather appealed to Sarah Bernhardt. When the celebrated actress swept into town to perform at McVicker's Theater, she was accompanied by a hundred pieces of luggage, her pet tiger cub and her lover of the day, a handsome young Italian known only as Angelo. Chicago's *grand dames* refused to receive her, but despite their snubs she said she 'found the city vibrant and exciting'. Not everyone agreed. George Curzon, touring America in 1887, thought Chicago 'huge and smoky and absorbed in the worship of Mammon in a grim and melancholy way', though that did not prevent him from subsequently marrying Levi Leiter's daughter.

By 1887, having driven Mr Fleming to early retirement, Harry

Selfridge was appointed retail general manager of the store. His increased salary enabled him to move his mother from Jackson to Chicago, and they both settled into a house in the city's Near North Side. Mrs Selfridge now had a maid to do her housework. She also had a carriage, whose groom drove a pair of matched chestnut horses to take her around town. The carriage was nowhere near as glamorous as Potter Palmer's imported French *char-à-banc* with its leopard-skin covered seats, nor as distinctive as the brothel-owner Carrie Watson's famous snow-white equipage with bright yellow wheels that was pulled by a team of four glistening black horses, but for Lois Selfridge, it was more than she had ever dreamed possible.

Her son meanwhile made impressive improvements to his own habitat within the State Street store, where he furnished a spacious office. By contrast, Field's office was so small and bleak that George Pullman called it a 'cubby-hole'. Field's routine never varied. He arrived by carriage each morning – setting down two blocks away so he could be seen walking to work – and spent most of the morning going through paperwork before touring the sales floors. He lunched at the Chicago Club, sitting at the 'millionaires table' with friends such as George Pullman and Judge Lambert Tree, and would then walk to the Merchants Loan and Trust Bank – an enterprise in which he held most of the shares – before calling in at the wholesale headquarters, housed in a magnificent seven-storey building covering a whole city block.

For all his tacit support of the retailing enterprise, it was the wholesale division that interested Field the most – mainly because it made the most money, but also because his travelling sales force reported back from far-flung towns in the Midwest on everything from the state of transport to local politics, land prices and immigration. Distilling this information gave Field an invaluable insight into commercial progress in rural America, which proved crucial to the investment strategy of his own portfolio. On most days, Field would spend an hour with John Shedd, by now manager of the wholesale department and already, in Field's eyes, a masterful merchant.

In 1888, John Shedd and Harry Selfridge were sent on a two-month business trip to Europe. They went to Germany, France and England, where Marshall Field now had offices in Nottingham as well as Manchester. For Selfridge the trip was a catalyst. He was impressed beyond measure with Au Bon Marché in Paris, where he filled two notebooks with ideas, and captivated by the merchandise on sale at Liberty's, particularly the ultra-modern, floaty chiffon 'teagowns' and other aesthetically inspired embroideries much loved by Liberty's more bohemian customers. In fact he was so entranced by the Arts & Crafts movement that when he returned to Chicago, he badgered Marshall Field to allow him to open a William Morris department.

In London, the two men lunched at the Criterion, dined at the Café Royal, attended the famous Gaiety Theatre and visited several English stately homes. It seems likely they went to Compton Verney in Warwickshire, where Marshall Field's daughter Ethel lived with her husband Arthur Tree and their young family in a mansion rented from Lord Willoughby de Broke. Here Harry Selfridge could stroll in gardens laid out by Capability Brown and admire the distinctive hand of Robert Adam who had remodelled the property in 1762. It was all a far cry from Chicago, not to mention Ripon, Wisconsin, and it almost certainly marked the beginning of what would ultimately become his grand passion for living in 'the stately homes of England'.

Back in Chicago, Selfridge determined to make sweeping changes and dreamed of opening branches in New York, Paris and, most importantly, London. Field indulged him – up to a point – but he refused to entertain any ideas of expansion abroad. He did, however, extend the store in Chicago, acquiring three buildings along State Street between the original store and the Central Music Hall, enabling Selfridge to open major new departments. The first was dedicated to children's wear and was partly inspired by the 'Kate Greenaway' collections that Selfridge had seen in Liberty's and by the middle-class trend for formal children's clothes spawned by the runaway success of Frances Hodgson Burnett's bestseller *Little Lord Fauntleroy*. Next came 'Fine Shoes' (mass-produced quality shoes were a recent innovation thanks to the American invention of a 'last-cutting' machine) which stocked shoes and boots in coloured leathers as well as basic black. The store also started to sell paintings, gifts and picture frames, and Selfridge opened service departments to clean customers' gloves, mend their glasses and restring their pearls.

The only thing missing was somewhere to sit, which Selfridge resolved by persuading Marshall Field to agree to an in-store restaurant. Given that there were so few places in Chicago where women could eat out by themselves, it isn't surprising that the store 'tea room', as it was first called, was a runaway success. Originally set up with just fifteen tables served by eight waitresses, within the year it was enlarged to cope with the 1,200 customers who ate there daily. It did not make a profit in the strict sense of 'numbers', but the add-on value in terms of service and keeping the customer in the store was incalculable. The lunch menu, devised by Selfridge with the assistance of a young Chicago cook called Harriet Tilden, was simple but delicious: chicken-pot pie, chicken salad, corned beef hash, cod fishcakes and Boston baked beans, and orange fruit salad served in the orange shell. When the original kitchens could no longer cope with demand, Miss Tilden co-ordinated a group of home cooks who pre-prepared the dishes and delivered them each morning. As the in-store restaurant expanded, so did the kitchen space, but Harriet Tilden's cooks were later put to good use when she opened her own business called 'The Home Delicacies Association', which catered for parties, receptions and society dinners throughout Chicago.

The restaurant was busy from the minute it opened for coffee in the morning, and the ritual of 'Afternoon Tea' at Field's became ever more fashionable. Tiny sandwiches were served in a basket trimmed with a ribbon bow, and the menu included gingerbread slices and the house speciality, Field's Rose Punch (ice-cream with a berry sauce), which came with a red rose on each plate. This was a typical Selfridge touch. The symbolism of flowers was an important part of nineteenth-century sentimentality. Magazines and the endlessly popular etiquette manuals were full of features on 'the meaning of flowers', and the most admired flower of the day was the full-blown, gloriously rich and sexy red American Beauty rose, named after the equally curvaceous, gloriously proportioned stage star Lillian Russell.

The increased activity in the store soon paid dividends. During the six years of Harry Selfridge's management, retail turnover increased from $4 million to $6.7 million. This, Selfridge reasoned, was fine for Mr Field, but he now wanted more for himself. Emboldened by his success, he audaciously asked Field to make him a partner in the business. The atmosphere in Field's office must have been electric as the elderly, reserved owner faced his cavalier, conceited young manager. Realizing 'mile-a-minute Harry' might otherwise leave, Marshall Field bowed to the inevitable. He made Selfridge a junior partner and personally lent him the $200,000 needed to 'buy himself in', while allocating him a share of just under 3 per cent of the total annual profits and increasing his annual salary to $20,000. The combined package meant that at the age of 33 Harry Selfridge was now making today's equivalent of $435,000 a year.

Harry revelled in his new position. He had always been beautifully dressed, but now his frock coats with their silk-faced lapels became even more immaculately tailored. He loathed dirty shirts, changing his at least once and sometimes twice a day. He had special high-cut wing collars made to disguise his unusually thick neck and he always wore the widest possible silk tussore ties with a very large, soft knot. A gold fob watch on a chain, a gold-rimmed pince-nez and a rose boutonnière, carefully chosen from the vase of fresh blooms placed on his desk each morning, completed his outfit. Some of his colleagues found him unbearably conceited – indeed, the only modest thing about him was his height – but he was still head and shoulders above most people working in the retail business.

Selfridge's private life at this time remains a mystery. His mother was his main companion and they were often noted in the press as 'attending the theatre'. Who else kept him company we do not know, but it seems likely that he paid for his sexual pleasures. Vice in Chicago being organized with the same efficiency that characterized more legitimate activities, there were any number of extremely elegant 'houses' which men like Harry Selfridge could frequent without the slightest scandal ever being attached to their name. Any of the celebrated Carrie Watson's twenty girls would have been delighted to welcome him, as would those working at Lizzie Allen's famous 'House of Mirrors' or 'The Arena', blatantly operating on Michigan Avenue where the local millionaires – and their sons – could make convenient visits.

Then, quite suddenly and unexpectedly, Harry became engaged to Rosalie Amelia Buckingham. His bride-to-be has been described as a 'Chicago debutante'. She was indeed a debutante when a teenager, but by the time she met Harry she was nearly 30 and had spent several years working as a successful property developer. Rosalie had learned her craft from her father, the property investor Frank Buckingham, who was also a member of the exclusive Chicago Club. Mr Buckingham had died in the early 1880s, leaving his 23-year-old daughter enough money to venture into development herself.

In partnership with her brother-in-law, Frank Chandler, Rosalie bought land on Harper Avenue in Hyde Park, then a rural outpost of the city. This was no small venture. Rosalie planned and oversaw the building of forty-two villas and 'artists' cottages', the villas each with a 45- or 50-foot frontage and a driveway to reach the stabling at the rear. It was an enlightened development, including a business block with a drugstore, a family grocery store, a café, a reading-room and even a public hall for lectures and concerts. The houses looked out on the park lagoons and lake, with the east side of the development being built sixty feet away from the railroad tracks, which the railroad company was expected to landscape in harmony with the general plan. The architect for the development was Solon S. Beman, the designer of the famous 'Pullman model town', where George Pullman corralled his employees. But Rosalie's villas were not intended for factory workers. They were elegant, spacious middle-class homes in what was the area's first planned community. Miss Buckingham was no giddy debutante.

Harry and Rosalie married on 11 November 1890. He was 34 and she was 30. Harry Selfridge was not a religious man in the conventional sense. Brought up a Presbyterian, as an adult he leaned towards Unitarianism. He believed deeply in 'salvation through good character and hard work' and championed 'improvement through education': his favourite motto was 'Life is what you make it.' In Rosalie, he found a like-minded spirit. The wedding ceremony gave her a foretaste of what life with a showman would be like. It was held at the non-denominational Central Church, housed in the Central Music Hall, just down the road from Marshall Field and one of the few venues in Chicago capable of seating the thousand guests on the happy couple's list. A choir of fifty – whose musical programme was conducted by the Director of the Chicago Musical College, Dr Florenz Ziegfeld – sang to the sound of the music hall's impressive organ, backed up by an orchestra of strings and harps. A display team had laboured to create the central aisle and roof as an exact replica of Ely Cathedral – a romantic curiosity which the newspaper reports failed to investigate but which they would have discovered was in honour of the bride's ancestors who had arrived in America from Cambridgeshire – and the hall was filled with the scent of 5,000 roses. More roses and a mass of lilies and foliage were wired around the pillars and the tiered boxes. The whole event was as spectacular as those later staged by Ziegfeld's son – also called Florenz – when he became the impresario behind Ziegfeld's Follies in New York. Indeed, many at the wedding thought the whole thing was a folly, but Harry Selfridge loved every glorious minute of it. His bride wore an ecru *duchesse* satin gown with exquisite antique lace cuffs falling from elbow-length sleeves. It wasn't made by Worth, but it was a beautiful dress, set off by an impressive necklace of blue diamonds – her gift from the bridegroom.

The couple left on their honeymoon accompanied by Lois Selfridge – a fact which didn't seem to perturb the new Mrs Selfridge in the slightest. It was just as well the two women got along because they would live together in various homes for the rest of their lives. An impressive array of wedding presents reflected the couple's status – not to mention the size of the guest list – and included a valuable parcel of land on the shores of Lake Geneva, a wealthy enclave ninety miles north of Chicago, presented to them by Rosalie's sister and brother-in-law, who owned a summer house next door. There Harry and Rose – as he always called his wife – would build a mock-Tudor country house with large greenhouses where Harry tended his favourite roses and prize orchids. Harry Selfridge now had two women to idolize, and they in turn both loved him unconditionally.

~

FULL SPEED AHEAD

'We live in an age where unnecessary things are our only necessities now.'
Oscar Wilde

On some days it seemed to Harry Selfridge that he was riding the crest of a wave, on others that he had crashed to the beach. At home, there was sadness for Rose and Harry when their first child – a daughter they named Violet – died a few months after her birth. Selfridge masked his grief by throwing himself even more energetically into his work, while Rose recuperated quietly. Having excelled herself with the development of Rosalie Villas, it might have been expected that she would continue working. But she didn't. In an era when women craved their independence, Rose seems to have been content at home. She had married a tornado of energy and at times seemed to find it all rather exhausting.

City officials were buzzing with plans following Chicago's coup in winning the bid to host what was officially known as 'The World's Columbian Exposition', America's celebration of the 400th anniversary of Christopher Columbus arriving on its shores. Chicago had flourished its cheque book to beat off stiff competition from New York, Washington and St Louis. In April 1890, President Harrison approved an Act of Congress to provide for 'an international exhibit of arts, industries, manufactures, and the products of the soil, mine and sea, in the city of Chicago', and invited the 'nations of the world to take part'. In much the same way that London's Great Exhibition of 1851 had launched the emergent trend of consumerism, Chicago's World Fair would establish it as an irrevocable part of daily life.

This was the event Chicago had been waiting for – not least the property speculators who rushed to buy land. Harlow Higginbotham (the senior partner in charge of finance at Marshall Field) was appointed as President of the Fair, and Daniel Burnham was designated as overall Director of Works. They knew when the Fair was going to be – 1892 – and they soon decided where, selecting a vast 630-acre site on the South Side, covering Jackson Park and the Midway Plaisance. How it would all happen was less easily decided. A group of the country's leading architects convened to plan the buildings. Headed by Burnham, the group included Richard Morris Hunt (of Astor, Vanderbilt and Field house fame), Charles McKim of the hallowed New York partnership McKim, Mead & White, Frederick Law Olstead (who had laid out New York's Central Park), and Chicago's own celebrated Louis Sullivan. They apparently started to argue at their very first meeting, with the eastern group advocating classicism and Chicago's Louis Sullivan, modernism. Furthermore, it soon became clear that the plans laid down couldn't possibly be completed in time, and the public opening of the Fair was postponed to 1893.

There being a lot to do, Chicago's great and good set to work. First, Mayor Carter H. Harrison had to get re-elected. He had already served a straight four terms, so the city's residents knew what they were getting – Harrison was a hard-drinking, keen gambling man. Sure enough, when he won, albeit by a narrow margin, he announced he had 'laid down two hundred barrels of good Chicago whiskey that could kill at the distance of a mile' for official hospitality. In New York, Mrs Astor's arbiter of etiquette Ward McAllister was horrified, writing in *The World* 'that it is not quantity but quality that visiting New York society will care about'. Uneasy about the menus, not to mention the wines, McAllister advised the city to 'import a number of fine French chefs as a gentleman who has been accustomed to terrapin and pâté de foie gras would not care to dine on mutton and turnips'. His pronouncements on Chicago's seeming inability to organize a banquet caused a furore, with the local press calling him a 'head butler' and a 'New York flunky'. McAllister, not to be outdone, unleashed a further barrage of criticism: 'It takes nearly a lifetime to educate a man how to live. These Chicagoans should not pretend to rival the East in matters of refinement – their growth has been too rapid for them to acquire both wealth and culture.'

McAllister, who had originated the concept of Mrs Astor's famous 'Four Hundred' (in reality the number of people who could comfortably fit in her ballroom), was obsessed with decorum, dancing and décor. Convinced that the rich of Chicago couldn't dance a quadrille, he was particularly caustic about the design of the millionaires' mansions, where the ballroom was often relegated to the third floor and, worse, accessed by an elevator: 'In New York, the opinion is that the approach to the ballroom should be as artistically effective as the room itself. We don't go to dance by going up in an elevator.'

Chicago, proud of its meaty menus and its elevators, ignored most of his pontificating, but jibes about dancing touched a nerve. Help was on hand courtesy of Eugene A. Bournique's Dance Academy where Mr Bournique, more used to teaching children their first ballet steps, was kept busy teaching the intricacies of ballroom etiquette to their parents. The city echoed to the sound of construction. New hotels were built, existing ones redecorated; new restaurants opened and, as the city's gaming dens hastily planned an expansion of their floor space, demand for roulette wheels rocketed and a new factory had to be opened to cope with the orders.

Mrs Potter Palmer, as the city's leading lady, was appointed chairman of the Board of Lady Managers in charge of their own Women's Building. Even in the face of the growing influence of the women's movement, such a project was a radical step for America, and Mrs Palmer determined it would be noteworthy. The Lady Managers hired a female architect, Sophia Hayden, to create their pavilion, planning a series of rooms to show everything from cookery demonstrations to the latest in home technology, interior design, arts, crafts and even a model kindergarten. It was agreed that concerts in the auditorium would only feature the work of women composers and that exhibitions would display the achievements of women in the arts and sciences and in the professions. Last but not least, the pavilion would exhibit the very latest in fashion trends, together with exhibits of rare jewels and antiquities borrowed by Mrs Palmer from her wealthy, titled friends in Europe. Everything in fact that a woman could want or need – except cosmetics.

Not that entrepreneurs involved in the embryonic business of beauty didn't want to exhibit. Madame Yale, famous for her lectures on 'The Religion of Beauty, the Sin of Ugliness', was keen to promote her products. But Mrs Palmer and her committee were utterly determined that she should not. Rouge and lipstick were, said Mrs Palmer, 'not things we wish to dwell on or emphasize'. In banning Mrs Yale, Bertha Palmer was following the mores of the day, which determined that cosmetics were 'not respectable'. Ladies like Mrs Palmer took care of their skin with soap, water and a face-mask made with old-fashioned oatmeal. They may have tried Harriet Hubbard Ayer's exclusive 'Recamier' cream – Mrs Ayer herself being from a good Chicago family – but more often than not they were content with a greasy lanolin-based cream made up by the local pharmacist. Given Chicago's brutal winter weather, they would almost certainly have used lip salve (one excellent local recipe included hog-fat, a useful by-product of Chicago's stock yards), and eyebrows were plucked and waxed. Finally, a light dusting of fine powder would have been applied to avoid shine. Further than that, they would not go.

As a consequence, in smart stores like Marshall Field's, the toiletries department was of minor significance. It sold hand mirrors, brushes and combs, hair accessories, eau de cologne and a wide range of beautifully packaged scented soaps. Neither did Field's attempt to enter the business of hairdressing or offer beauty treatments such as manicures and massage, which were the fiefdom of small, individual beauty parlours. Field's held out against the onslaught of cosmetics for a long time, though others soon succumbed. As early as 1897, the

Sears catalogue offered its own line of cosmetics, including rouge, eyebrow pencils and face powder, while Harry Selfridge himself would famously go on to open England's first major cosmetics department in 1910.

With 25 million visitors expected to attend the Fair, Marshall Field astutely set a retail expansion plan in motion. Early in 1892 he began to buy buildings to the east of the store, commissioning Daniel Burnham to design a new nine-storey annexe, which had to be ready in eighteen months. Despite his awesome workload overseeing the erection of more than two hundred buildings for the Fair, Burnham managed to bring the new Field project in only two months over deadline, and by August 1893 it was open for business.

Harry Selfridge became minutely involved in planning the layout and fitting of this new space of more than 100,000 feet, which ultimately gave the store an overall total of nine acres. Under Burnham's expert tutelage, he received a master class in building, lighting and shop-fitting. Technical innovations included the installation of thirteen high-pressure hydraulic elevators and twelve separate entrances with revolving glass doors. Interior fixtures included lavish hand-carved mahogany counters trimmed in bronze and, in a welcome first for shoppers, a majestic suite of ladies' lavatories. There were now a hundred different departments at Marshall Field's, all of them dressed to the nines to welcome the international visitors who were touring the Fair and who, inevitably, were also drawn into the store.

For Selfridge, 1893 was a momentous year. In addition to the World Fair and the expansion of Field's, he and Rose had a baby daughter, Rosalie, born on 10 September – which explains why Rose was absent from most of the festivities connected with the Fair: when pregnant, ladies of the day never socialized in public.

Harry was among the welcoming committee that greeted the Duke of Veragua – a direct descendant of Christopher Columbus – and his Duchess when they arrived in Chicago in May for the opening celebrations. Despite his lofty titles, among them 'Admiral of the Ocean Sea', the Duke was a man of modest means who bred Arab horses at a stud farm outside Madrid. Flattered at being met by an escort of the United States Cavalry, and delighted by the lavish hospitality and media attention accorded him and his Duchess, the Duke began to overstay his welcome. Two weeks grew to three and then a month. The organizing committee, panicking at the cost of hosting the ducal couple, suggested it was time to leave. The Veraguas finally agreed to go, but not before the Duke had intimated that the same military escort that had met them on arrival should also see them off at the station. The organizing committee, with no remit to provide a second escort, were saved by an enterprising member who kitted out a team of amateur actors as hussars, mounting them on black horses and equipping them with swords. It did the trick nicely.

Running the Fair involved considerable diplomacy as tempers flared and egos exploded. The mighty Steinway Piano Company had refused to exhibit, so the committee banned its pianos from being used by any of the dozens of orchestras playing throughout the Fair. This didn't worry the young musician Scott Joplin, who was practising his new 'rag-time' tunes on a rickety upright in a local saloon, but it did alarm the great pianist Ignacy Paderewski who refused to play on anything but a Steinway. The impasse was broken when the Fair's musical director had the foresight to smuggle in a Steinway, resulting in such a row that the poor man was forced to resign.

The next Spanish grandee to sample Chicago hospitality was HRH the Infanta Eulalia – daughter of Queen Isabella II and a haughty young woman who was fond of remarking that 'in Spain there is Nobility – or nothing. We do not recognize the middle classes.' With the World Fair being targeted at exactly that group, her visit was destined to be tricky. Eulalia and her husband Prince Antoine arrived at the station in George Pullman's own private railway car – somewhat late having made an unscheduled stop in Pennsylvania, where Eulalia had sent out for a fresh supply of Spanish cigarettes. To the delight of Chicago's booming tobacco industry – and the distress of Bertha Palmer who loathed smoking – the Infanta puffed prodigiously, even enjoying a cigar after dinner. Her much-publicized habit prompted an enterprising local firm to box up Cuban cigars with her picture on the lid, unfortunately promoting her to 'Eulalia, Queen of Spain' in the process.

The Royal party was allocated a glorious suite at the Palmer House Hotel, stuffed full of antiques and tapestries to make them feel at home. Legend has it that the Infanta at first refused to meet Mrs Palmer on the grounds that she was merely 'the wife of my innkeeper'. What is certain is that wherever the Infanta went, she was always late. Keeping Spanish-style hours, she didn't arrive at the gala reception held at the Palmers' home in her honour until 10.15 p.m. Once there, however, she was invited to take up position on a velvet throne set on rugs impregnated with rare perfumes where she held court until the small hours, while John Sousa's band kept the party entertained.

Chicago's South Side had blossomed into a glorious mass of pearly-white grandeur, shimmering by the lake like Camelot, with the gilded domes of its 'Court of Honour' (as the classically styled principal building was called) twinkling in the sunlight. The team of artists and architects who had created this model 'White City' as an awesome show of corporate power and consumerism allowed themselves to be described as 'the greatest meeting of minds since the Renaissance'. In reality, apart from the central, anchor buildings in stone, the whole was mainly done by smoke and mirrors. Most of the buildings were temporary edifices made from a mixture of plaster, cement and jute fibre, all painted white. Critics called them 'decorated sheds' but even the sternest opponent couldn't fail to be secretly impressed. Thousands of daily visitors travelled on the newly built South Side 'L', an elevated railroad that dropped them off at the Jackson Park Terminal where they could walk through Louis Sullivan's monochrome, futuristic Transportation Building before touring the Fair on its own elevated electric railway.

An off-site 'amusement area' in the Midway Plaisance, segregated from the exhibition halls but an integral part of the concept, offered round-the-clock excitement. The most thrilling was a ride on the 'Giant Wheel' built by the brilliant young design engineer George

Ferris. The Fair's organizing committee had long wanted something to 'top' the Eiffel Tower, which had dominated the 1889 Paris International Exposition. After months of indecisive bickering, they eventually settled on the Ferris concept with the proviso that George Ferris should fund not only the plans and specifications (which alone cost him $25,000) but also the construction costs. Ferris and his team worked round the clock through the severe Chicago winter. When they had finished, his triumphant wheel towered majestically to a height of 266 feet, giving the passengers who paid 50 cents to ride in one of its 36 carriages – each big enough to hold 40 people – a view of three different States from the windows. During the nineteen weeks the Ferris wheel operated, it carried nearly one and a half million people and was the greatest single attraction at the Fair. Tragically, the strain of raising the cash and the stress of building the wheel exhausted Ferris. He died destitute and alone in a Pittsburgh hospital just three years after his prototype wheel had astounded the world.

Other than the Ferris wheel, the biggest draws at the Midway Plaisance were Buffalo Bill Cody and his 'Wild West Show', and Fahreda Mahzar, an exotic dancer who called herself 'Little Egypt' and who performed her signature belly dance – the 'hootchy-kootchy' – wearing layers of transparent chiffon which, as one eager reporter noted, 'showed every muscle in her body rippling at the same time'. 'Little Egypt' wasn't the only one flexing her muscles. Assigned to tour Europe to procure military bands to play at the fair, Florenz Ziegfeld Jr, showing his potential for showmanship, had brought back the acclaimed German strongman Eugen Sandow, who subsequently became the father of modern-day body building. Flo put him under a management contract and masterminded his performance at the Fair. Sandow started his act lying in a black velvet-lined box, his body dusted in white powder, and then slowly rose from it like a muscled classical God, dressed in little more than a leopard-skin loincloth. Some women were so overcome at the sight that they fainted – even Bertha Palmer was persuaded to 'touch' Sandow's rock-hard muscles, pronouncing them 'very impressive'.

During the six months of the Fair, there wasn't a visiting VIP who didn't make their way downtown to Marshall Field, where Harry Selfridge personally conducted them around the store. Field himself was usually nowhere to be seen when these celebrity visits were made, finding them as distasteful as he did talking to the press. Field neither liked nor trusted journalists, whereas Harry instinctively understood the power of publicity, giving them all the help he could. Harry was now being described in the newspapers as the 'genial personality in charge of the retail division of Marshall Field', and his job there fitted him like a second skin.

As the Fair drew to a close, visitors could reflect on what they had seen. First and foremost, they had been exposed to the wonders of electricity, in itself an icon of technological advance. They had drunk the world's first carbonated drinks, eaten the world's first hamburgers, and admired the world's largest cheese – which weighed in at thirteen tons. Visitors had sent picture postcards to friends using the world's first commemorative stamps, enjoyed cookery demonstrations involving new products such as Quaker Oats and Aunt Jemima's Pancake Mix, and fallen in love with the bicycle. Some had heard Dvorak's 'New World Symphony' which he composed for the Fair, while others had seen Anschutz's 'electro-tachyscope' project the world's first moving images. Mayor Harrison, receiving the plaudits of his colleagues on Mayor's Day, 28 October, must have felt justifiably proud, but the ebullient Mayor didn't live long enough to enjoy the plaudits. He was assassinated that night by Eugene Prendergast, who in his defence subsequently pleaded insanity. Prendergast lost his case and was executed.

The World Fair had a profound impact on Harry Selfridge who, having witnessed at first hand how to entertain a crowd, later became devoted to showing all manner of technical innovations to a capti-vated audience in London. The Fair itself, quite apart from being the precursor of global theme parks from Coney Island to Disney World, also so enchanted the young writer L. Frank Baum that he turned its 'White City' into his 'Emerald City' of Oz.

The World Fair was symptomatic of changes taking place everywhere in the western world, particularly in women's lives. The World's Congress of Representative Women had met in Chicago during the Fair, where over 150,000 women flocked to listen to Elizabeth Cady Stanton and Lucy Stone speak. Fresh ideas poured forth from a huge number of newly successful women's magazines. Women in Chicago now travelled alone on the cable street cars and elevated trains. There were changes too in fashion. Women would have to wait another decade to abandon their corsets, but there was an important shift in the shape and weight of clothes as more and more women took to wearing two-pieces and blouses.

The 'jacket-and-skirt' combination had first been seen in America during the Civil War. Women in the intellectual and professional classes had continued to wear it, calling it their 'emancipation suit'. Dress reformers also adopted front-buttoning soft underwear as pioneered in fine knit by Dr Jaeger and in cotton by Dr Kellogg. The leisured classes and newly rich, however, had relentlessly clung to the formality of the back bustle both by day and by night, until the 'two-piece' with its faintly military cut and gored skirt was given a huge boost when it was adopted by the Prince of Wales's beautiful wife, Princess Alexandra, whose every move in fashion was eagerly watched in America. For once the trend hadn't originated from Worth. It was the British tailoring genius Charles Poynter of Redfern who made the suits for the Princess – in tweed for shooting parties and in navy blue and white grosgrain for yachting. The waist was still cinched, but the bustle had disappeared, and the sleeves were puffed from shoulder to elbow and then narrowed from elbow to wrist.

The trend for what the stores referred to as 'tailor-mades', along with the ornate, high-necked blouses that went with them, triggered the mass production of much better-quality ready-to-wear. Marshall Field's still had its own in-house workrooms for hand-made clothes, but bulk stock, for them as for other stores, was now sourced from the clothing factories and sweat shops of New York and Chicago.

America's 'new woman', as the media styled her, energetically took to sport, particularly tennis, which in itself created a fashion trend. Players wore softer skirts, with a plainer 'shirt-waist' blouse and an unbuttoned cotton-drill jacket. Nothing typified this image more than the drawings of the graphic artist Charles Dana Gibson. The 'Gibson Girl' was officially launched in 1890 and for the next twenty-five years she came to represent the ideal female form in the United States. The tall, rangy and patrician young woman styled by Gibson, with her casually up-swept hair and *sportif* clothes, had a huge impact on fashion. Women wanted to look, dress and live their lives like her.

Women also took enthusiastically to dance as an acceptable form of exercise, in particular adopting the 'stretch and body poses' movement programme originally pioneered by the Frenchman François Delsarte, which became a huge craze in America. Not that 'doing Delsarte' meant breaking a sweat, it was more about grace and control. His system was the precursor of contemporary dance as pioneered by Loie Fuller and her disciple Isadora Duncan, who naturally chose Chicago – acclaimed as the most progressive city in America – to launch her professional career in 1895. When she auditioned at Chicago's leading variety house, the Masonic Temple Roof Garden, Isadora so impressed its manager Charles Fair that he booked her on the spot. Knowing his audience, however, the cigar-chomping Mr Fair doubted that her dance programme would hold them. 'You might do the Greek thing first,' he suggested, 'then change to something with petticoats and frills so you can do kicks.' With only her 'Grecian' shift in her luggage – and no money for shopping – Fair sent Isadora to see his friend Selfridge.

Selfridge was enchanted with Isadora, overseeing her selection of red gingham, white organdie and lace ruffles for her outfit. Billed as 'the California Faun', Isadora was a sensation, and, having dressed her, Selfridge was in the audience to watch. Some people later said he undressed her too – she was after all a believer in free love, and Harry was an attractive man, with a tendre for dancers and a wife who was often to be found 90 miles away, supervising the construction of their imposing mock-Tudor house on the shores of Lake Geneva. Whatever the case, Isadora Duncan and Harry Selfridge remained friends until she died.

Field himself continued to add to his property portfolio, one particular acquisition having a certain poignancy. In 1898, Levi Leiter's only son Joe, who so far had excelled himself solely in playing high-stakes poker, decided to gamble on making his own fortune by attempting to corner the world's wheat market, buying all he could on margin. When the Chicago meat baron P. D. Armour needed 9 million bushels in a hurry he contacted young Leiter, who refused to sell. Armour wasn't going to be pushed around by 'an uppity kid'. He sent a fleet of ice-breaking tugs over the frozen lake north to Duluth, buying wheat for himself and an extra 9 million bushels, which he poured into the market. Young Joe Leiter's margins were called in and he ended up owing $10 million. With his son facing certain bankruptcy and possibly prison, Levi Leiter had to liquidate assets fast, among them a valuable parcel of land on the corner of State Street, housing the site of department store Schlesinger & Mayer, for which Field paid his ex-partner $2,135,000.

The Leiters' financial disaster had a dramatic impact in London, where Leiter's daughter Mary, now Lady Curzon, was putting together the sumptuous wardrobe required for her forthcoming position as Vicereine of India. It wasn't only her clothes and jewels that were needed. George Curzon required an impressive wardrobe of uniforms, and the couple were also expected to pay the outgoing Viceroy for his wine cellar, horses, carriages and silver plate. Curzon, who had little money of his own, had always assumed his rich father-in-law would be able to provide everything necessary. All he got from Levi Leiter was £3,000 and a new tiara for Mary, leaving him in the embarrassing position of having to request an advance on his salary.

Back in Chicago, by 1900, 14 million tons of cargo were passing through the port. Over 500 miles of street-car tracks – called 'street railroads' – threaded their way through the city, and the elevated railroad was packed every day. Automobiles were also slowly beginning to make an appearance, though to visitors it must have seemed as if everyone was riding a bicycle as the new craze for cycling swept the nation. Happily for women cyclists their skirts didn't sweep the ground. When Lillian Russell took to cycling – on a custom-made Tiffany gold-plated machine, with mother-of-pearl handlebars and her initials worked in diamonds on the wheels – she wore a cream leg-of-mutton sleeved cycling suit with the skirt shortened by three inches, which set an unstoppable fashion trend.

Fashion also had a huge impact on Marshall Field. Since the World Fair, Field's had imported over $3 million worth of goods annually from around the world. By 1900 the retail division alone turned over an astonishing $12.5 million. With the store severely short of space, that year Field acquired the rest of the buildings in the block, including the Central Music Hall where Harry and Rose had married, enabling him to demolish the building on the original site and replace it with an enormous twelve-storey structure, retaining only the comparatively new annex. Once more Daniel Burnham and his team swung into action, and once more Harry Selfridge was flying with excitement. At every stage of the development he booked advertisements to inform shoppers about progress, at the same time reassuring them that Field's was 'committed to fair prices and good value'. Selfridge was busier than ever at work, and Rose was busy at home with their two daughters – Rosalie's sister Violette was born in 1897 – and their son, Gordon, who was born three years later. Their fourth child, another daughter called Beatrice, born in 1901, would complete their family.

Advertising had become a major tool in the promotion of retail. The industry with which Selfridge had experimented in the early days was now virtually unrecognizable. Nationally, the biggest spenders were the food companies and the tobacco industry, but businesses producing toiletries and soft drinks were not far behind. By 1899, eighty companies were making, or beginning to make, automobiles, and advertising agencies were keenly anticipating the day when cars would appear on the pages of influential magazines. In the meantime, they had to make do with the bicycle, and for the first time ever women were shown outside the home in a non-domestic setting riding their bicycles.

Advertisements for Marshall Field were, like most retail pages, booked locally rather than nationally, with newspapers being the biggest beneficiary. Indeed, the growth of retail advertising paralleled the growth of the big city newspapers, which created arts, event and fashion features by way of reciprocal editorial. Following company policy, Marshall Field pages never appeared on Sunday, this being still a day devoted to family, friends and Church.

The first phase of the six-year building programme opened in 1902. Marshall Field's was a monument to new technology with over 50 elevators, 15,000 fire-sprinklers, and a cold storage vault with room for 20,000 fur coats. There was a library, a first-aid room with a trained nurse, an information bureau, a concierge service to book theatre tickets and hotel rooms, a crèche where mothers could leave their children in the care of trained nannies, and seven restaurants. Harry Selfridge had supervised every inch of the project from the miles of carpets to the hundreds of mirrors. He hadn't forgotten the staff either. Now numbering 7,000, they had a special canteen, recreation rooms, locker rooms, a gymnasium and their own library. He instigated a three-day training system whereby new salespeople were given an intensive course in manners and in how to make the customer feel at home.

John Wanamaker, the famously enlightened Philadelphia retailer – regarded as the originator of ethical advertising – who then owned America's largest emporium, came to visit, and even he was impressed. In the first three days of business, more than 150,000 people came through the doors and were given special celebration souvenirs costing over £10,000. Marshall Field's old mentor Potter Palmer wasn't there to share his triumph. Palmer had died that year, leaving an estate worth over $8 million to his wife Bertha, even setting aside a sum for her next husband 'because he'll need it'. In the event, Bertha remained a wealthy widow. Field was dumbstruck when he heard that

Palmer's fortune had passed directly to his wife, bypassing their son. 'What on earth does she need with all that money?' he asked. 'One million dollars is quite enough for any woman.'

Field was increasingly isolated. His estranged wife was dead. His brother Henry was dead. Many of his friends were dead. He never entertained in his vast, empty house. His children and grandchildren lived in England. He eschewed the poker circle at his club – gambling, in his opinion, was a weakness. His only activity was work – and playing the occasional round of golf. Peter Funk, a colleague who had the courage to speak his mind, said to him: 'Marshall, you have no home, no family, no happiness, nothing but money.'

Harry Selfridge had played a huge part in masterminding the development of the retail division and in helping to create Marshall Field's fortune, but despite his lavish lifestyle, he was still merely a salaried man. When the business was incorporated as a private limited company in 1901, Field allocated 6,000 shares to Harry, but John Shedd got more, which irked him.

In the winter of 1903, with the retail division's annual turnover now at $17 million, profits a shade under $1.5 million and the next phase of development being planned, Selfridge lobbied Marshall Field for more. It wasn't just about money. He craved recognition. Gambling on the fact that Field would give him what he wanted (including the renaming of the business as 'Marshall Field & Selfridge') he made his bid – and lost.

Field turned him down, and with that, Harry Selfridge made plans to leave.

~

GOING IT ALONE

'Our deeds determine us, as much as we determine our deeds.'
George Eliot

In the early 1930s, Harry Gordon Selfridge had his portrait painted by Sir William Orpen RA. The artist captured his subject looking contemplative and dignified, pen in hand, studying what might perhaps have been a financial statement. Among the large collection of treasured family memorabilia packed away into trunks and boxes at the home of Simon Wheaton Smith, Harry Selfridge's great-grandson, is that same portrait turned into a jigsaw puzzle. Nothing could be more apt in trying to fathom Harry Selfridge. The man was puzzling indeed.

In 1903, he was living in considerable comfort with his wife and family in their imposing house at 117 Lake Shore Drive, and at their even larger weekend home on Lake Geneva. He was a respected member of the business community, running what was virtually his own fiefdom at Marshall Field where he was doing a job he loved and receiving ever-increasing profits by dint of his shareholding. Selfridge had great faith, indeed an almost messianic belief, in what *he* thought was the right way forward commercially. But he forgot one salient fact. It wasn't his business.

Nancy Koehn of Harvard Business School, one of the world's leading authorities on entrepreneurial history, has made an extensive study of Marshall Field & Co. 'Selfridge,' she says, 'deserves a lot of credit for bringing Field along, and helping him understand new developments in retailing.' On the topic of Harry's complex personality, Professor Koehn says: 'He was pushy, exuberant, with panache and vision.' However, she adds that what killed the partnership was Harry's overweening ambition. 'Field would have looked at his extravagances with a pursing of the lips – everything from the size of his office to the scale of his lifestyle – all this from a man with no visible investments, who lived solely off the business.'

Chief among Harry's ambitions had always been that Marshall Field should expand beyond Chicago. Disillusioned by Field's refusal to open in New York, Selfridge set his sights even higher. Having made several buying trips to England, and being increasingly enamoured with the business opportunities he saw there, he lobbied Field to open a branch in London. Marshall Field himself knew England well. Indeed, his daughter Ethel (recently divorced and now married to naval officer David Beatty) lived there, as did his son Marshall II. Visiting them was one thing, opening an overseas business quite another.

Harry also wanted to adjust the system whereby the store buyers had first and foremost to source from the wholesale division, to whom they paid a 6 per cent levy on all goods. In the early days, there had been advantages in sourcing bulk goods – especially household linen, hosiery and other basics – from the division. It was quick, easy and, even with the levy, cost-effective. But fashion and accessories were a different matter. Selfridge had long felt that the wholesale offerings were simply too conservative, too 'safe', and not in keeping with the needs of Chicago's increasingly sophisticated shoppers. He wanted the store's retail buyers to have a free hand in where – and from whom – they ordered their stock. The idea was anathema to Marshall Field and, unsurprisingly, won little support from John Shedd, the altogether calmer, more conservative favourite of Field, who ran the wholesale department.

Finally, there was the question of a change in name for the store. Field was growing old and his son played no part in the business, while Selfridge had poured every ounce of energy he had into the store. His achievements had been spectacular – in his own mind he *was* part of the store – and he wanted his name over the door.

There were few colleagues Harry Selfridge could talk to. He wasn't a man who shared his intimate fears and feelings easily. The hierarchical structure at Marshall Field was dominated by the original, elderly partners who were Field men to the core, and he was at odds with his one potential ally, John Shedd. There was, however, one person who was always ready to listen and offer shrewd advice. His best and most loyal friend was his mother. To outsiders, Madam Selfridge seemed to be merely gentle, dignified and kindly. To those who knew her better, however, she was something else entirely. The costume designer and artist Grace Lovat Fraser, who later became close to the Selfridge family in London, wrote: 'Madam Selfridge was white-haired and tiny. Always dressed in black with lots of exquisite lace, she seemed the embodiment of a classic sweet old lady. But her appearance was misleading, for though she looked frail she was strong and hardy, had a keen brain and was an excellent business woman. For all her deceptive fragility, she could be unobtrusively formidable and was a very important influence in her son's career.'

Harry's mother's support was crucial. No doubt buoyed by her belief that he should strike out on his own, when Harry heard that the nearby store being built for Schlesinger & Mayer was discreetly on the market, he made a spontaneous decision to raise the funds and buy it himself. The formal records of the transaction have vanished. Some say he raised enough money from bankers to buy the freehold for $5 million. That seems unlikely given that Marshall Field himself was the freeholder. Field rarely, if ever, sold investment property, and he certainly wouldn't have sold it to Harry Selfridge. Others infer that Selfridge simply took over the lease, which at the time was owned by David Mayer and the retail magnate Henry Siegel, who had bought out Leopold Schlesinger a year or so earlier.

What is certain is that Harry's new store was, and remains today, a beautiful building. Designed by the pioneering commercial architect Louis Sullivan – who numbered Frank Lloyd Wright among his staff

– in collaboration with the engineer Dankmar Adler, the twelve-storey, terracotta-clad corner site, with its elaborate ironwork ornamentation on the lower façade, had taken five years to complete. By the time it was finished, Adler had died, Sullivan's practice was in decline and Mayer was broke.

In the spring of 1904, as building work neared completion, Henry Siegel must have been only too pleased to consign the lease. For Selfridge, it was a huge step. He was risking everything on a single throw, but for a man with a gambler's soul, who lived and worked in the then capital city of gambling, it was worth it. Selfridge was now faced with the task of stocking and staffing his own store, as well as finding tenants for the upper floors. He also had to explain his decision to Marshall Field. The atmosphere in Field's office that day must have been icy. Having admitted that he was leaving, and that he had bought Schlesinger & Mayer, Selfridge offered to stay and train his replacement. Field's chilly reply to the man who had worked for him for twenty-five years was: 'No, Mr Selfridge, you can leave tomorrow if it suits you.' With that, Harry cleared his desk.

When the paperwork involved in his settlement from Marshall Field was completed, Harry Selfridge had liquid assets of well over a million dollars as well as ownership of two substantial houses. His plans made news, but neither he nor Field gave much away about what had happened. Interviewed by the media, Selfridge merely talked about 'his great desire to become head of a business of my own', saying he was 'absolutely confident of success' and that it was 'time to take the step as he had just turned 40' – shaving eight years off his age. Marshall Field remained tight-lipped when journalists questioned him about the loss of his star executive. Indeed, he rarely talked about it even to his own colleagues, other than saying to John Shedd, 'We'll have to get another office boy.' Selfridge was more gracious. Field had been a huge part of his life, the dominant albeit distant father-figure he had craved to please. He never forgot him. When he opened Selfridge's in London, a portrait of Marshall Field took pride of place in his office.

With a fanfare of brass-band music and flags flying, Harry G. Selfridge & Co., Chicago, opened its doors on 13 June 1904. It was an auspicious time to be opening a new business. Affluent consumers had taken to the road in their new automobiles and were driving them out to newly opened country clubs where they eagerly took up the fashionable game of golf: both hobbies necessitated extensive, not to mention expensive, specialist wardrobes. Automobiles had hit the city like a whirlwind. In 1900 there had only been 100 permits issued for motor vehicles, but by the time Harry Selfridge opened his store, there were nearly 1,500 registered drivers in Chicago. The City Council, perturbed by the trend for 'scorching', as driving fast was called, set a speed limit of ten miles per hour and required drivers to have 'full use of arms and legs and be free of a drug habit'. In a city where rich and poor alike enjoyed their drink, no mention was made of alcohol.

Selfridge had long specialized in store windows that presented a themed story. Now his beautifully dressed opening displays paid homage to the latest fashion in ladies' and gentlemen's 'motoring clothes'. Female mannequins were dressed like the subjects of Sir William Nicholson's exquisite painting *La Belle Chauffeuse*, in duster coats, huge gauntlet gloves and big hats tied under the chin with a chiffon stole, while the male mannequins were shown in 'go faster' goggles and belted tweed driving jackets. Picnic hampers and leather-strapped luggage completed the picture.

Selfridge must have gone through a great deal of anguish in the run-up to the opening. It would have been hard for him travelling to work each morning, walking into his own elegant building, but wishing it was the bigger one down the road. Twenty-five years at Field's were not easily forgotten. Bonds had been forged which could not easily be broken. He later explained his emotions during those troubled times to a journalist from the *Saturday Evening Post*: 'I was extremely miserable competing with my own people – the people with whom I had spent so many happy and gloriously exciting years. I tried to beat down the feeling, but my unhappiness increased.'

Selfridge tried everything he could to energize his new staff but they simply couldn't meet his impossibly high standards. 'There's no one here who knows *how* to do it,' he told his wife sadly, perhaps only now realizing how skilful the vast back-room team had been at Marshall Field.

After being forced to leave so abruptly – no presentation, no gifts, no party, no recognition *at all* for what he had done over twenty-five years – Selfridge became a man dispossessed. Always the eternal optimist, now he became depressed. Suddenly, life at Harrose Hall, his country house on Lake Geneva, where he could tend his green-houses full of rare orchids took on a new allure. Just three months after starting his new business, he made a spontaneous decision to sell up and retire. He called his ex-colleague John Shedd for help and advice. Shedd came up with the reputable retailers Carson, Pirie & Scott, who were anxious to relocate, and arranged a meeting between Sam Pirie and Harry Selfridge. The canny Mr Pirie struck a hard bargain, offering Selfridge – who had wanted a $250,000 premium over and above the original cost of his lease – $150,000 plus his supplier liabilities. Desperate to get out, Harry accepted.

Not unsurprisingly, Harry found retirement dull. He pottered around the grounds at Harrose Hall, tending his roses and orchids, and spending time with his young family. But it wasn't enough. He bought himself a steam yacht which apparently rarely left its moorings, and attempted to take up golf, a game which he played abysmally badly. His friends urged him to take up public office, which in Chicago would have been a challenge in itself. The idea didn't appeal. 'No politics for me,' he said, 'it's too much like being put in the pillory.' He would probably have agreed with a reporter from the London *Daily Mail* who, after visiting the city, had written: 'Chicago presents more splendid attractions and more hideous repulsions than any city I know. Other places hide their dark side out of sight – Chicago treasures it to the heart of the business quarter and gives it a veneer.' He couldn't have put it better himself. Chicago's tycoons were ruthless. Harry Selfridge was never really part of their world.

Despite being a manager *par excellence*, to most of them he would always remain 'Field's ex-office boy'.

Selfridge had a cavalier attitude towards money. He lived extravagantly, spent prodigiously on those he loved and had a belief that all would always be well – regardless of what he owed. In later years, when his personal overdraft had reached monumental proportions, one of his bankers in London remarked, 'Mr Selfridge seems to enjoy the sensation of debt.' In Chicago, with his family and perhaps his age in mind, he took out a high-level life insurance policy. He also tried his hand at investments. Invited to put money into the White Rock Soda Company – carbonated drinks being all the rage – he turned the offer down as being too closely associated with diluting whiskey. However, he did decide to invest in a gold mine. In the winter of 1904, he became President of the Sullivan Creek Mining and Milling Company, providing the finance to drill for gold at the Calico mine in Tuolumne County, California.

It all started off rather well. The Chicago firm of Allis-Chalmers – then the world's largest manufacturer of mining equipment – was on board advising Selfridge as to what equipment would be needed, and the mining expert William Chalmers seemed impressed with the initial geological data from what was a rich gold area. Drilling tests and surveys went on throughout the spring of 1905, with Selfridge paying all the costs.

That summer the Selfridge family left to spend a season on the French Riviera. There, letters arrived from America requesting more money for equipment and wages. Then came the news that Selfridge had longed to hear. They had found gold at 190 feet – enough to send for assay, and enough to convince Selfridge that he was about to become very rich. Late in August, he settled his family at the Ritz in Paris, while he went to London on business. He had a meeting to attend.

At the age of 71, Marshall Field suddenly had a spring in his step and a smile on his face. He'd put a smile on the face of Europe's most important jeweller's too as he shopped for a sumptuous collection of diamonds and pearls – presents for his new bride, Delia Caton. Mr and Mrs Arthur Caton were friends of Marshall Field who, it was always said, had long held a *tendre* for his neighbour's attractive, elegant wife. When Arthur died in 1904, Field seized the moment and proposed to Delia. They sailed to England in July 1905 and were married on 5 September at St Margaret's, Westminster. Selfridge's trip to London was timed precisely so he could visit Field – and not just to congratulate him on his new marriage.

Two earlier biographies of Selfridge have claimed that he went to see his old boss with an audacious offer to take over the Chicago store. Nancy Koehn flatly rejects the idea: 'Selfridge could never have raised that amount of money, and even if he could, Field would never have sold.' However, the talk at the time was that Harry Selfridge had the support of the mighty J. P. Morgan himself in his planned acquisition, and that Field was sufficiently intrigued to agree to 'look at' his proposals. Whether Selfridge was looking at London in his own right, as he later claimed, or whether he was proposing an outpost of Marshall Field there, we'll never know. But one way or the other, any hopes of doing business with Mr Field were about to be destroyed.

The newly-wed Fields returned to Chicago early in October that year, taking with them Marshall's son, his wife Albertine and their young family. Also en route back to America were the Selfridge family. By the time they got home on 10 October, news had arrived that the gold mine was barren. What little gold there was would be too expensive to excavate. By the time the company was wound up, Selfridge had lost $60,000 or, in today's money, just under $1,200,000.

In November, tragedy of a far greater kind struck the Field household when Field's troubled son died in hospital from a gunshot wound to the stomach. Not unnaturally, the family claimed one of his guns had been discharged accidentally. Others said he had committed suicide, while the talk of the town was that he had been shot by one of the girls at the city's most notorious brothel, the Everleigh Club. Owned by two genteel Kentucky sisters, Minna and Ada Everleigh, the brothel was the ultimate in luxury. The sisters had been just 21 and 23 when they opened their 'house', dedicated to servicing the desires of Chicago's wealthy men. Ada did the hiring. 'I talk with each applicant myself,' she said proudly in the promotional brochure she circulated. 'Girls must have worked somewhere before coming here – we do not take amateurs.' Indeed they didn't. The Everleigh Club girls were not merely beauties in ball gowns. They were expertly trained in the art of flattery, good conversation and even better sex, and several of them married extremely well. The Club had Silver and Copper Rooms for the mining kings, and the Gold Room was refurbished each year with real gold leaf. An ensemble of violin, cello, piano and, occasionally, a harp provided soothing music. The kitchen was run by superb chefs, and the cellar stocked with the finest champagne – Minna didn't serve red wine, reasoning it made the customers sleepy. On Christmas Eve, the sisters would give a special party exclusively for the 'gentlemen of the press'.

The Everleigh Club of course also offered gambling, and the stakes were high. Minna, who was convinced men preferred gambling to girls, placed a thirty-minute limit on roulette and dice. The club was never raided – the sisters paid the police well for their protection – and its opulent tranquillity was rarely shattered, except on one memorable occasion, when the rabidly anti-smoking campaigner Lucy Page Gaston stormed in yelling, 'Minna, you can stop your girls from going straight to the devil – you must stop them smoking cigarettes.'

Although father and son had never been close, Field was grief-stricken. He carried on working – supervising the next phase of the momentous rebuilding programme at the store – and playing his weekly round of golf. On New Year's Day 1906, though it was bitterly cold, he and three friends played eighteen holes, traipsing knee-deep through the snow in search of their special red golf balls. By the next day he had developed a sore throat but insisted on travelling to New York with his wife and valet. By the end of the week he had contracted severe pneumonia from which he never recovered, dying in his suite at the Holland House Hotel.

Field had planned his will very carefully. Determined there would be no squandering of his hard-earned fortune, he had set up complex trusts. On the death of the immediate beneficiaries, the capital would revert to the Field estate, and his grandchildren would not receive the bulk of their money until they were 50. His daughter Ethel meanwhile became seriously rich, enabling her to spring to her naval husband's defence when he was threatened with disciplinary action following the straining of his ship's engines. 'What, court martial my David? I'll buy them a new ship!' she exclaimed. In the event, the Navy relented, but Ethel's $6 million inheritance did buy her husband a Scottish grouse moor, a hunting lodge in Leicestershire, a steam yacht and a mansion in London. Four years later, at the age of 39, David Beatty became the youngest admiral in the Royal Navy since Horatio Nelson.

Harry Selfridge mourned Marshall Field deeply. Whatever low points their strained relationship had reached, Field had been Selfridge's mentor. His death marked the end of the great era at Marshall Field. Potter Palmer was dead. Levi Leiter was dead (leaving Mary Curzon a very rich woman). As specified in Field's will, John Shedd became President of the store, continuing with the expansion plans laid down by the founder. For Harry Selfridge, at the age of 50, the time had come to consider his future.

~

BUILDING THE DREAM

'L'Angleterre est une nation de boutiquiers.'
Napoleon Bonaparte

In 1906, no one meeting Harry Selfridge for the first time would have dreamt he was 50. He looked a decade younger, talked with endless enthusiasm and exhausted people half his age with his boundless energy. Not that he exercised to keep fit. 'Thinking is enough physical exercise for me,' he used to say. When he was pondering some major – or even minor – decision, he would sit in his swivel chair, turn it towards the window, lock his hands behind his head, and stare into the distance. No one ever dared interrupt him. When he'd decided on the outcome, he'd swing round quickly and say, 'Right, here's what we'll do, let's get on with it.' And that was that. Once he'd made up his mind, he never changed it.

Craving a new challenge, and encouraged by his close friend Walter Cottingham, of the Sherwin-Williams Paint Company (an enterprising firm whose motto was 'Cover the Earth'), Selfridge made up his mind to move to London and open his dream store. The awesome Selfridge energy swung into operation. Letters were written, cablegrams sent, telephone calls made to friends and acquaintances, meetings arranged. He was back at work and loving it. As far as his family were concerned, if he was happy, they were happy. They were probably relieved to see him so energized, and didn't mind at all when

he took off for London, staying first at the Savoy Hotel and thereafter renting an elegant furnished apartment in Whitehall Court,
an imposing mansion block with a spectacular view over St James's
Park.

One of the essential requirements for gracious living in Edwardian
London being live-in servants, a Scottish couple, Mr and Mrs Fraser,
moved in during March that year, Mrs Fraser as housekeeper and
Mr Fraser first as valet and later butler. The Frasers were to be part
of the fabric of Selfridge family life for the next two decades. Fraser
fitted the stereotype of the British butler perfectly. Depending on
his mood, his manner would swing between the unctuous and the
supercilious: a family friend described him as 'a cross between Disraeli
and Micawber'. In 1921, when the Selfridge family had just moved
into the palatial splendour of Lansdowne House, Fraser answered
the bell and found a distinguished elderly gentleman on the doorstep
proffering a flat box. The visitor was Monsieur Pierre Cambon, the
ex-French Ambassador to the Court of St James, who on his return
visits to London always called first at his old friend Lord Lansdowne's
house, bringing with him a gift of a very ripe Brie. Confronted by a
strange servant, Monsieur Cambon asked if Lord Lansdowne was at
home. 'I've never heard of him,' said Fraser, suspiciously sniffing at
the parcel, 'and he certainly doesn't live here.' Monsieur Cambon –
and presumably his cheese – beat a hasty and confused retreat.

From the moment he arrived in London, Selfridge was determined
not to be thought of as a 'flash Yankee', a type viewed with grave
suspicion by London's business community, who were still reeling
from the dubious antics of the transport tycoon Charles Tyson Yerkes,
known to have been a contemporary of Selfridge in Chicago.

Backed by American money, Yerkes had arrived in London in
1900, aiming to feather his nest by developing the city's underground
railway system. Having manipulated his way into gaining control of
the Metropolitan District Railway, Yerkes audaciously mounted a
'rescue' bid for the half-completed Bakerloo line. The Bakerloo had
been left stranded when its original founder had committed suicide

by swallowing cyanide following his conviction for fraud. Yerkes (the inspiration for Theodore Dreiser's trilogy on corrupt financiers) subsequently added the Charing Cross, the Euston & Hampstead and the Great Northern, Piccadilly and Brompton Railways to his portfolio, as well as financing the building of the Lots Road power station to supply the burgeoning electric lines. Discovered to have been falsifying the accounts – his speciality being to pay massive management charges into his private bank account – Yerkes fled to New York, where he died in 1905. He left behind him a network of deep tunnels yet to be completed and, in many circles, a deep-rooted mistrust of American methods of business. It was all close enough for Selfridge to be alarmed at being thought of as anything less than punctilious in his business dealings.

Anxious for the business of retailing to be taken seriously, and partially as his own armour against a potentially hostile environment, Selfridge adopted a formal style, dressing as though he was a merchant banker rather than merely a merchant. He didn't retreat into frock coats, but the pearl-grey, braided morning coats he had favoured in Chicago were now toned down to darker shades of charcoal and black, worn with either striped or plain trousers. He remained faithful to his signature high-cut stiff collars and added a classic white 'slip' to frame his waistcoat, and in the evening he was immaculately kitted out in white tie and tails. There was always a sense of formality about his clothes – no one could ever remember seeing him dressed in anything even remotely casual.

Knowing what he wanted to do was all very well. Knowing where to do it was the next challenge. His criteria were space and easy access. Bond Street as a location was fleetingly considered and then rejected as too narrow to suit his craving for scale. Regent Street was dismissed due to restrictions on size imposed by the Crown Estates. He seriously considered the Strand, finding a site that appealed, but negotiations over a lease apparently collapsed. Being a man obsessed with beautiful buildings, the allies he found to search for the ideal site were all acquaintances involved in building and architecture. Among them was the young architect Delissa Joseph, who not only designed stations for the Underground Electric Railway Company but who also had a friend called Samuel Waring – who was interested in meeting Harry Selfridge.

By 1906, Samuel Waring was not only Chairman of the leading furniture manufacturer and retail business, Waring & Gillow, but also a director of a specialist building firm called Waring & White, a business run in association with the noted American construction engineer, James G. White. For Harry Selfridge, who needed an investment partner, Waring offered an irresistible combination of technical expertise and much-needed cash. Waring & White, under the skilful direction of the architects Charles Mewes and Arthur Davis, had just completed construction of the Ritz Hotel, London's first steel-framed building. Selfridge, like Waring, was a guest at the hotel's splendid opening-night dinner, where no doubt they discussed their plans to shake up London's retail establishment. The two men, both spontaneous, super-charged, insomniac workaholics, quickly – in hindsight perhaps too quickly – agreed terms. In June that year they formed a company called Selfridge and Waring Ltd with capital of £1 million in 100,000 preference shares at £5 each, and 500,000 ordinary shares at £1 each. Selfridge had 150,006 shares and Waring 150,001.

The partners settled on a site towards what was at that time the 'dead end' of Oxford Street, where Waring owned some properties he was prepared to see demolished. Selfridge saw the potential of the site immediately. It was conveniently placed for the mansions of Portman Square, near enough to the fashionable *demi-monde* residents of St John's Wood, and ideally placed to capture the public travelling on the Central Line which, having opened six years earlier, now carried 100,000 people a day between Shepherd's Bush and Bank. With stations at Holland Park, Notting Hill Gate, Queen's Road (renamed Queensway in 1946), Lancaster Gate, Marble Arch, Bond Street, Oxford Circus and beyond to St Paul's, the Central Line was the dream line for West End retailers.

From the very beginning, Selfridge visualized his store as stretching from Duke Street to Orchard Street – as it does today – although he had to wait until 1928 until that happened. But he also hoped it would reach right back to Wigmore Street, forming a double island site. To begin with, however, he had to make do with what they could get, which meant acquiring the leases of the adjoining jumble of small shops, tenement housing and a much-loved local pub, the Hope Arms, adjacent to some run-down warehouses and a busy stable-yard on the corner of Duke Street. Above all, they needed the consent of the landowners, the Portman Estate, as well as planning permission from St Marylebone Council. There was an enormous furore when plans were announced. From the fuss the locals made – especially those who drank in the Hope Arms – one would have thought Harry Selfridge was demolishing Buckingham Palace. Instead, he planned to build a palace of his own.

Selfridge moved into offices on the opposite side of the road at 415 Oxford Street and started to plan his development. He was never happier than when poring over architectural drawings. When it came to turning them into reality, however, he faced obstacles on a daily basis. He was used to the speed of Chicago where building regulations and permissions were quickly settled with a handshake – albeit one often accompanied by a wad of money. Now he had to face London's ponderous bureaucrats.

Selfridge was his own project manager, beating a regular path to see both the Chairman of the St Marylebone Borough Council works committee, Edward Hughes, and his colleague, the district surveyor Mr Ashbridge. Turning on the full power of his affability and charm, Selfridge impressed them enormously, particularly as he attended each meeting in person. Hughes would later say: 'He would bring his persuasive powers to bear and he often succeeded in convincing us that his was the correct view.'

Selfridge's original concept was a neoclassical six-storey building with a dramatic central tower. The first drawings were prepared by a young American trainee architect called Francis Swales, who had studied at the Ecole des Beaux Arts in Paris and served as an intern at the offices of the revered Jean-Louis Pascal. Selfridge, enchanted with the result, carried the drawings with him everywhere. 'I fingered them so frequently that they got dog-eared. I had frontal elevations and side elevations and floor maps – I couldn't bear to be parted from them. The result was I almost wore away the pockets of every suit I possessed.' Copies of the beautiful drawings by Swales were sent to Daniel Burnham in Chicago, who was retained as the originating architect.

Busy completing an impressive new twelve-storey store for John Wanamaker in Philadelphia, Burnham was not told that planning restrictions in London at the time forbade any building higher than a modest 80 feet from pavement level. Burnham's elevations were proudly presented to the council – who promptly rejected them. The reaction back at the great man's office was predictable. Young Mr Swales was quickly replaced by the London-based architect Robert Atkinson, who was well versed in the 'Chicago School' having worked in America but who also knew enough about the complexities of London planning regulations not to make any more expensive mistakes. Out went the six floors and tower and in came an 80-foot-high building with five vast upper floors and a deep basement that would provide additional trading space beneath them. Selfridge now had the best team of architects that money could buy. The trouble was his money was running out.

It had cost a lot – in excess of $500,000 – to get to the starting-block. Buying out the leases of surrounding properties had been much harder, and taken far longer, than Selfridge had thought possible. It had also been expensive, yet at no time did Samuel Waring put his hand in his pocket. All the money was Harry's, and he was feeling the strain. Not that anyone could tell. He smiled, joked, hosted dinners, went to the theatre and commuted to America to see his family. The publisher Charles H. Doran met Selfridge several times on transatlantic voyages during that period. Selfridge was delighted to be in the company of a fellow American who listened patiently to his new friend's woes about archaic planning laws and complex fire regulations.

After what Selfridge himself described as 'an interminable time spent in lawyers' offices' and nearly a year after Selfridge & Waring was formed, the site was finally cleared and excavations began. The foundations were dug deep enough to support extra floors or even his tower should regulations change, and Harry Selfridge dug deeper into his pockets to pay for it all. Still Sam Waring hadn't parted with a penny. He was even making money from Selfridge, who had by now cashed in one of his last remaining assets, selling his Lake Shore Drive house. Harry had also donated his precious orchid collection to Chicago's Lincoln Park and had moved his family to England, where they leased Waring's magnificent country estate, Footscray, in Sidcup, Kent.

Waring & Gillow were commissioned to make Harry an imposing desk, but the building programme was so slow Selfridge began to doubt he would ever have an office in which to put it. One chilly November day, in a move intended to obtain publicity as much as to inspire progress, Selfridge arranged for a band to play outside the building site. For months now he had talked to the press about his plans – how exciting they were, how big the store was going to be, how daring it was. His 'music while you work', however, succeeded in making headlines of the wrong sort. The police arrived, claiming that the band was creating a public nuisance, and ordered it to stop playing.

For Sam Waring, it was the last straw. From the beginning he had baulked at the scale of his partner's plans. When he first saw the drawings he offended Selfridge by asking if it was to be a shop or a Greek temple. Some of his frustration is understandable. As Harry's grandiose schemes progressed, the various architects produced over 12,000 blueprints. For Waring, the project was becoming more trouble than it was worth. The relationship between the two egotistical personalities, which for months had existed at a level of simmering hostility, now collapsed completely, with the inevitable result that Waring abruptly withdrew from the partnership. For Harry Selfridge it was a catastrophe. He was left with a deep hole in the road into which he had already sunk over a million dollars and he simply didn't have the money to continue alone. As building came to a halt, Selfridge was left looking bleakly at what the press described as 'the largest building site London has ever seen'. Disputes between the ex-partners led to litigation that was subsequently settled out of court. Selfridge said little in public, only remarking to a journalist that 'We had crossed the Rubicon, and my money largely paid for the ferry.'

London's established retailers must have been delighted at Selfridge's embarrassment, but Selfridge himself remained composed, never doubting for a moment that he would find a way through. He carried on compiling data on London and its inhabitants – how they travelled, where they lived, what they read, where they shopped. Huge ledgers in the Selfridges archives show how methodically he undertook this research. Every newspaper and magazine is listed with its price, readership and ownership. Reports were compiled on the stock and sales techniques of rival retailers. He gathered information obsessively, so much so that by the time Selfridge's opened to the public, there wasn't much he didn't know about the demographics of his customer base. He called it 'scientific' planning. Today we would call it the cutting-edge of market research.

Looking back at the brief years of the Edwardian era, it is all too easy to think life was just a round of country house parties, endless servants and extravagant living. To a certain extent it was all of these things. But while the rich led a seemingly charmed life, a great swathe of the populace lived in poverty and the middle class had not yet fully succumbed to the temptations of shopping for anything other than what they needed. Much of this was changing fast – and Selfridge knew it. A new group of men were finding their way into the inner circles of power – men like the grocery tycoon Sir Thomas Lipton, the trade magnate Arthur Sassoon and the financier Sir Ernest Cassel. There was already talk about the newly elected Liberal Government's plans to 'tax the rich', and intense political discussion about helping the poor. Most significantly, elements of the middle class were beginning to break established boundaries. Shopping for them wasn't just about formal clothes, mourning clothes, maid's uniforms and other household necessities. They wanted luggage to take on their travels, fashionable clothes to pack, photographic equipment to record their activities, sporting equipment and all the things associated with a more mobile life. This was the target audience Selfridge had envisioned for his altogether more egalitarian store. It was also a group many of London's existing retailers had not yet identified.

No one who met Selfridge at the time would ever have known he was a whisker away from financial disaster. He always put on a show, never more so than when money was tight. The end of 1907 was a difficult time in which to raise money. Wall Street was in disarray due to the collapse of the Knickerbocker Trust Company. In Britain high unemployment and unease on the London Stock Exchange sent share prices tumbling and pushed up the bank rate to 7 per cent. There was also a widely held view that London already had enough shops. Harrods, D. H. Evans, Whiteley's, John Barker, Debenham & Freebody's, Swan & Edgar *et al.* already catered for London's shopping needs. Could there possibly be room for yet another store?

Buoyed by his almost divine belief in financial salvation, Selfridge believed there was. Relief came just three months later in the shape of the genial tea tycoon John Musker who, along with his partner Julius Drew, had made a fortune through the Home & Colonial grocery chain which had originated in Liverpool. Musker had happily acquired the trappings of wealth, indulging in the expensive hobby of owning and breeding racehorses and acquiring a beautiful house called Shadwell Park in Thetford, Norfolk, where he maintained a fine stud. Musker was happy to invest in what Selfridge eagerly described as 'London's first custom-built department store'. In March 1908, Selfridge & Co. Ltd was formed, with capital of £900,000, made up of 400,000 preference shares and 500,000 ordinary shares at £1 each. Curiously the arrangement was finalized by a deed executed in France over a sixpenny stamp, a move reported by the *Financial News* rather cynically as 'saving Mr Selfridge the sum of £2,000 in stamp duties'. Selfridge, a firm believer in the adage 'all publicity is good publicity', ignored the sarcasm.

Builders were back on site within the month. Interestingly, Selfridge continued with Waring & White, for the benefits of the talented Mr White far outweighed any lasting resentment towards Waring. He also employed the Swedish engineering firm of Kreuger & Toll, along with their innovative structural engineer Sven Bylander – although communicating with the genius 'man of steel' was tricky as he spoke barely a word of English. Ivar Kreuger happily translated for Selfridge, who delighted in keeping the press up to date about progress on what was described as 'the first fully steel-framed retail building in England'. Since working with steel was much quicker than with iron, he also anticipated 'an exceptionally fast ten-month building programme'. Architects today owe a great debt to Harry Selfridge and his team of construction experts. Largely thanks to their endeavours, the antiquated 1894 London Building Act was rewritten to sanction steel-framed construction, and from that point onwards steel became the pre-eminent structural material.

While sightseers thronged Oxford Street to watch the giant crane lifting 125 tons of steel a week, Harry Selfridge set about recruiting his senior management team. He meticulously planned an 'organizational chart' – essentially the entire structure of the business at a glance – showing who was responsible for what, from the shop floor right through to the staff rest-rooms. Nothing, absolutely nothing, was left to chance. There was to be a staff doctor, a visiting staff dentist and a 'supervisor of staff athletics'. Transport departments were set up with 'motor drivers' as well as horse-drawn vans. Glove cleaning (just one of the many services to be offered by the store) would be out-sourced. All this and more was recorded on the massive document pinned to the wall in Harry's temporary office.

Three key posts were filled by Americans: C. W. Steines became controller of merchandise, William Oppenheimer directed the store's interior layout and fixtures, and Edward Goldsman took charge of the window displays. Before Selfridge, window-dressing in London had been haphazard. Some of the bigger stores had a nominal display manager, but visual presentations were rarely planned to a theme and never colour co-ordinated. In most cases, it was merely a case of showing the diversity of stock, which often involved putting one of everything in the window. The result, as Andrew Carnegie had said, was 'just jumble'.

Exactly as he had done at Marshall Field, Selfridge broke the established practice of folding merchandise away behind glass cabinet doors. Goods were to be freely on show throughout the internal floor space. The store's windows would tell their own story. There were twenty-one of them, twelve of which contained the largest sheets of plate glass in the world, and as far as Selfridge was concerned, each was a blank canvas waiting to be painted to perfection. Edward Goldsman was allocated enough studio space to house props and given sufficient staff to cope with what was listed on the organizational chart as 'flags & scenic work; interior & side aisle displays; main windows; flowers & palms'. The resulting displays – some of which wouldn't look out of date today – were visual masterpieces that defined the concept of creative window-dressing ever after.

The other senior management executives taken on in those heady, pre-opening months were all British. Selfridge interviewed them at length, caring less for references than for his own judgement. He had his foibles. He wouldn't employ men who were too tall or had a skinny neck, and he loathed scruffy shoes or anything less than perfectly manicured hands. Those who passed the test included Frank Chitham, who came from the Scotch House to oversee the launch of men's 'quality ready-for-wear coats and suits' – imported from the USA and in themselves a revelation – while the chief accountant Arthur Youngman was recruited from Debenham's. The staff manager Percy Best came from Hayes & Candy, and the systems manager (not a modern title as one might think, but actually used by the store in 1909) Alfred Cowper from the 'delivery & receiving' sector of Whiteley's. For all of them, leaving jobs with established firms to join the maverick American was a gamble, though perhaps less of one in the case of Whiteley's, where the once great business was in disarray following the founder's much publicized death earlier that year, William Whiteley having been murdered by a deranged young man called Horace Rayner, who claimed to be his illegitimate son. Given Mr Whiteley's habit of exercising *droit de seigneur* over the female staff, the surprise is that there was only the one claimant for paternity.

Despite the temptations of running a store that eventually employed over 2,000 young women – some of them exceedingly attractive – there was never the slightest suggestion that Harry Selfridge ever flirted with his female staff, never mind having an affair with any of them. The idea would have horrified him. To him, the staff were an army to be marshalled onwards to victory. He revelled in their adulation, but intimacy of any sort was out of the question.

Nonetheless, in the autumn of 1908, Harry found time for the occasional pleasurable, lingering lunch or supper with several women, among them the beautiful ex-Gaiety Girl Rosie Boot – the Marchioness of Headfort – who became a lifelong friend, and Lady Sackville, the châtelaine of one of England's great Elizabethan houses, Knole. Victoria Sackville, who had captivated Harry when the Selfridges were living in Samuel Waring's house, Foots Cray, in Kent, had a penchant for rich men, especially rich American men. She was also politically adept, articulate and devastatingly attractive, having inherited her Spanish dancer mother's dark, sultry eyes and sensual mouth. Her daughter, the writer and gardener Vita Sackville-West, would later say: 'If ever the phrase "to turn one's heart to water" meant anything, it was when my mother looked at you and smiled.' Lady Sackville also owned a charming gift shop called Spealls, in South Audley Street, where she sold expensive lamp shades and pretty bric-a-brac at inflated prices to enthusiastic American visitors.

On his regular theatre outings, however, Harry was generally accompanied by his wife Rose who, along with their children and Madam Selfridge (as Lois was always called), were now living in a palatial eighteenth-century house at 17 Arlington Street, leased from the Countess of Yarborough. Selfridge may not have wanted to be thought of as flash, but he was more than happy to be thought of as rich. Surrounded by the impressive Yarborough sculpture collection – including masterpieces by Bernini – and their even more impressive library, London's most talked-about American family blithely settled into British life in the grand manner.

Arlington Street was an aristocratic enclave, colonized by the scions of Britain's finest families, where their Robert Adam and William Kent houses were known by name – Rutland, Wimborne, Zetland, Yarborough – rather than by number. In general they viewed change with suspicion – Ivor Guest, Lord Wimborne, had grumbled furiously at the disruption caused by the building of the Ritz, which overlooked his gardens – but taxes were taking their toll and Lady Yarborough for one needed the rent. Not all the Selfridges' neighbours were as tolerant as the charmingly unorthodox Duchess of Rutland and her daughters, Marjorie, Letty and Diana Manners, who lived next door in an equally beautiful house, today the site of the Caprice. The Duchess, quickly realizing that Mr Selfridge intended to staff his private office with well-connected young men of impeccable background, suggested her great friend Viscountess de Vesci's nephew Yvo as being 'just right for the job'. He was hired within the week.

Of course, no one really knew how much – or how little – money Selfridge actually had. It was said that his wife's family were rich and it was known that he had worked with Ethel Beatty's father, Marshall Field, and had been in business with Lord Curzon's father-in-law, the late Levi Leiter. (Leiter's other daughters, Daisy and Nannie, had become respectively the Countess of Suffolk and the Hon. Mrs Colin Campbell.) Selfridge, master of illusion, would simply smile and say they had all been 'marvellous people'.

That autumn the press eagerly reported on progress, fed by daily bulletins. The *Daily Graphic* quoted Selfridge as saying, 'We have broken all previous building records and without any overtime of consequence ... we built 80 square feet on the corner to the top of the great columns, including the steelwork of the storey above, in two weeks and five days.' It was an awesome sight and a frightening climb for those invited by Selfridge to tour the site. Among them was the publisher Evelyn Wrench, who noted in his diary: 'I climbed the girders with him and felt dizzy doing so.' Wrench, a distinguished traveller who would go on to found the Overseas League and the English-Speaking Union, was tremendously impressed with Selfridge. 'He certainly is one of the most forceful Americans I know. I feel sure that, granted good health, he will revolutionize the drapery and large store business in this country.'

Not all the press reports were positive. The drapery trade press were particularly sceptical about the size of the project and the sales turnover needed to sustain it, while other reports were frankly scathing about Selfridge's concept. Most criticisms had a distinctly anti-American bias. The *British Weekly* wrote: 'A crusade has been started to force on London superfluous luxuries such as those over-stocked across the Atlantic.' But in the main, the press warmed to Harry Selfridge because he, unlike virtually any other British businessman, courted them assiduously.

Selfridge had arrived in London at a point when the popular press was becoming ever more powerful. Lord Northcliffe, in particular, had astutely recognized what the growing reading public wanted out of their daily newspaper. His *Daily Mail* was appealingly priced at just a ha'penny and packed with a unique mix of scandal, social gossip, competitions and opinionated features by some remarkably fine writers. Northcliffe was not the first proprietor to discover this potent combination. George Newnes had started his phenomenally successful pictorial weekly magazine *Tit-Bits*, featuring short news 'bites' peppered with pictures, in 1881, and it soon had a circulation of over half a million.

Just as Northcliffe felt that a newspaper intended for mass readership had to be exciting, so Harry Selfridge felt the same about his shopping venue. From his earliest days in business, Selfridge had understood, as few other men really did, the value of constant publicity and how to make the best use of it. While doing so, he forged relationships with reporters, gossip-writers, editors and proprietors alike. One of his closest friends – a fellow Wisconsin-born American who had settled in London – was Ralph Blumenfeld, an ex-*Daily Mail* man and now editor of the *Daily Express*. Rarely a week went by when the two men didn't lunch or dine together, and rarely a day passed without them exchanging a letter or telephone call. Selfridge respected the press and perhaps even feared them. He once told his advertising manager: 'Never fight with them, never fall out with them if you can possibly avoid it, they will always have the last word.' He was right to be cautious, and his caution paid off. Years later, when he was deeply in debt, his life in shocking decline, the media largely left him alone.

Selfridge astutely hired an ex-journalist called James Conaly as his press officer and set up a special 'press club room' for reporters to use when they were in the West End. Invited journalists had their own keys, and the room was equipped with typewriters, telephones, stationery, a fully stocked bar and the guarantee of some sort of human-interest story for them to phone through to the news desk on a daily basis. Editors were given hampers at Christmas, flowers at Easter. There was even a diary kept that listed birthdays so a special gift could be sent, and wives were always guaranteed the best table in the store's Palm Court Restaurant. But it wasn't merely efficient media handling that endeared much of Fleet Street to Harry Selfridge – his unwavering belief in advertising meant they also made money.

During the opening week of his store, Selfridge hit London with an advertising campaign the like of which it had never seen. Thirty-eight richly illustrated advertisements drawn by some of the most well-known graphic artists and cartoonists, including Sir Bernard Partridge of *Punch,* appeared on 104 pages in 18 national newspapers. The campaign caused a sensation, with even *The Times* declaring it marked an epoch in the history of British retail advertising – perhaps regretting having vetoed Harry's attempt to book its entire front page for the launch. The cost of such a campaign was enormous. The store spent an astonishing £36,000 in just seven days – in today's terms nearly £2.35 million! That excluded production costs – and Bernard

Partridge didn't come cheap. To the chagrin of London's advertising agencies, all the work was handled internally. The in-house creative department produced the artwork and Harry Selfridge personally selected the space, insisting that he receive the 10 per cent discount usually given to agencies.

In those days most stores merely booked a modest series of quarter-pages. Harry Selfridge created a whole new source of income for news-papers – and they loved him for it. It wasn't just the sheer volume of his spending that made waves. Uniquely, his advertisements weren't about products: they were a mission statement about his philosophy of shopping. Not everyone liked them. One advertising trade paper called them 'high-falutin' nonsense' while another dismissed them as 'piffle'. Other reactions ranged from admiration to derision at Harry's sentimental, idealistic text:

> We have every pleasure in announcing that the formal opening of our premises – London's newest shopping centre – begins today and continues throughout the week. We wish it to be clearly understood that our invitation is to the whole British public and to visitors from overseas – that no cards of admission are required – that all are welcome – and that the pleasures of shopping as those of sight-seeing begin from the opening hour.

In promoting the 'pleasures of shopping', in calling the store a 'shopping centre' and, more significantly, in talking about 'sight-seeing', Harry Selfridge was putting into place things we take for granted today. Art exhibitions in-store? Selfridge did it in 1909. Cookery demonstrations in the kitchen equipment department? Selfridge did it in 1912. But nearly a hundred years ago, these were visionary ideas. It was almost as if H. G. Selfridge was being advised by his new friend H. G. Wells. He made mistakes of course. Given the rising tension between Britain and Germany, his advertisement headed 'Greetings to the Fatherland' was perhaps unwise. All in all, though, his advertisements, with their lack of pressure to buy and their reassuring messages about fine quality, convenience and comfort, superb service, fair prices and above all fun, broke new ground.

Against all the advice from his army of technicians scrambling to finish the store interiors in time, Selfridge fixed the opening day for Monday, 15 March 1909. No one believed the store would be ready. Indeed a journalist escorted round the premises reported that 'disorder reigned supreme'. The 1,800 staff worked throughout the weekend until midnight on Sunday, frantically unpacking and arranging stock in over a hundred different departments. In the store's magnificent windows, hidden until the opening by ruched silk theatre curtains, Edward Goldsman had created exquisite fashion displays inspired by Watteau and Fragonard. The staff gasped with admiration – and then gasped in horror when the newly installed sprinkler system erupted, flooding most of them.

Water was the biggest problem. Outside there was too much – on the opening day it poured with rain – and inside there soon wasn't any at all. As thousands of people streamed through the store, doing everything from using the impressive bathrooms to drinking water with their lunch, the 400-foot-deep artesian well pumps gave way under the strain. In desperation, the manager of the hairdressing department fled upstairs to the restaurant, commandeering all the soda siphons to rinse out shampoos.

Staff positioned by the Oxford and Duke Street doors counted in 90,000 people on the opening day. In a nice theatrical touch by Selfridge, who always got on very well with the local constabulary, over thirty policemen were on hand outside to handle the crowds. For the most part those who came were just looking. Actual sales totalled a meagre £3,000, well under target. Selfridge himself didn't mind. Or if he did, he didn't show it. As far as he was concerned, the opening day was a bit like the opening night of a play. It was the reviews he was waiting for. Did people like the store? Would they return? Would it be a long-running success?

There wasn't much not to like. The place was a marvel. There were six acres of floor space with no internal doors. Instead there were wide, open-plan vistas – perhaps not quite as open as Selfridge had wanted but, given onerous fire restrictions, still a revelation for London retailing. Nine Otis lifts, each six foot square, whisked passengers from the toy, sports and motoring departments on the lower ground floor to the restaurant on the top floor. The store was brilliantly lit and flooded with the scent of fresh flowers. Floors were carpeted in the house 'signature green' which was also used for everything from the commissionaires' uniforms to the smart delivery vans. There was a library, fully stocked with all the latest magazines and newspapers; a silence room (for respite between exhausting bouts of shopping); a branch post office (for mailing letters and cards written on complimentary store stationery); an information bureau; and, in a forerunner of today's concierge services, staff on hand to book everything from train tickets or seats at a West End show to a hotel suite or a steamship state room on a passage to New York. There was a first-aid ward with a uniformed nurse in attendance (her clothes supplied by the in-store nurses' uniform department); a bureau de change; parcel and coat drop-off points; sumptuous ladies' and gentlemen's cloakrooms; a barber's shop; a ladies' hairdressing salon that also offered a manicure service; and even a chiropodist. The huge restaurant served lunch to people entertained by an orchestra, while men – though not women – could escape to their own smoking room. Harry Selfridge had thought of everything.

His competitors were dumbfounded at the amount of space given over to services. Surely the point of a shop was for people to buy things? The Selfridge philosophy, however, was first to get them in, then to keep them there. Thereafter they would buy. As he said in one of his advertisements, the store sold 'all merchandise that Men, Women and Children wear' and 'almost everything that enters into the affairs of daily life'. At that point, he meant more or less everything other than food and wines. Those would come later. Neither did he sell furniture, or at least not beds, wardrobes or dining-tables and chairs. Some thought this was the result of his 'deal' with Waring who, after all, was also a furniture retailer. In reality, as Selfridge later said, it was because margins were better on decorative home furnishings such as lampshades, glass, china, silver, cutlery, lacquer screens and rugs. Waring meanwhile had sent over the impressive desk destined for the Chairman's impressive fourth-floor corner site office. He also sent a bill, which Selfridge avoided paying for the next three years.

Lord Northcliffe himself visited that week, shopping incognito, and was so pleased with the service he received that he wrote to Selfridge praising the skill of the salesman, saying that the chap in question – a young man by the name of Puttick – 'was destined to go far'. Selfridge quickly dictated a reply, signing it for the first time with what thereafter became his business name: H. Gordon Selfridge.

Looking at earlier letters, it is evident his signature changed too. It was almost as if he'd been practising a brand-new sweeping flourish of letters. Now he had a new name, new handwriting, a new store and a new life. But old habits remained.

Somehow, in all the frantic months of preparation, Selfridge had found time to become initiated into that select band of brothers, the Freemasons. He joined Columbia Lodge 2397, whose membership was exclusively made up from the American community in London. Among the distinguished list of Columbia Founders was Henry S. Wellcome, the American pharmaceutical millionaire, who cordially received 'Brother Gordon Selfridge' to the Lodge. Brotherly love however would soon be irrevocably strained when Wellcome's wife Syrie and Harry Gordon Selfridge started their tempestuous affair.

TAKE-OFF

'A store which is used every day should be as fine a thing and,
in its own way, as ennobling a thing as a church or a museum.'
H. Gordon Selfridge

Over a million people were counted into Selfridge's during the opening week. From that moment on, both the store and the man became famous. 'Selfridge', wrote one columnist, 'is as much one of the sights of London as Big Ben. With his morning jacket, white vest slip, pearl tie-pin and orchid buttonhole, he is a mobile landmark of the metropolis.' There was always a small crowd waiting outside to see him arrive at work each morning at 8.30 a.m. An observer recalled that 'he was received in respectable silence by the bystanders, who always waved at him'. Selfridge would doff his hat and proceed inside. He took his private lift to the fourth floor and walked briskly down the corridor lined with framed press editorials and advertising tear sheets to his north-east corner office suite. There his personal staff – Thomas Aubrey, his private secretary, and two typists – would already be going through the first post.

Harry's morning unfolded in a series of rituals, each performed with precise timing. Though he usually shaved at home, in the store the American-equipped barber's shop sent up an assistant to give him a scalp rub and trim and hot towel wrap, and to lightly wax his moustache and eyebrows, while a manicurist buffed and filed his fingernails.

The young salesman from the menswear department who acted as his in-store valet would bring up several freshly laundered cream silk shirts and hang them in the cedar-wood closets, where a second set of dress clothes was ready in case he wanted to change at work before going out for the evening. His high, Cuban-heeled black patent boots – made to order by Alan McAfee of Duke Street, with in-built 'lifts' to give him an extra half-inch – were rubbed with a chamois cloth and, finally, his black silk top hat was carefully brushed.

The restaurant supervisor delivered a pot of weak China tea and a bowl of fruit, pausing to discuss the menu for any guests due for lunch in his private dining-room. A florist arrived from the flower department with a selection of roses and orchids from which Selfridge carefully selected a rose for the crystal vase on his desk and an orchid for his boutonnière. Three times a week, huge vases of flowers were carefully arranged in his inner and outer offices and the dining-room. Selfridge adored highly scented flowers and was fastidious about their care, always checking the water to ensure it was topped up and pausing to snap off a dead bloom.

Refreshed, he would then deal with the early morning post, the first of five enormous batches that arrived daily from the Remittance Office, which handled all the store mail. He would go through important letters with Mr Aubrey and then, at 9.15 a.m., run through the day's engagement diary with his Social Secretary. At precisely 9.30 a.m. he would don his hat and walk the store's six acres, the monarch of all he surveyed.

Department managers frantically telephoned ahead to alert staff, who would instinctively straighten up and smooth their clothes, trying not to look self-conscious. Harry would stop and have a word here, ask a question there. He never asked anyone how they were, loathing any mention of even the mildest ill-health. 'Tell me …' was always his opening question, 'how is this selling?' or 'has this gone well?' He knew *exactly* how it had been going, for the previous day's sales reports were on his desk first thing each morning, but he wanted to hear it from them. On his instruction, staff always called him 'Mr Selfridge' to his face, never 'Sir'. He actively disliked that formality.

Any letters signed 'I remain, sir, your most obedient servant', in the manner of the time, made him wince. For the most part, his staff referred to him as 'the Chief'.

As he made his rounds, he would scribble notes about things that annoyed him or queries to be followed up on his shirt cuff in pencil: not for nothing were there spares in the office. He never criticized anyone in public – and rarely praised them either – but he would nod and smile faintly when he heard good news. Then, looking at his watch – always set five minutes fast 'so I've got five minutes longer to live' – he would move on to the next department. Nothing escaped his eagle eye, from a stain on the carpet to a blunt pencil. If he found dust he simply paused and wrote HGS with his fingertip, just as he had always done at Marshall Field. It wouldn't be there for long.

His presence, however, lingered long after he'd left and the staff would talk about his 'walk' for the rest of the day. Sometimes they would get a reminder, by way of a yellow telegram envelope that arrived at their work station. Originally, Selfridge had reasoned that they would jump to open the envelope thinking they had been sent a telegram. Once the staff had figured out the system they were even quicker to open it, never knowing if it was good news or bad but aware that it was a personal message from 'the Chief' exclusively for them.

Harry's tour took more than an hour. By the time he got back to his office he had seen over a thousand people. Within a decade that number had grown to well over three thousand and ultimately it would rise to over five. He engaged with them all. For a lot of them, it was the highlight of their day. The man himself – imbued with a glamour lacking in any other retailing chief – was why they worked at Selfridge's. The store was a theatre, with the curtain going up at nine o'clock every morning. Like every impresario before or since, Harry Selfridge was checking that his cast was in order, with the stage set for the next performance.

The rest of the morning was spent studying buyers' reports and stock inventories, meeting the advertising department staff, planning window displays or on the telephone. The store had 120 lines to the Mayfair Exchange and 600 internal extensions. Selfridge regarded all embryonic telecommunications systems as an essential business tool. He had offered the National Telephone Company the opportunity to open a branch exchange in the store, but they turned him down, instead giving the store the distinctive telephone number 'Gerrard One' by way of compensation. As telephones spread through London, Selfridge's was the first store to sell the equipment and also the first to advertise on the cover of the telephone directory – no one else had thought of it.

Harry's office door was – in theory – always open for people who wanted to see him. In reality, Thomas Aubrey carefully guarded the inner sanctum. Generally affable, Selfridge could at times be tetchy. Executives called to meetings would get a signal from Mr Aubrey, who used a coded system – 'North Wind', 'North East Wind' or 'Gale Force Wind' – so that they knew what to expect. They also soon learned that he hated, absolutely hated, long meetings. In a move designed as much to unnerve people as to structure his time, he would place a large hour-glass upside down the minute someone entered his office. Turning towards them with his vivid blue eyes fixed in a pene-trating gaze, he would ask 'What can I do for you?' Fifteen minutes, he reasoned, was long enough for most issues. It wasn't so much that 'time is money', more that 'time is precious'. He was fixated by it. He was 53. He wanted to be 30 again.

Given the *froideur* with which London's established retail busi-nesses had reacted to Selfridge's grand opening, it is curious how many of them swiftly recalled anniversaries of their own to celebrate that year. Peter Robinson, D. H. Evans, John Barker, Swan & Edgar and Maples all staged events that enabled them to send out elaborate cards and entertain their customers. Even the mighty Harrods succumbed, deciding they couldn't wait a minute longer to celebrate their 75th Jubilee by hosting a series of grand concerts led by the London Symphony Orchestra. Selfridge was hugely amused at their arithmetic, for though their founder Henry Harrod had opened his original small shop in Stepney in 1835, he hadn't acquired ownership of the Knightsbridge site until 1853. Sir Alfred Newton, the Chairman of Harrods, visited Selfridge to pay his compliments. Their meeting, seemingly friendly, ended with Sir Alfred saying: 'You'll lose your money.'

Selfridge may have remembered that remark some weeks later when the store was deserted for days at a time and takings were meagre. A reporter from the *Evening News*, who found himself virtually alone on an upper floor, bumped into Selfridge himself who, full of bravura, simply said: 'We've not provided half enough lifts – it doesn't do to keep people waiting.' While the *Evening News* remarked on 'his unconquerable optimism', there were other, less appealing, press notices. The *Anglo-Continental Magazine* puritanically observed: 'Selfridge's employs every art to lure the feminine element into those extravagances which work ruin and misery at home.'

In some respects the magazine had a point. In an era when the average household rarely had access to credit, many families still only bought what they could afford. Selfridge's, more than any other store in England, spearheaded the revolution that changed people's perception of shopping, perhaps most significantly by involving his customers less in 'ruin and misery' than in the real pleasure of purchasing something, however modest, and being made to feel special while doing it. When the store opened, all visitors (as he preferred to call customers) received miniature silver keys as a gift 'so they would feel at home'. 'I want to serve the public courteously, efficiently, expeditiously and with absolute fairness,' he told the respected American journalist, Edward Price Bell. As a consequence, his customers lacked for nothing. Lord Beaverbrook, not an easy man to impress, would later remark that 'Gordon Selfridge pioneered the art of pampering.' He was right. People went to Selfridge's to buy something they wanted rather than something they needed.

What Harry Selfridge himself needed at this point was money. He had an annual payroll bill of over £120,000 to meet, interest to pay on his £350,000 loan from John Musker, an annual ground rent of

£10,000 and increasing National Insurance costs, not to mention a huge promotional budget to underwrite. It was hardly surprising that his finances were precarious. Discussions were under way with interested parties about a stock issue, but it was proving hard to finalize. Frank Woolworth, the American 'dime store' multi-millionaire, was in London at the time, exploring his own planned expansion in England. He wrote to colleagues back in America:

> Stores here are too small and shallow. Customers do most of their shopping from the windows. The moment you go in, you are expected to buy and to have made your choice from the window. They give you an icy stare if you follow the American custom of just going in to look around. Selfridge's is the only department store that looks like an American establishment. He has spent an enormous amount of money and may make a success in time. He has been trying to float some stock in his corporation but without much success. Most Englishmen think he will fail. There seems to be a prejudice against him – in fact against all foreigners invading this territory. We will have no walkover here.

Selfridge himself was saddened by what he felt was 'a certain hostility, originating with our competitors'. It was said that several senior staff had specifically applied for jobs at the behest of rivals and were reporting back on new systems and turnover figures. Certainly, some members of staff were fired abruptly within a matter of months. Selfridge hotly denied that this was due to commercial espionage, explaining that those let go hadn't 'responded to our training methods or house rules'. These were carved in stone: no gratuities or suppliers' kick-backs were to be taken, punctuality and presentation were of paramount importance, and staff were expected to adhere to a strict dress code.

There were no second chances at Selfridge's. One mistake meant instant dismissal. The staff didn't seem to mind. There were five applicants for every available job, wages were a little higher than elsewhere, staff facilities were unique for the time and – significantly – there were no fines. An early employee, who worked there for over thirty years, recalled: 'There was a feeling of kindness pervading the store right from the start – it was always a happy place.'

Selfridge may have upset a lot of people in London, but he genuinely wanted to make Oxford Street the pre-eminent shopping street in the world. It was proving harder than he had thought and he admitted his ideal would be to have 'Harrods on one side of us, Whiteley's on the other, and Swan & Edgar facing us. Then we should all do better.'

There were daily discussions about how to increase footfall. Determined to attract men into the store – either accompanying their wives and girlfriends or shopping themselves – Selfridge opened a rifle range on the roof terrace. Paintings that had failed to be selected for the Royal Academy's Summer Show were exhibited in the store. 'Artists have a hard enough time making a living,' said Selfridge, 'and anyway, there might be some undiscovered treasures amongst them.' As it happened, there weren't, but he was always keen to explore new ideas. Even his children weren't allowed to leave the breakfast table until they had each made at least three suggestions. Rosalie, Violette, Harry Gordon (always called Gordon Jr) and Beatrice were now 15, 12, 9 and 8 respectively. Their upbringing was unusual to say the least. Their contemporaries didn't breakfast with their parents, let alone discuss business ideas, nor did their fathers own stores that provided the unheard-of treat of ice-cream sodas for tea.

Grace Lovat Fraser, a friend of Rosalie's, spent a lot of time at Arlington Street. The atmosphere was 'lively and informal, with the house always full of young people, of whom gentle Mrs Selfridge was very fond'. Grace became very close to the children, often joining them on trips to matinées organized by their grandmother, whom she described as 'unobtrusively formidable' and 'unquestionably the head of the household'. Rose Selfridge didn't share her husband's passion for London or its nightlife. Neither did she care for the rigid formality of the era. Even Jennie Jerome, Winston Churchill's mother and an early 'dollar princess' who was a member of Edward VII's set, wrote in her 1908 diary: 'In England, the American woman is looked upon as a strange and abnormal creature with habits and manner something between a red Indian and a Gaiety Girl.' Admittedly, Jennie had a snake tattooed around her wrist and a penchant for lovers younger than her own son, whereas Rose Selfridge wasn't in the least flashy and loved nothing better than being at home with her family. Rose missed Chicago, travelling back there three, or sometimes four times a year to see her sister.

The children had very different personalities. According to Grace, 'Rosalie was quiet and gentle, like her mother, while Violette was outgoing, pretty and given to improvising unexpected amusements which were indulgently regarded by the rest of the family.' Violette, the 'wild child' of the family, once famously bluffed her way into her father's office, disguised in a blonde wig, and solicited a fairly generous cheque from him for a fake charity.

The girls went to Miss Douglas's school in Queen's Gate, had dancing classes at Mrs Wordsworth's, and learned to curtsey and to speak 'very pretty French'. Young Gordon meanwhile was sent away to prep school. Groomed from an early age to join the business, his holidays filled with private tuition, even as a child he often appeared at his father's side for photo opportunities. The store was the children's playground. The three girls were treated like little princesses in the toy department, the pet department, the girls' clothes department and especially the confectionery department. Gordon Jr and his friends probably preferred the vast lower basement, where men stoked the coal furnaces that heated the steam radiators throughout the store, or Irongate Wharf in Paddington, where the delivery vans, carts and horses were kept.

The children led a very international life compared to many of their classmates. Summers were spent in Chicago, while in winter they went to St Moritz to ski and skate. In London, they cycled around town, played tennis and took judo classes, activities for which they were dressed by the store where sports clothes and equipment were stocked in depth.

While sportsmen now wore lighter clothes, women were still covered from chin to ankle, or from chin to knee in the case of swimwear. In 1909, Mrs Charlotte Cooper Sterry, who had previously won the Wimbledon Ladies' Championship five times, said: 'To my idea nothing looks smarter or more in keeping with the game than a nice white skirt – about two inches off the ground – white blouse, white band and a pale coloured silk tie and white collar.' What she didn't say was that she was – as all women were – still wearing a corset, although the newly introduced 'sports corset' was a smaller affair, made in cotton, shaped like a waist-cincher and much more lightly boned. It took what had originally been introduced as a child's garment – the ribbed cotton liberty bodice – to liberate sportswomen from corsets when an enterprising manufacturer made them in adult sizes, marketing them as a lighter-weight cover-up.

Women who played golf fared little better. The struggle between the new woman's enthusiasm for golf and her clothes became so acute that special golf courses were laid out with short holes as they couldn't hit a long drive wearing a tightly cut jacket. At this point, Burberry – having made their name with special weather-proofed motoring clothes – came to the rescue with their 'Ladies' Free-stroke Coat with patent *Pivot* Sleeve and adjustable skirt'.

There's little evidence to suggest that the Selfridge girls enjoyed country pursuits – understandably, given that their father didn't even own tweeds, once famously annoying his hostess by turning up for a weekend in the country still wearing his usual formal coat and striped trousers.

Above all, the family talked together, with Madam Selfridge marking up interesting passages in the morning and evening newspapers for daily discussion round the dining-table. Selfridge was a fond father, indulgent towards his children and himself indulged by his devoted wife and mother. Edward Price Bell, who knew them in both Chicago and London, observed that his home and family 'provided [Selfridge] with emotional riches of astonishing affluence'. Despite all this, it wasn't enough. Selfridge had a compulsion for conquest – whether in work, or with women.

Financial security came three months after the opening of the store when, despite some scepticism in the City, Selfridge succeeded in raising money through the company's share offering. The originating £900,000 capital was split into £400,000 worth of 6 per cent cumulative preference shares at £1 each, and £500,000 worth of ordinary shares at £1. Selfridge himself owned well over 200,000 preference and 300,000 ordinary shares. There was a further offer of £400,000 worth of 5 per cent first mortgage debentures at £100 each. Selfridge, having alerted investors 'not to expect dividends for a year or two', immediately went out and bought sixteen adjoining buildings, increased his advertising budget and hired 200 new members of staff.

Though the store was too new to have earned a place in London's fashion hierarchy, customers were drawn by the depth of accessories beautifully displayed in individual departments: parasols, coq feather boas, trimmed millinery, handkerchiefs, gloves and lace. Selfridge's also specialized in shoes, sold the most mouth-watering tea gowns and had some of the best-stocked children's wear and corsetry departments in town. Servants' liveries, nurses' uniforms, even clothes and dog-collars for the clergy – Selfridge's sold them all.

It was a good beginning, but it wasn't enough. Existing stores already had an established customer base. Harrods served 'society' and the classier end of the artistic world – Oscar Wilde, Lillie Langtry and Ellen Terry had been among the first to sign up for monthly credit accounts when Harrods launched them as early as 1884. Swan & Edgar was the store of choice for actresses, dancers and the *demimonde*, all of whom ordered delicious clothes made in their workshops under the supervision of the talented Ann Cheriton. Swan's real claim to fame came when W. Somerset Maugham used it as a model for his fictional 'Lynn & Sedley' in *Of Human Bondage*, paying the floorwalker Gilbert Clarke 30 guineas to give him a blow-by-blow description of the rigours of retailing, right down to the depressing and dirty staff hostels.

Older established firms were invariably steeped in dark mahogany and staffed with imperiously mannered floor-walkers. There was very little of the theatrical about Debenham & Freebody, whose chilly Carrara marble halls in Wigmore Street were an oasis of genteel respectability serving upper-middle-class women who booked in at 'Madam Pacard's Dressmaking Department' for their special gowns.

Virtually all these clothes were hand-sewn, machines only being used for linings and petticoats. Selfridge's, like all the 'better stores', had their own workrooms where seamstresses specialized in different sections – sleeves, bodices or skirts. 'Made on our own premises' was the benchmark of quality, although ever-increasing demand put additional pressure on production space and staff costs, leading to a marked increase in 'sweated labour'.

There were very few prestigious ready-made clothes available, other than cloaks and capes, which didn't need fitting. The one exception was that mainstay of the Edwardian wardrobe, the beautiful blouse, which retailed at an average price of 2 to 3 guineas. Small, specialist manufacturers made up most of the lace and pin-tucked blouses and provided most lingerie – robes, lace-trimmed petticoats and camisoles. Such establishments might employ anything from a dozen to fifty girls, usually young, almost always immigrants, who earned somewhere between 5 and 15 shillings a week. The girls often worked in appalling conditions, and the poor light and close work ruined their eyes. *Makers of Our Clothes*, published after the 1906 Anti-Sweated Labour Exhibition organized by the Cadbury family's *Daily News*, describes the gruellingly long hours and low pay of people in workshops or at home, whose skills with a needle were the only way they could keep a roof over their head. Very few customers stopped to think how the clothes they were buying had been made.

A lot of women used the department stores to buy part-made pieces, particularly unhemmed skirts and dresses with an open seam at the back, as clothes were not yet graded by size. Those with sewing skills or good local dressmakers bought 'dress lengths' or 'blouse lengths' ready cut, and of course all the trimmings from the haberdashery department, while the more affluent had made-to-measure 'Paris models' replicated by the store's workshops. Whether the gown in question was a paid-for model from Paris or simply been lifted from the pages of a magazine rather depended on the store in question, but regardless, a woman fond of fashion had to be 'fitted and pinned', devoting hours each week to the process.

Selfridge's never set out specifically to target the grander women of the Edwardian era, who still sourced their clothes in the more rarefied, opulent surroundings of court dressmaking establishments such as Redfern, Reville & Rossiter and Mascotte in Park Street, the latter owned by the socially well-connected Mrs Cyril Drummond. Arguably London's first famous designer was the equally well-connected Lady Lucy Duff Gordon – known as Lucile – who had her own fashion house. She created her own distinctive look and had a flair for publicity – helped by the fact that her sister was the famously risqué author Elinor Glyn.

Lucile eagerly adopted celebrity dressing, designing a wardrobe for the actress Lily Elsie in her role in *The Merry Widow*. She was also the first London designer to use live models, to colour co-ordinate accessories to outfits, and to deliver clients' orders packaged in bold striped boxes with ornate labels almost as sumptuous as the clothes inside. Selfridge's, with its 'house green' used on everything from the colour of their delivery vans to the store carpets, came closest in such stylish co-ordination.

The department stores were quick to copy Lucile's ideas. Harrods promoted 'a display of gowns on living models' for their 1909 Jubilee shows in their 'Costume Department', but while the store called itself the 'Shrine of Fashion', the truly fashionable worshipped at Lucile's. No record exists of the full guest-list for Lucile's ground-breaking show held earlier that year, which she called 'The Seven Ages of Women'. Her house mannequins included the statuesque beauties Hebe, Phyllis and Florence, as well as the incomparable Dolores who went on to become a famous Ziegfeld showgirl in New York. Among the audience were Queen Marie of Romania, Lillie Langtry, Queen

Ina of Spain, Bertha Potter Palmer, Ethel Field Beatty, Margot Asquith and what the media called 'every society woman in London'.

Change in fashion had been a long time coming. For over a decade Edwardian ladies had been poured into their favoured boned 'S-Bend' corsets, which created a lush embonpoint and a curvy *derrière*. The beautiful Mrs Keppel, the King's mistress *en titre*, had herself now swelled to Junoesque proportions, whereas the Queen, at 64, still had a hand-span waist and porcelain complexion, albeit one liberally covered in make-up The Queen's use of cosmetics was unusual. Lipstick, eye-shadow and mascara were still generally taboo and worn only by show-girls and good-time girls. Stores sold toiletries, which included scent, hairnets, brushes and combs, cold cream, face powders, tiny booklets of *papier poudre* sheets and even the odd pot of rouge, but such things were generally tucked away in a discreet part of the building – at Selfridge's at the back of the lower ground floor, next to 'trusses and bedpans', and at Harrods up on the first floor. All that was about to change.

Fashion was being disseminated with increasing speed, spilling out of the pages of the ever-growing number of magazines and newspapers. In Paris the new 'lean line' had just been launched by Paul Poiret, whose influence ultimately banished frilled and flounced petticoats and whose hobble skirts heralded the reinvention of what went underneath. Out went curved corsets and in came underpinnings specifically made to contour a long, lean and straight body. Poiret was fond of saying he had 'liberated women' by introducing the brassiere and banishing boned bodices. In reality, real Poiret devotees wore long, hip-hugging foundation garments under skirts so tight they could hardly walk.

Poiret found an enthusiastic following among the British fashion élite. The Prime Minister's wife Margot Asquith invited him to present his collection at a special show for her friends at No. 10 Downing Street, where Helena Rubinstein herself was on hand to supervise the models' make-up and apply some rouge to Mrs Asquith, who had a penchant for cosmetics. Unfortunately the press took violent exception to this French invasion, creating such a furore that questions were raised in the House of Commons. The media were equally critical: 'Not only does Mr Asquith refuse his own people the right of protection, but he facilitates the intrusion of foreign merchandise by allowing exhibitions in the residence which has been paid for by the nation's trade.' The Prime Minister's wife, for once unusually subdued, was subsequently to be found at Lucile's, while Monsieur Poiret basked in the publicity and department stores furiously copied his designs.

One fashion that didn't change was big hats. If anything, they got even bigger and were trimmed with a profusion of feathers and flowers. Big hair on the other hand was being toned down. Selfridge's sold a huge selection of false hair-pieces but the latest trend, thanks to Charles Nestle's Permanent Wave Machine, was for waving. 'Girls Prefer Curls' said the ads, which meant that at the store's hairdressing department – featuring the most modern equipment in London – the ten senior stylists were kept busy curling. They were also colouring, thanks to the Frenchman Eugène Schueller's new hair dyes.

Clothes had also changed colour, no longer confined to a palette of sweet-pea tones or Royal Mourning Mauve. Thanks to the Fauve movement in Paris, strong, bold shades had finally swept back into fashion.

In July 1910, London's grandees were treated to a Russian *divertissement* hosted by Bertha Potter Palmer at her palatial home in Carlton House Terrace. Harry and Rose Selfridge were among the guests who saw Anna Pavlova and her partner Michel Mordkin perform, with Pavlova wearing a sumptuous scarlet satin and gold tissue appliquéd robe designed by Ivan Bilibine. Dance in various forms inspired huge fashion trends, just as dancers like Anna Pavlova, Isadora Duncan and the notorious Maude Allan – famous for writing an illustrated sex manual for women – became style icons. When Maude Allan made her debut in *Vision of Salome* at the Palace Theatre, a production loosely based on Oscar Wilde's equally notorious *Salome*, she wore what Lady Diana Manners described as a 'wisp of chiffon'. Maude also wore ropes and ropes of faux pearls, triggering a craze for fake jewels. Selfridge's hastily opened a large costume jewellery department, which annoyed their Mr Dix and Mr Tanner, who presided over real stones in the store – but the fashion for fakes became an unstoppable trend.

The biggest impact on fashion through dance, however, undoubtedly came from Sergei Diaghilev's Ballet Russe, launched in Paris in the summer of 1909. The stunning sets designed by Alexandre Benois and Leon Bakst prompted a sea-change in home décor, triggering vibrancy in everything from paint colours to curtains and cushions and Selfridge's dedicated their entire run of windows to a promotion for the Ballet Russe when Diaghilev brought the company to London in 1911.

Selfridge's was in the right place at *exactly* the right time. Daily it seemed the press was reporting a new invention or feat of bravura, but nothing captured the public's imagination more than aviation. In the six years since Wilbur and Orville Wright had first taken to the air at Kitty Hawk in North Carolina, the thrill of flight had taken hold. Newspapers – in particular Northcliffe's *Daily Mail* and George Holt Thomas's *Daily Graphic* – saw aviation as a means of boosting circulation, between them offering thousands of pounds in prizes to those who could make or break flight records. The fact that most entrants were opportunist self-publicists, with little hope of getting their machines off the ground, didn't matter. It all made good copy.

The French, having invented the hot-air balloon in the eighteenth century, were understandably keen to set their own aviation records. By 1907, the Voisin-Delagrande biplane had made it into the air, while in 1910, the colourful self-styled Baroness Raymonde de Laroche became the first woman in the world to receive a pilot's licence. Most exciting of all, the Frenchman Louis Blériot flew into the history books as the first man to fly over water. On a cloudy day in late July 1909, he soared into the air above Calais in a monoplane driven by a three-cylinder engine, attached to a two-bladed propeller, and headed for England.

Blériot's epic journey – which lasted just forty-three hair-raising minutes – was sponsored by the *Daily Mail*, who had enticingly offered £1,000 as prize money. Waiting on the Kent coast was an enthusiastic French reporter waving the *tricolor*, a *Daily Mail* photographer and newsman – and Harry Gordon Selfridge. A deal was struck. Louis – grateful apparently for some hard cash – agreed that Selfridge could exhibit his plane in his store for four days. It has been said that Selfridge was conveniently motoring in Kent that morning and just happened by. His son, however, said he had planned the coup like a military exercise, driving down to Kent having already made arrangements to transport the plane back to London. Whatever the case, young Gordon, confined to bed with a bad cold, missed the excitement. It seems unlikely that Lord Northcliffe would have allowed his prize-winning pilot – not to mention his plane – to be whisked away so promptly unless he had agreed in advance. Given his acquaintanceship with Selfridge and the publicity that a four-day exhibition offered the *Mail*, he had nothing to lose.

Blériot's plane, so fragile-looking that one observer said it seemed to be 'all leather straps and balsa wood', left Dover on an open railway wagon and arrived at Cannon Street Station at four in the morning. There was no motorized delivery van large enough to carry it, so the aircraft made its journey somewhat ignominiously by horse and cart to the store, where it was installed in the hastily cleared 'bag and trunk' department on the lower ground floor, protected by a wooden barrier and guarded by six reserve police constables around the clock. Having spent hours on the telephone to Fleet Street, Selfridge was assured of headline-breaking news that would coincide with the store's opening that morning. He had also booked advertisements, styling them like news announcements: 'Calais – Dover – Selfridges,' screamed the copy. 'The Blériot aeroplane, which flew the Channel yesterday, is on view, free of charge of course, on our lower ground floor. The Public are cordially invited to see this wonderful epoch-making machine.' Anticipating a rush of hot-blooded males, he tactfully added 'Reserved space for lady visitors' underneath.

It was the best show in town. Blériot's plane was seen by 150,000 people, among them MPs who were given a special viewing, as were members of the House of Lords. On Thursday that week, the store stayed open until midnight to accommodate the crowds. Competitors called it a 'cheap stunt'. Stunt it was – but it certainly wasn't cheap. It was a classy, clever, extravagant, *glorious* piece of marketing genius, which at a stroke established Harry Gordon Selfridge as the showman of shopping. From that point on, his business started to take off.

~

LIGHTING UP THE NIGHT

'Dance, dance, dance, till you drop'
W. H. Auden

For a trend to develop credibility and profitability, it has to become something that everyone is doing, however briefly. In 1910, 'trend-spotters', as today's consumer consultants are called, would have had a field day. Science was sexy. Almost all the inventions or technological refinements that were emerging in the late Edwardian era acted as a trigger of change: the aeroplane, the motor car, the telephone, colour printing, the advertising poster, graphic design, product packaging, refrigeration, processed food, recorded music, electricity, the camera, the embryonic cinema, even the six-hour boat to France. And of course there was the all-powerful popular press which, by promoting each one, helped create new consumer demand.

In 1910, the public were dancing to big-band music, smooching and sighing to the lyrics of songs such as 'I wonder who's kissing her now' and then buying phonograph wax cylinders to play the music at home (the cylinders were often sold with recording attachments, which gave the added excitement of being able to make a voice message). Professional musicians grumbled about the quality of the sound which had a tinny echo – John Sousa, by now a world-famous band-leader, scathingly called the cylinders 'canned music' – but it didn't stop them flying out of the new phonograph department at Selfridge's. Obsolescence being the life-blood of retailing, however, the complex cylinders were soon superseded by pressed discs in paper sleeves, courtesy of Columbia Records: the big hit of 1910 at Selfridge's was 'Land of Hope and Glory', recorded by Clara Butt.

For young couples, music and dancing were an escape from stifling restrictions at home. Increasingly, independence came simply from having somewhere else to go, such as the Lyons tea shops where a respectable young man could take his girl. Yet the morality of the time still insisted that men and women should not be featured together. When Selfridge's advertised their restaurant with a picture of a couple looking seductively at one another over the cutlery, it broke new ground.

Independence also came through transport. In London this included the expanding Underground system and the newly introduced motor buses which were rapidly replacing their horse-drawn predecessors. On the route down Oxford Street, the conductor would shout out 'Selfridge's' as the bus pulled up at the stop outside. Selfridge's booked bus-panel advertising, but there was never any name on the façade of the store. Selfridge, believing that signs would interfere with its architectural symmetry, reasoned that by now everyone knew his building. Instead, there were just two discreet plaques at each end of the window bays. He had long hoped that the Bond Street tube station might be renamed 'Selfridge's', and constantly lobbied his close friend, Albert Stanley, the influential Managing Director of the Underground Electric Railway Company. Mr Stanley would smile indulgently whenever Selfridge raised the topic and then gently reject the idea.

The store was now lit until midnight each night, shining like a beacon in the dark smoggy street, the window displays advertised as 'being part of the city's entertainment', designed to 'introduce the new art of window shopping'. Unfortunately, the vast piles of tantalizing merchandise freely displayed inside – dozens of sponges, mountains of scented soap, layer upon layer of embroidered handkerchiefs – also encouraged shoplifting. As more and more thieves were arrested, local magistrates accused Selfridge's of 'pandering to kleptomania'.

Selfridge himself was curiously uncommunicative about shoplifting. It was almost as though he refused to believe people could steal and wanted the whole messy business to go away. He hated being associated with it. When a thief was on trial, his public relations staff were instructed to call the newspapers and ask them not to mention Selfridge's by name but merely to write 'at a West End store'.

Dance continued to enchant and enthral, as did the dancers. When Anna Pavlova made her first public appearance in London at Shaftesbury Avenue's Palace Theatre in April, it was rumoured that Selfridge was *à deux* with the queen of the *pas de deux*. He had first met her the year before and went to see her perform several times, sending her baskets of flowers that were as tall as she was, if not taller. They were seen having supper together, Selfridge immaculate in white tie and tails, and Pavlova in a 'magnificent sable wrap', the inference being he had provided it – though since she was being paid £1,200 a week, she could easily have afforded to buy her own. Selfridge's certainly stocked sables in the fur department, and the couple's lingering tour of the store was later vividly recalled by a staff member. But then 'the Chief' was often to be found escorting famous women, a visit to Selfridge's being a sine qua non for visiting celebrities who all signed their names with a diamond-tipped stick on a specially dedicated glass window panel in Harry's office. His advertising manager, A. H. Williams, who later wrote a book about his two decades at the store, was adamant that not all these liaisons were of an intimate nature, claiming that Selfridge was merely a generous host and escort, albeit one hopelessly captivated by fame. Yet the rumour that he was a roué refused to die.

Royalty's own roué, King Edward VII, died in May 1910 and was deeply mourned. Thousands of people got up before dawn to line the route of the funeral procession, hoping to catch a glimpse of his coffin. As the cortège wound its way through London, with his dog Caesar faithfully following behind, many members of the public wept. No one was really in the mood for shopping, and business slipped back at almost every shop and store, except ironically at the grand fashion houses where staff were busy making elaborate dresses for Royal Ascot in, to paraphrase Henry Ford's slogan for his Model T car, 'every colour, so long as it's black'. There were some who felt Ascot should be cancelled that year, but the race meeting went ahead in what famously became known as 'Black Ascot'.

A few weeks earlier, Selfridge's had published their figures, which revealed a mixed year. The Blériot effect had by now worn off. Selfridge dipped into his personal funds to the tune of £28,500 to pay the 6 per cent interest due to preference shareholders. The store's figures were not well received, even though it was clear that the enormous sums invested in the store would obviously take time to recoup. Many stores in Oxford Street – even crusty old Marshall & Snelgrove – admitted that their business had 'dramatically improved since the opening of Selfridge's'. Yet the man himself got a poor financial press.

Fortunately for Selfridge, his new best friend Sir Edward Holden, Chairman of the Midland Bank, chose to ignore it. Sir Edward, having become the Midland's General Manager in 1891, had spearheaded such an aggressive expansion programme that at the peak of his friendship with Selfridge in 1918, he was presiding over what was then the largest bank in the world. Sir Edward's vision for international expansion meant he frequently travelled to America, a country he admired and where at one point during the early 1900s he had considered opening branches in New York and Chicago. While that idea never materialized, in 1905, uniquely among British banks, he had the foresight to open a foreign exchange department. Sharing Harry's belief in the lucrative prospects of the widening travel market, Sir Edward was an enthusiastic supporter of his grand plans.

It wasn't just the store's cash deposits that impressed Sir Edward – although on busy days the counting-house staff shuttle 'over the street' from the store to the Midland branch opposite was very gratifying – it was the unstoppable faith, the fanatical enthusiasm with which Selfridge embraced the new era's potential.

As always, Harry's arguments were persuasive. He had a masterful command of statistics, using them in a way rarely seen in business at that time. He gathered impressive evidence from his staff, many of whom were sent out daily armed with notebooks and pencils to record everything from the number of people getting off buses outside to the numbers entering rival stores. Rarely a day would pass without Selfridge talking to Sir Edward about his plans, his hopes, his dreams. He couldn't do any of it without money, and Sir Edward Holden and the Midland Bank had plenty of that to offer. The staff, meanwhile, were becoming used to the mercurial personality of 'the Chief' who didn't hesitate to make spontaneous decisions about dramatic departmental changes.

In 1910, fresh from a visit to Paris where he saw ranges of cosmetics and perfumes openly on sale in the stores, Selfridge decided to expand the beauty department, which until then had been part of the pharmacy department. The cosmetics industry had already begun to form an identity beyond the stage and the street. Independent young women were experimenting with make-up, although since coloured cosmetics were still controversial, the problem wasn't so much about wearing it but rather not wearing too much. New, better-quality products were now being made by Richard Hudnut, Helena Rubinstein and Bourjois, all producing finer-ground, purer-tinted face powders and rouge. The *London Journal of Fashion* noted that 'rouge, discreetly put on, forms a part of every *toilet* as worn by fashionable women, although some amongst these are beginning to use their face powders somewhat too heavily. The startling effect of contrast, by making the lips vividly red and the face very pale, greatly ages a woman. Still … almost everybody uses scarlet lip-salve.'

Even though an unstoppable trend was underway, Selfridge's sold very little red lipstick, and then only discreetly. The initial purpose of the relocated department was to sell perfume. Selfridge, who adored scent, could identify most of those on the market, and one of his undoubted attractions to women was that he enjoyed talking about such things. He knew if a woman was wearing Houbigant. He loved Guerlain. Firmly believing that perfume heightened the senses,

Selfridge wanted to offer the experience to everyday shoppers. Placing perfume inside the front doors of the store was a master-stroke, having the added advantage of disguising less pleasant odours: not everyone made personal hygiene a priority, and the smell of horse manure and exhaust fumes from the street could be overwhelming.

Selfridge wasn't the first to perfume a public place. In 1870 at the famous Gaiety Theatre, where the impresario John Hollingsworth had presided over a glamorous chorus line of 'Gaiety Girls', the perfumer Eugene Rimmel, otherwise known as 'The Scenter of the Strand', perfumed the pages of the theatre's programmes. More erotically, he installed special nozzles to perfume the water in the foyer fountain. A night out at the Gaiety was heady stuff in more ways than one.

Selfridge's set about putting boxes of face powder side by side with rouge, and swansdown powder puffs next to manicure sets, but above all at that time, they sold perfume. Pure perfume was still vastly expensive. A crystal bottle of fine fragrance could cost up to £3 or even more, an impossible amount for those earning 10 shillings a week. But thanks to the chemist Georges Darzens's discovery of the 'glycidic method' of synthesizing aldehydes, delicious smells could now be replicated at affordable prices. This meant that Selfridge's could sell bottles of 'Lily of the Valley' priced at 1/6d. The customers of course knew nothing about synthetic chemicals – they were just happy it smelled nice.

All this interest in femininity meant that Selfridge himself became a figure of fascination for all sorts of women. He was an avid 'first-nighter', always sending flowers to a favoured actress. There was no difficulty in choosing what to send as a gift to his favourites – he had a store full of such things. He was also gaining the reputation of being generous when the women in his life had financial troubles. Late in 1910, it seems the flame-haired author Elinor Glyn turned to Selfridge in her own hour of need.

Harry had met Elinor not through her sister Lucile but through their mutual friend and her neighbour in Essex, Ralph Blumenfeld, the *Daily Express* editor who not only championed her work but also paid well to publish it. Unhappily married, Elinor had for some time been having an affair with Lord Curzon, himself now a widower after the untimely death of his wife Mary Leiter in 1906. It was always an affair destined to end in pain. Curzon had great political ambition, three young children and an expensive lifestyle to maintain. Glyn was married in an era when divorce was unthinkable, and worse, she earned her income writing outré novels. When Curzon ended their relationship in the late autumn of 1910, Elinor was desolate. She was also broke and owed money to Curzon – a debt he expected to be repaid.

Throughout his life, Selfridge was attracted to successful, independent and famous women. He responded to a brittle sense of humour, was susceptible to girls in gorgeous clothes and, one suspects, was sexually aroused by being 'treated mean'. Elinor Glyn pushed every button.

Elinor met up with Selfridge in Paris that autumn. In her diary she called him 'the American Napoleon', admitting that she treated him with indifference despite being flattered by the attention he paid her. He took her out, made a huge fuss of her, no doubt paid all her bills, and ensured she lacked for nothing. It must have amused Selfridge to hand over money that would repay Lord Curzon. He always enjoyed the web of connections with his past.

A quintessential 'sugar and sin' Edwardian character, Selfridge never let his true devotion to his family get in the way of collecting beautiful arm-candy. While he was seeing Elinor Glyn, he also began an affair with Syrie Wellcome, the fall-out from which would come home to haunt him.

Syrie was the daughter of Thomas Barnardo, the pious philanthropist who established the Dr Barnardo's Homes for orphaned children. In 1901, at the age of 22, Syrie exchanged a controlling father for an equally controlling husband when she married the dour 48-year-old American pharmaceutical millionaire Henry Wellcome. Theirs was a bitterly unhappy and violent marriage, which left her physically as well as mentally scarred.

As Masons, Wellcome and Selfridge subsequently became part of the same close-knit circle. In the manner of the day, men of a certain social standing often dined out without their wives. They had their clubs – Selfridge joined the Reform – and attended endless dinners and speaking events connected with their business interests. But from time to time, wives joined husbands at formal banquets. Syrie, more inclined towards fashionable and bohemian society, and bored by such gatherings, must have been grateful that Harry Selfridge was often on hand to relieve the tedium. He wasn't a man known for his sense of humour but he did have a sympathetic ear and gave women his undivided attention. He also liked spoiling people. The combination was irresistible.

When her troubled marriage finally collapsed in 1909, Syrie, armed with a generous annual allowance of £2,400, set about launching herself in society. Beautifully dressed, brittle and, although no beauty, an attractive woman with a flawless complexion, she was 30 and ready to have fun. Officially, she was chaperoned by her widowed mother, a woman who was quite prepared to see her daughter enjoy herself whatever the cost to her reputation. Syrie herself was beginning to form the disciplined good taste that would ultimately evolve into a career as an interior decorator. Initially, however, she spent money rather than made it – and her tastes were expensive. Even an allowance of £2,400 a year wasn't going to go far, so when Harry came calling, she was happy to see him, gladly accepting his gift of the lease of an expensive house in York Terrace West where she lived with her mother. Their three-year on-and-off affair wasn't just about the money he generously provided. Harry had wonderful contacts which undoubtedly helped her career.

People close to Selfridge always believed that it was the chase and possession of his beautiful companions that Selfridge enjoyed, the act of conquest being more important than that of sex. Whatever the case, Syrie and Selfridge entered the relationship with their eyes wide open, perfectly matched in what they wanted and needed from their liaison. There was talk that Syrie was frigid, but Rebecca West, who knew a thing or two about sex herself, was dismissive of such rumours. 'Their relationship,' she said, 'was certainly a love affair. But they were lovers only when it suited them.' For a while it suited Harry very well. But there was never any suggestion that Syrie was his sole companion – he was often seen in the company of other women.

None of the senior staff seemed aware of the curious double life that 'the Chief' was leading. That would come later. They did know he worked long hours, arrived early each morning, enthused about work above almost everything else, and was bursting with ideas. Though he maintained a dignified distance from his female staff, nothing about women escaped his attention. On one daily tour he noticed that a sales assistant had bad teeth. He arranged for her to see the staff dentist and his attention turned to toothbrushes. Disappointed with what was on offer in the store, he found the best bristle brush supplier in Europe and bought up the entire stock. Selfridge always bought in large quantities. Suppliers gave him good prices and the press gave him good headlines.

Keen to popularize book-buying, he opened a huge 'popular' book department, run in conjunction with W. H. Smith. Selfridge ordered 60,000 velveteen-covered copies of the Book of Common Prayer, pricing it at 1 shilling. Next came the Selfridge Bible, then the Selfridge World Atlas, the Selfridge Dictionary, the Selfridge Encyclo-paedia and the Selfridge Cookery Book, all bought in blocks of at least 50,000 at a time and keenly priced. The department was designed to have the feel of a library, with tables and reading lights for customers. In a move rare for the time, Selfridge advertised his book department, calling it 'the most comfortable bookshop in all Europe'.

In an attempt to emulate the success of budget shopping at Marshall Field, Selfridge's opened their 'Bargain Basement' in 1911. It was promoted as the 'place where the thrifty housewife can shop to her advantage', and though it didn't have the impact of its American predecessor, slowly but surely it generated a steady profit. The Basement stocked legitimate 'seconds', bought-in bargain lines, discounted sale stock from the upper floors and occasionally truly wonderful hats marked down in price – all piled on tables where customers scrambled to find a bargain. Nothing was individually wrapped and removed for delivery. Bath salts for example were simply poured into a brown paper bag with a big scoop and handed over. The main difference between the Basement and the upper floors was not one of price – there were good-value lines on sale elsewhere in the store and good-quality things on sale in the Basement. But upstairs there was premium staff service and goods were delivered. Downstairs, customers generally served themselves and took home what they had bought. That in itself was unusual. If there was one thing that stood out in the golden age of retailing as practised by the great department stores, it was that everything, absolutely everything, was delivered. Customers never had to carry anything themselves. Purchases were taken to the dispatch department, marked up with an address label and delivered to wherever they had to go.

In the sweltering heat of 1911 – the hottest year in living memory – came the Coronation of King George V and Queen Mary. Selfridge regarded the event as being as important as the World Fair in Chicago. This was his opportunity to make Londoners take the store to their hearts, to tap into the natural affection that the people held for the Royal Family and to prove to everyone that here at least was one American with a heartfelt respect for great British traditions.

Selfridge intended to decorate the exterior of his store as if it were a civic building, not just with bunting and flags, but in a grandiose scheme that would reflect both the glory of the monarchy and the glory of shopping at Selfridge's. He spent hours consulting with the Royal College of Heralds over every minute detail, planning the elaborate décor that would symbolize and honour the concept of royalty past and present. The result was an astonishing sight. A plush red velvet frieze edged with thick corded gold ran along the top of the Ionic columns. The new King's monogram was embroidered in gold thread in the middle of each section and hung with gold-embroidered medallions emblazoned with royal emblems. Twelve-foot high shields bore the arms of previous kings, and each shield was surrounded by helmets and gauntlets, halberds and flags, while gilt papier-mâché lions guarded the base of each column. Waxed red and white roses symbolized the houses of Lancaster and York, and at the junction of Duke Street and Oxford Street there was a colossal gold crown. Every shield and portcullis was illuminated, and an astonishing 4,500 light-bulbs lit up the night sky. It cost a fortune and hopefully impressed Sir Edward Holden.

The press were certainly impressed, especially since Selfridge had invited the younger members of the extended Royal Family to watch the show from the first-floor balcony. As the royal procession returned from St Paul's Cathedral, came down Oxford Street and drew level with the store, the King and Queen turned and waved to assorted members of the Teck and other German grand-ducal families, as if the store itself was receiving the Royal seal of approval. The newsreels particularly enjoyed this *coup de théâtre* and the staff were so puffed up with pride they talked of little else for weeks. Whether courtiers were as enthusiastic is doubtful. The British were pretty good at putting on their own show. They didn't need an American shopkeeper to do it for them.

Selfridge was becoming known for making too much noise. He tried too hard, and the new Royal couple were traditionalists. Though an avid shopper, Queen Mary preferred to patronize Harrods, John Barker and the very sedate Gorringe's in Buckingham Palace Road. Despite Selfridge's yearning for Royal patronage, she never once visited the store in his lifetime.

That Selfridge himself was a snob is undeniable. Nothing delighted him more than when his wife's application for member-ship of that august body, the Daughters of the American Revolu-tion, was accepted, proving her family's long American lineage. Yet his snobbery was complex. He genuinely sought recognition for his staff as members of the 'profession of retail' and he was bitterly upset when, for example, the store director Percy Best sought member-ship of his local golf club and was rejected. But his passion for self-aggrandizement was too much for the establishment. Being in trade was one thing. Being publicly proud of it was something entirely different.

Not that Selfridge himself was particularly concerned about criticism from establishment figures. By now he had his own, increasingly influential circle of friends: Albert Stanley (now Lord Ashfield), Ralph Blumenfeld, Thomas Lipton and Thomas Dewar, whom he fondly called 'Tom Tea' and 'Tom Whisky'. He discussed spiritualism with Sir Oliver Lodge and played poker with Sir Ernest Cassel, dealing his own heavily embossed cards and using his own beautifully engraved mother-of-pearl chips. His admiration for Sir Oliver Lodge extended to his being given his own reserved table in the store's Palm Court Restaurant, where on most days he would take tea and meet informally with his fervent admirers. Lodge spent his time in distinguished company. Friends and 'believers' of the noted physicist – a brilliant scientist and inventor who was also deeply involved in psychic phenomena – included Sir Arthur Conan Doyle, H. G. Wells and Jacob Epstein. The restaurant staff would hover uncertainly around his table, in part curious, in part nervous, for the great man readily admitted he believed in the spirit world and was known to take part in séances.

By nature more practical than spiritual, with his interests firmly rooted in the present – and the future – Selfridge seems unlikely to have shared Sir Oliver's zeal for the afterlife, although he did have a 'near death' experience early in 1911 after a serious car crash in the Lake District. He was unconscious for over forty hours – long enough for his family to be gravely concerned – but then woke up quite suddenly, pronounced himself 'fit as a fiddle' and two days later, to the astonishment of colleagues who later said he had 'wished himself well', went straight back to work.

After the accident, perhaps feeling more in touch with his own mortality, he seemed even more hyper-charged than usual. From that point on, he developed insomnia, rarely sleeping more than four or five hours a night, although he did take brief cat-naps during the day. Time was the thing. Like the White Rabbit, he rushed around looking at his watch. He was always very nearly late, creating havoc with travelling companions by seemingly enjoying arriving at the boat train just as the departure whistle was being blown. There just weren't enough hours in the day to get everything done. Things were planned to the last second and he was a brilliant judge of timing, in more ways than one. When the *Daily Mirror* invited eighteen well-known figures to see if they could judge precisely how long a minute took to pass, only two of them got it right. One of them was Harry Gordon Selfridge.

Selfridge was always keen to investigate anything new. As he was a regular commuter to America as well as a devotee of the White Star shipping line, it might have been expected that he would have considered joining the maiden voyage of the *Titanic* in April 1912. His daughter Rosalie was by this time at Finch in New York, in those days a smart 'post-graduate' finishing school which offered the daughters of the rich a grounding in art and music, lectures on world affairs and advice on hiring and firing servants. Rose and Harry had in fact crossed the Atlantic in January and had plans to go again in June. Selfridge himself often went over every couple of months, but in April that year, assisted by their faithful butler and housekeeper Mr and Mrs Fraser, they were busy moving from Arlington Street to their new house at 30 Portman Square. As always with Selfridge's English homes, it was a house with a history, having been the family home of George and Alice Keppel throughout 'Mrs George's' affair with Edward VII, who had been a constant visitor.

The sinking of the *Titanic* stunned the world, not least because it shattered people's faith in advanced technology. Among the 1,523 people who died in the catastrophe was Isador Strauss, the owner of Macy's in New York, who had visited Selfridge in London just a few days earlier. The elderly Mr Strauss went to his death accompanied by his devoted wife who, having been offered a place on a lifeboat, refused to leave his side. Harry Selfridge also mourned his friend W. T. Stead, the editor of the *Pall Mall Gazette*, who had often dined with the family at Arlington Street. Stead was another member of Sir Oliver Lodge's coterie and himself a great believer in psychical research. He had often dreamed about drowning, and just before boarding the ship he wrote to his secretary, 'I feel as if something is going to happen and that it will be for ever.'

Among the survivors were Lucy and Cosmo Duff Gordon who were bound for Lucile's New York showrooms. Elinor Glyn was at her house in Green Street when news of the catastrophe started to filter through. Desperate for news of her sister and close to hysteria, she immediately rang Ralph Blumenfeld's office. She needn't have worried. Lucy and her husband had managed to get into a lifeboat, despite the convention of the day that priority should go to women and children. More disturbing was the subsequent news that the boat wasn't even full and did not turn back to pick up other passengers. The Duff Gordons were bitterly attacked in the press, and gossip-mongers had a field day. Some said Duff had hastily piled on some of his wife's exotic clothes and masqueraded as a woman to secure his place (unlikely, given that he had a full beard). Others claimed that Lucy had insisted he stay with her, which is more plausible. When the Duff Gordons were called to account for their actions at an inquiry, they were vindicated, but Lucile's reputation in London never really recovered and she moved the hub of her fashion business to New York. Duff and Lucy soon separated, but both were haunted by the experience. For years afterwards, the accusation that they had deserted a sinking ship followed them wherever they went. Only today, ninety-five years later, has the truth come out with the publi-cation of a letter from her maid, proving that luck had been on their side in being ushered by a crew member on to a virtually empty boat.

Social responsibility was high on Harry's agenda, and he regularly hosted charitable events in the store. An auction or fashion show held in the name of a good cause had the added attraction of bringing the rich, the titled and the famous together. That April, a fund-raising auction in the Palm Court Restaurant was held in support of the *Titanic* 'Disaster Fund', hosted by the celebrated actress Marie Tempest. Theatrical stars were a natural choice for Selfridge who was addicted to the stage. They attracted the right sort of press attention and they were happy to sign customers' autographs.

One of Harry's favourite plays – not least because its theme was fashion – was *The Madras House*, written and produced by Harley Granville-Barker. Selfridge admired the young, ultra-fashionable playwright/producer enormously, buying blocks of tickets for all his productions and distributing them among the staff who felt compelled to attend whether they wanted to or not. For Granville-Barker, whose intriguing work often received mixed reviews, Harry's generosity was a boon. For the store's staff it was a mixed blessing.

By now store turnover was up and profits were slowly but steadily rising: in 1912 to £50,000, in 1913 to £104,000, and in 1914 to over £131,000. Selfridge, having made a bet with Sir John Musker on meeting targets, was soon proudly driving a new Rolls-Royce. The financial press attacks had eased. *The Economist* commented on the latest figures: 'Not a roaring success, but the business is increasing.'

At the morning meetings, the ideas were still coming thick and fast. 'Merchandise' or gift vouchers were introduced. Sluggish morning trade was improved by special price-point promotions that ended at noon. A pet department opened, with special emphasis on the Selfridge family's favourite pug dogs. During the 1912 eclipse of the sun, customers were invited to watch the excitement from the roof garden. Though they were given coloured glasses for protection, most preferred to watch the reflection in the well-stocked fish ponds. Roger, the boiler-room cat – perhaps divining the fish – padded eight floors up from the sub-basement but then fell off the roof. Thousands of Londoners mourned his passing.

The death of the 'company cat' had been announced by 'Callisthenes', Harry Selfridge's new pet. The pseudonym appeared at the foot of a column which was published each day in the *Morning Post*. The column also appeared at random each day in various other newspapers, particularly *The Times*, the *Daily Telegraph*, the *Evening Standard*, the *Daily Mail* and the *Daily Express*, as well as the late Mr Stead's *Pall Mall Gazette*. 'Callisthenes,' explained Selfridge, 'was the original Public Relations man' – in fact a relative of Aristotle who, having caught the eye of Alexander the Great, was invited to join him on his expeditions as official historian.

The 'Callisthenes' column, usually about 500 words long and discreetly signed off with 'Selfridges & Co. Ltd', reflected 'the policies, principles and opinions of this House of Business upon various points of public interest'. All sorts of topics were covered, from Harry Selfridge's grand passion for a Channel Tunnel to the store's concern at the volume of traffic in Oxford Street. From time to time the column was given over to a celebrity pleading a cause: one early writer was Elinor Glyn.

Most other retailers were bemused by 'Callisthenes', unable to understand why Selfridge paid for such oblique advertising. In reality, the columns were often fascinating, sometimes sweetly sentimental but always sincere, and they drew people into the Selfridge's 'family'. *New Age* magazine howled with laughter, calling them 'utter cant', but 'Callisthenes' forged a place in the daily life of Londoners until 1939.

'Callisthenes' was even bold enough to tackle female suffrage. Selfridge himself supported their cause, ensuring the store advertised regularly in the suffrage magazine *Votes for Women*, specifically promoting merchandise such as ribbons, belts and handbags '*in the Movement Colours*'. The store stocked stationery overprinted with the suffrage slogan 'Votes for Women' – and even sold Suffrage Christmas Crackers! When suffragettes went on the rampage in 1912, throwing bricks through West End store windows, they wreaked havoc, causing thousands of pounds' worth of damage. The store director of Liberty's mournfully told the *Evening News*, 'Women have regrettably turned against the shrines at which they usually worship.' In the mêlée, Selfridge's remained untouched. Perhaps Harry, as a sympathizer, remained immune – either that, or they knew the vast plate-glass windows were virtually impregnable.

The retail industry is often cited as being among the first to offer women career opportunities. In reality, most women only worked on the shop floor – though in Selfridge's, charmingly dressed in white pantaloons and faux-Russian tasselled boots, they also operated the lifts. There were of course lady buyers among the staff at Selfridge's, and several of them were in charge of substantial budgets. Indeed, Madam Selfridge herself unveiled a charming bronze plaque on the roof terrace which stated: 'This plaque is a tribute to women's work in the establishing of this business and is set up as a permanent record of their splendid loyalty and the quality of the service they have rendered'. Despite the fine sentiment, however, during Harry Gordon's lifetime and for long afterwards, no woman ever got anywhere near executive level, sat on the Board of Directors, or was involved in investment planning.

The night before Christmas Eve 1912, a musical revue called *Hello Rag-Time!* burst on to the stage at the London Hippodrome. It was a storming success, appealing to all tastes – Rupert Brooke admitted to seeing the show ten times. Its thumping music and its snappy, sexy chorus girls parading down the 'joy plank' through the cheering audience heralded the dawn of dance mania. The sell-out show was a display of uninhibited, unashamed fun. Rag-time was American through and through, as American as the two ice-cream soda departments that opened that season at Selfridge's, where on an average day they got through 4 gallons of lemon squash, 4 gallons of chocolate, the same of coffee and 240 quarts of cream. The two departments were equipped with brand-new brine ice freezers and a new piece of technology called a Lippincott carbonator that whipped up 100 gallons in less than an hour. There were soon queues of customers standing in line for seats. There were queues too at the Hippodrome the following year when *Hello Rag-Time!* was replaced by *Hello Tango!* This was an altogether different type of show. The Latin American dance became just as much of a craze, but its unashamed eroticism attracted criticism from many who felt it was sleazy.

Selfridge's hosted a charity costume ball on the roof, where the social set enthused over a tango demonstration by Maurice and Florence Walton, London's premier dance duo. Selfridge's were quick to stock tango shoes and tango dresses, slit high up each side. The Bishop of London denounced the new craze as 'shocking', but respectable ladies soon started to host 'tango teas'. Those yearning for something even more decadent went to the Cave of the Golden Calf, a breathtakingly avant-garde nightclub just off Regent Street, decorated with exotic murals painted by Wyndham Lewis, where a Negro jazz band played in a smoke- and dope-filled haze and customers danced as if the music would never stop.

~

WAR WORK, WAR PLAY

'One should never give a woman anything she can't wear in the evening.'
Oscar Wilde

One morning early in 1914, Lord Northcliffe swung round from the desk at which he terrorized his secretarial staff at *The Times* and snapped: 'How are we going to pay for a war?' Warming to his theme about the need for economy, he declared that women were 'spending too much on nightdresses!' Word that the increasingly eccentric Northcliffe was about to launch an anti-consumer crusade flew around the building. *The Times*'s advertising manager, James Murray Allison, having just set in motion a sales initiative to secure more revenue from retail advertising, was so alarmed he found the courage to visit the inner sanctum and plead his cause. The last thing he wanted was for his irascible boss to turn against shopping. Northcliffe's outburst had been triggered by a Board of Trade report citing an increase in consumer spending and a commensurate increase in the manufacture of women's clothing, an industry in which nearly 800,000 women themselves were now working.

Fashion was making news and the stores were making money – stores in the West End, that is: those in the suburbs were suffering. The *Financial World*, picking up on their plight, noted that 'before the advent of Mr H. Gordon Selfridge and the perfecting of the motor-bus, much money now taken in Oxford Street was spent in the suburbs'.

Financed by the Midland Bank, Selfridge had repaid Musker's

loans and bought him out. With investment capital at his disposal, he spent a quarter of a million pounds acquiring not merely the 'fancy goods' shop William Ruscoe at 424–426 Oxford Street, but also the eight adjoining shops that had belonged to the long-established draper's Thomas Lloyd & Co. in order to begin his grand expansion plans.

Not everyone was pleased. People bemoaned the passing of Lloyd's, one elderly customer fondly recalling, 'It was the sort of place where ladies bought antimacassars for their horsehair furniture.' Negative editorials appeared about large stores crushing small shops, a criticism that in one form or another still rumbles on today. Selfridge himself countered the criticism, saying that investment was essential to create jobs and, as he put it, 'to diffuse as much sunshine as we can among all people, whose combined loyalty and labour make business possible'.

The wholesalers who made a lot of business possible were less keen on his methods. Selfridge's was beginning to bypass the middle-men and go straight to the manufacturer, where the sheer volume of their orders ensured enormous discounts. Selfridge himself was fond of making grand statements about the business of retailing, and about his own store – proudly boasting that it was now 'the third biggest attraction in town after Buckingham Palace and the Tower of London'. Adamant, as always, that his business existed not merely to make money but to bring a whole new experience to women shoppers, he declared: 'I want them to enjoy the warmth and light, the colours and styles, the feel of fine fabrics.'

There were those who sneered – in particular G. K. Chesterton, who took every opportunity to mock what he called 'the sentimentality of Selfridge'. Yet those close to Harry never doubted he meant every word. Arthur Williams later recalled: 'I don't remember *ever* hearing him utter an insincere remark.' His staff, now totalling nearly 3,000 people, never doubted him. They had gladly contributed to the cost of a bronze bust cast by the noted sculptor Sir Thomas Brock as a gift for 'the Chief' to celebrate the store's fifth birthday, presented to deafening applause at a huge gathering held at Queen's Hall, Langham Place.

Harry's affair with Syrie Wellcome meanwhile was waning. Syrie had recently met the writer W. Somerset Maugham and was now juggling her affections between Maugham, Selfridge and a dashing army officer called Desmond FitzGerald (who subsequently dumped her to marry Millicent, the Duchess of Sutherland). Her complex love life imploded on the first night of Maugham's play, *The Land of Promise*, which Syrie had promised to attend as his guest, not realizing that the date clashed with the grand house-warming party she was hosting to celebrate her top-to-toe redecoration of the Regent's Park house provided by Selfridge. Having had to deal with florists and caterers, she was late for the theatre, putting Maugham in a foul mood which worsened when he found Selfridge holding court at the party afterwards. A persistent story, much used by Maugham's biographers, is that Selfridge, still besotted with her and disconcerted by the appearance of a rival, offered the astonishing sum of £5,000 a year for her upkeep, the inference being he wanted fidelity. It is more likely that Syrie was trying to save face. There had never been any suggestion that she was his sole possession. That wasn't Selfridge's style. The truth is that her benefactor had fallen for the charms of the petite French *chanteuse* Gaby Deslys.

Usually cheerful around the store, where one of his favourite sayings was 'there's no fun like work', Selfridge could be moody. He was capable of going off people very quickly for no apparent reason. This habit was generally confined to his girlfriends or the beaux of his daughters, but he did occasionally turn on members of his growing staff. A case in point was Miss Borwick, an elegant and extremely competent senior knitwear buyer whose department was always in profit. Selfridge called her into his office and – so the story goes – fired her abruptly. After years of service, the weeping Miss Borwick was given a month's pay and told to leave. It was the same with Syrie Wellcome. Uneasy about her talk of divorce, and tiring of her temperamental moods, he left her in her luxuriously appointed house, filled with the expensive furniture he had provided, and moved on to pastures new. Maugham was left to pick up the pieces.

Sir George Lewis, Oscar Wilde's solicitor and an old friend of Maugham, tried to warn the writer that there would be a scandal. 'You're to be the mug to save her,' he wrote, explaining that Selfridge had left her and, worse, that she was deeply in debt. When divorce proceedings were initiated by Henry Wellcome the following year, Selfridge, who could easily have been cited as co-respondent, escaped unscathed. Wellcome would never have put a brother mason through that indignity, and in any event, Syrie was now pregnant with Maugham's child.

The prospect of war with Germany hung in the air. The media was full of disturbing stories. Sir Maxwell Aitken, the thrusting Canadian-born British MP who was energetically buying his way into the Pearson-owned *Daily Express*, regularly lunched with Ralph Blumenfeld and Selfridge. They talked of the growing threat in Europe, the terrible, unresolved violence in the Balkans, the bitter unrest in Ireland and, to Aitken's mind, the inadequacies of the Prime Minister, H. H. Asquith. Harry's increasing prominence came in part from the store's huge advertising budget, but also from his willingness to air his opinions on life as he saw it at a growing number of civic, charitable and educational conferences and dinners. He particularly admired the Rotarians, travelling on their behalf to Glasgow, Liverpool and Dublin, where he delivered his talks in a soft American accent, regaling the audiences with anecdotal observations based on topics often covered in 'Callisthenes'.

Invariably, he was asked about America and the mood in mighty Chicago. Selfridge kept in touch with his Chicago contacts, proudly sending his annual accounts to Harry Pratt Judson, President of the University, who wrote back saying: 'Your Chicago friends are following your English career with great interest.' Rosalie had made her debut there at the end of 1913, and the city's press was full of stories of the balls, receptions and teas held in her honour during her stay, all complimenting her on her 'American patriotism' in making her debut

1. Harry Gordon Selfridge married Rosalie Amelia Buckingham on 11 November 1890 in an extravagantly orchestrated ceremony held in Chicago. They spent their honeymoon in Newport, Rhode Island.

2. Lois Selfridge, Harry's mother, in 1906 at the age of 71. Friends remarked that 'she seemed the embodiment of a classic sweet old lady, but she was unobtrusively formidable'.

3. Harry Gordon Selfridge, seen here *c*. 1910, was always immaculately groomed and tailored. His taste was for formal clothes and he was rarely seen in anything remotely casual.

4. Oxford Street at the corner of Duke Street, *c.* 1907,
before the construction of Selfridge's.

5. Selfridge dreamed of building a double-island site, extending from Oxford Street,
flanked by Orchard and Duke Streets and stretching back to Wigmore Street.
The architects, Sir John Burnet and Frank Atkinson, executed a series of ideas
incorporating a dome, intended to be 'as important as that of St Paul's'.

6. One of the series of spectacular advertisements to launch Selfridge's, drawn by leading illustrators and artists of the day such as Byam Shaw (this drawing by Sir Bernard Partridge), which formed the biggest retail advertising campaign ever seen in England at that time.

7. Horse-drawn buses were a familiar site on London's streets until the end of 1911, when the London General Omnibus Company replaced the service with motor buses. Selfridge's name could be seen everywhere – except on the front of the store.

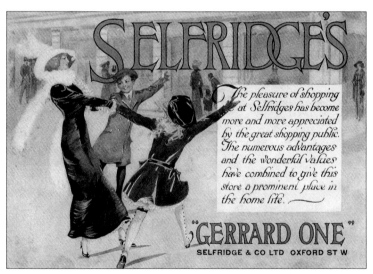

SELFRIDGES

The pleasure of shopping at Selfridges has become more and more appreciated by the great shopping public. The numerous advantages and the wonderful values have combined to give this store a prominent place in the home life.

"GERRARD ONE"

SELFRIDGE & CO LTD OXFORD ST W

8. Advertising copy often focused on family values – as well as good value – and promoted the concept of 'having a family day out at Selfridge's'. This image was part of a colour series created for popular women's magazines.

9. Harry Selfridge on the roof terrace of the store in 1911, with (*left*) the fashionable playwright Harley Granville-Barker and (*right*) the fashionably dressed author Arnold Bennett.

10. The store's famous roof terrace was always a focus of major entertainment including dance demonstrations and exhibitions. Closed during the First World War, the roof gardens re-opened with a series of afternoon fashion shows.

11. The light and bright store interiors, with high ceilings, spacious aisles and wide vistas, were unlike anything ever seen before in London. If Selfridge found dust on one of the glass counters, he scrawled his initials – HGS – on the surface. They wouldn't be there for long.

12. Selfridge's created the concept of visual display as we know it today. Their window-dressing, under the direction of the American display manager Edward Goldsman, was raised to a pinnacle of perfection.

13. Harry and his daughter Rosalie, photographed at Chicago's Grand Passenger Station in 1911. The family travelled back once, and often twice, a year to Chicago, where their arrival was always a local news item.

14. The First World War gave women the opportunity to take over jobs previously always undertaken by men. At Selfridge's, they cleaned windows, trained as firefighters, stoked the boilers and drove the delivery vans. Here, one of the smart bottle-green and gold-lettered delivery vans is dressed for a staff member's wedding – decorated with flowers to deliver the bride!

15. The French *chanteuse* Gaby Deslys, described by Arnold Bennett as 'the official *amant*' of Harry Selfridge in 1915, and as famous for her hats as for her singing and dancing.

16. From exhibiting aeroplanes such as Louis Blériot's to the Sopwith *Atlantic*, Selfridge's promoted aviation at every possible opportunity. In 1919, the year Harry Selfridge made the world's first commercial air flight travelling from London to Dublin, he also staged a fashion show of leather flying suits on the Observation Tower on the store's roof.

17. In 1928, Harry's daughter Violette and her aviator husband Jacques de Sibour flew in their tiny Gipsy Moth on a daring trip to go big-game hunting in Indo-China. En route they mapped a new trail over the Burmese jungle down to Bangkok. Obliged to travel light, Violette (seen off here by her father at Stag Lane Airport) still packed a black lace evening dress and a dozen pairs of silk stockings.

18. Highcliffe Castle, Christchurch, leased by the Selfridge family as their country home from 1916 to 1922. Selfridge spent today's equivalent of £1,125,000 on modernizing it to suit his tastes. Rose Selfridge and her daughters ran a hospital for wounded American soldiers at the castle during the First World War.

19. Harry Selfridge playing his favourite game of poker on board his yacht, *Conqueror*, c. 1930. He always used heavy, mother of pearl chips – thought to bring good luck – and his own, specially made cards embossed with his initials.

20. Harry's steam yacht, designed by Camper & Nicholson and first registered in 1911, weighed over 850 tons, was 211 feet long and slept twenty in considerable comfort. Used as an Armed Patrol Yacht in the First World War, Selfridge acquired the yacht in 1927, renaming her the *Conqueror*.

21. The Dolly Sisters – Rosie and Jenny – danced into Harry's life in the early 1920s. Whether his grown-up children approved or not, the 'Dollies' were part of the extended Selfridge 'family'. In Le Touquet in the summer of 1926, Harry looks fondly at the twins, shown flanking his daughter Beatrice. She looks less than amused.

22. Sports stars beat a path to the store to make personal appearances, often being handsomely paid to give master-classes to customers in golf, cricket and in particular tennis. Harry Selfridge – a lifelong tennis fan, albeit watching not playing – hired Wimbledon champion Suzanne Lenglen to endorse Selfridge's as 'the home of tennis equipment'. Innovative windows backed every in-store appearance.

23. Selfridge's famous window displays were show-stopping productions. From furs to food, toys to telephones, their visual mastery won countless awards for the creative visual display staff, who took inspiration from all aspects of art and design. One of a series of windows based on Surrealism, this is a typical sale window, promoting basic bath towels – with a twist.

24. In 1910, anticipating the emergent trend for cosmetics, Harry Selfridge opened the first dedicated perfume and cosmetics hall on the ground floor of *any* department store. Buyer Nellie Elt presided over what became the store's most profitable department and is seen here, *c.* 1925, standing by the Elizabeth Arden counter. The temperamental cosmetics tycoon and Mr Selfridge became life-long friends.

25. The Otis Elevator Company launched the first step-type escalator at the Paris Exposition in 1900. By 1921 their engineers had refined the system to create the design we know today. Escalators revolutionized customer-flow through department stores. This escalator was installed at Selfridge's in 1926, the most up-to-date model in a London store at that time.

26. In 1935, Harry Selfridge's last love interest was the Swedish-French actress Marcelle Rogez. When their affair ended in 1938, she moved to Hollywood, where she met and married the film director Wesley Ruggles.

27. Film director Frank Capra – in London for the opening of his film *You Can't Take It With You* in 1938 – signs the famous autograph window in the Chairman's office, observed by Harry Selfridge and his son Gordon Jr. Celebrity guests had been writing their names with a diamond-tipped pen since the window was inaugurated in 1911.

28. During the founder's lifetime, Selfridge's adorned the exterior of the store for the Coronation of King George V, the Jubilee of King George V and, most sumptuously of all, the Coronation of King George VI in May 1937, shown here.

in her home city and not in London. It might have been expected that Rosalie would, at this point, have taken a job, if not in her father's own store – that being exclusively reserved for Gordon Jr, now a pupil at Winchester – then perhaps in journalism. As a teenager, she had followed the family tradition by writing and producing her own edition of *Will o' the Wisp*, modelled on the newspaper once produced by her father. She even sent a copy to President Theodore Roosevelt, receiving a charming note on a picture of the White House in return. But none of the three Selfridge daughters ever took a paid job during their father's lifetime.

Early in 1914, Selfridge's hosted an enormously popular 'Dominions' exhibition featuring Canada, Australia, New Zealand and South Africa. So many people crowded into the Palm Court Restaurant that the press office calculated they would have made a single file stretching for twenty miles. Visitors saw at first hand the delights of life in these far-flung countries, and more than a few admitted they were thinking of emigrating to them. Rudyard Kipling used the exhibition as his theme for a lecture at the Royal Geographical Society, saying that in the not-too-distant future it would only take four days to fly to Australia. The topic of aviation was rarely far away: exhibition-flying at Doncaster aerodrome was all the rage; industrialists were busy planning the building of aircraft; and England's first acclaimed aviator, Claude Grahame-White, who ran the Hendon Flying Club, could hardly keep up with demand for lessons.

In March 1914, Selfridge's raised £300,000 with an issue of 6 per cent cumulative preference shares. The offer was so oversubscribed that it closed by midday. A delighted Selfridge told the *Evening News* that his wholly owned ordinary shares were 'not for sale at any price'. He was busy planning the opening of his first Food Hall at premises acquired on the opposite side of Oxford Street, and also devising yet more charts and graphs showing growth, stock turnover and depreciation. He even had a card index for every staff member, showing his or her personal capacity and performance.

The staff had become used to his exacting standards. As well as obligatory morning staff training sessions for the whole workforce, anyone under the age of 18 – and many were – had to attend compulsory evening classes four nights a week. They were given lectures, slide shows and demonstrations, and when they had 'qualified' in the sense of completing the course, certificates and prizes – usually a signed book – were handed out at a strawberries-and-cream garden party on the roof terrace. Proud parents were invited to witness the passing-out parade at which their young son or daughter received a ribbon-tied certificate from Mr Selfridge himself.

Interviewed about his staff training methods, Selfridge said: 'I consider it good policy, as well as good principle, to take your assistants as far as possible into mental partnership with you. Make them feel a real interest in the business. Pay a premium for good ideas and good suggestions from assistants. They should realize that they are part and parcel of a going concern, and sharers – definite sharers – in the success of that concern.' Warming to his theme he continued: 'Make their life as happy as possible. Feed and pay them well. Make them contented. To grind the life and soul out of a miserable white slave is sheer bad business policy.'

The wages paid seem ridiculously low. A 16-year-old in the cash department earned only 5 shillings a week. But if that same youngster's figures weren't out by more than a ha'penny for a month at a time, he or she would get a 10-shilling bonus. If the figures were still accurate after three months, that amount rose to 30 shillings – a huge sum at the time and one which certainly concentrated the mind. Junior sales staff averaged £1 a week before the First World War, with 3d in the pound on top in sales commission. Paid overtime was rare, there was no pension scheme, and sick pay was at the discretion of the management. But all staff had the opportunity to rise up the hierarchy. Selfridge left notes on the staff-room bulletin boards: 'Merit will win'; 'We want intelligent, loyal, happy, progressive employees'; 'Do unto others as you would have them do unto you'; and his favourite 'Do it now!' They usually did.

Meanwhile, the affair between the retail prince Selfridge and the showgirl Gaby Deslys was intensifying. He had always had a curiously juvenile attitude towards stage stars. A showman by instinct, he responded sensitively and sensually to the atmosphere of the theatre, where the women who performed sang him a siren's song.

Gaby Deslys was 31 when she met Selfridge, and already famous for a string of love affairs with rich admirers including the young (but by now deposed) King Manuel of Portugal, Prince Wilhelm of Germany and the original Wall Street Robber Baron Jay Gould's son, Frank J. Gould. She was a sensation both on and off the stage. Born in Marseilles in 1881, she had moved to Paris where she worked her way up the musical revue ladder until, at the time she met Selfridge, she was probably the most famous personality in show-business – in today's terms hovering somewhere between Marilyn Monroe and Madonna. Gaby was adored by shop-girls, chambermaids, secretaries, Lords, Ladies – and Harry Gordon Selfridge. Her dancing wasn't bad. Her singing was pretty mediocre. Her comedy acting was adequate. But somehow the whole added up to utter magic.

Deslys had first come into Harry's orbit when she launched the winter season of 1912 at Alfred Butt's Palace Theatre in Shaftesbury Avenue. Her review, entitled *Mademoiselle Chic*, involved her playing a *demi-mondaine* trying to choose between love and money, in one scene stripping down to her underwear. London's theatregoers hadn't had as much excitement since Maude Allan last took to the stage. Gaby was a material girl. Money mattered to her. She once famously said she would only dine with a man 'if they paid £50 for the pleasure of her company at supper' – sex not included. Rich men showered her with jewellery. Yet while she took a lot from them, she also earned a lot herself and was a tough negotiator. On one American tour she was paid $3,000 a week, and when she signed with Adolph Zukor's Famous Players Company to make a film in Paris, she was paid a fee of $15,000 plus 5 per cent of the gross. Not a bad deal for a fortnight's work.

Gaby Deslys was at the forefront of fashion, and her clothes made headlines. She wore Poiret's hobble dresses and Doucet's soft lace robes. Her extravagant show costumes were designed by Etienne Drian and lovingly made in Paquin's workshops. Drawn by Erté, photographed by Jacques-Henri Lartigue, endlessly written up by *Tatler*, Gaby was a celebrity before the word was invented. A youthful Cecil Beaton recalled being enchanted by her: 'She was a successor to the grand Parisian cocottes of the nineties on the one hand and, since she was such a famous theatrical figure, the precursor of a whole school of glamour that was to be exemplified twenty years later by Marlene Dietrich.'

Gaby's signature was her hats. She did big hats to such extremes – huge feathered and ribboned cartwheel confections – that she needed a second cabin on Atlantic crossings just for her millinery. The more outlandish the hats, the more the public loved them. Gaby's hats – indeed Gaby herself – so influenced Beaton that years later, when he was working on *My Fair Lady*, Audrey Hepburn's memorable millinery and the entire black-and-white Ascot scene were inspired by Gaby's hats.

Gaby's stage partner was the slick-haired and handsome Harry Pilcer. A superb dancer, Pilcer worked tirelessly on developing Gaby's skills. Their specialist routine, known as 'the Gaby Glide', was so athletic that on one memorable occasion her legs were wrapped round Harry's waist.

In those heady months before the war, young people were dancing as though their lives depended on it. Whether at smart supper-clubs in New York, in steamy nightclubs in Paris, or at tea dances at Lyons' Corner House, couples were perfecting their fox trot. The American vaudeville actor Harry Fox had invented what was originally called 'Fox's Trot', although it never made him any money. Poor Harry Fox drifted in and out of stage revues demonstrating his dashing steps, was briefly married to the dancer Jenny Dolly and then stood by while the celebrated international dancers Vernon and Irene Castle made his dance their own.

The Castles were the forerunners of all modern ballroom dancing. The idols of Fred and Adele Astaire, they had an immense influence on fashion. Irene was the first famous woman to bob her hair, wearing Lucile's floating dresses *sans corsette* as she whirled around the floor. The famous artists' agent Bessie Marbury had discovered the pair in Paris in 1914 and moved them to New York that year, establishing the elegant Castle House dancing school where society ladies learned to shed their inhibitions. The couple danced divinely to the new syncopated music that was sweeping New York, where everyone seemed to be humming the young composer Irving Berlin's 'Alexander's Rag-time Band'.

Back in London, the band in Selfridge's Palm Court Restaurant had to work hard to keep up with the pace, and the phonograph department could hardly meet demand. The store's latest gadget, their external 'electric moving news strip', flashed out details about the latest hits available in the store to the awed public watching from the pavement outside. The news strip also relayed everything from the weather forecast to the latest sports results, while ticker-tape machines inside punched out information on stock-market moves. Meanwhile, boys of all ages hovered around the newly installed seismograph in the hope that an earthquake would strike in some remote part of the world.

Tatler eagerly reported that Selfridge's had recruited some aristocratic new staff – albeit just for the day. Lady Sheffield, Lady Albemarle, Viscountess Maidstone and the Duchess of Rutland – helped by her daughter Diana – took up duty behind the sales counters, with all profits from their efforts going to benefit an educational charity for young mothers in Stepney. The 'divine Diana' Manners, having sold ribbons all morning, moved to silk stockings in the afternoon, demonstrating how fine they were by pulling them up over her arms, a sight of such fatal charm that one male customer bought a dozen pairs on the spot.

Education of a different sort was on offer when the store presented the latest state-of-the-art technology in what was called 'A Scientific and Electrical Exhibition – admission free'. Among the wonders on show were an automatic telephone exchange, a vacuum ice-machine, an X-ray machine and newly invented electric cookers. A complete installation of wireless telegraphy allowed messages to be sent to and received from Paris. Most thrilling of all, the young and eccentric inventor Archibald Low set up his latest gadgetry. Low had already demonstrated his 'Televista' at the Institute of Automobile Engineers in May that year, where an enthralled Harry Selfridge had been in the audience. Low's machinery was crude and underdeveloped, but it was the first demonstration of what would eventually become television. *The Times* reported that 'if all goes well with this invention, we shall soon be able, it seems, to see people at a distance'. Low never continued his experiments with television. John Logie Baird would have that distinction, and in 1925 the results of his pioneering work were also demonstrated at Selfridge's.

On 1 August 1914, Germany declared war on Russia and, two days later, on France. On 4 August, Great Britain declared war on Germany and so the long-anticipated war finally began. The British Army, with a reported strength of just over 700,000 trained men, was overwhelmed with new recruits. By the end of September 750,000 men had joined up. At Selfridge's, where 1,000 of the 3,500 staff were men, over half enlisted at once. Selfridge guaranteed that any male employee 'serving his country' would have his job back when he returned.

Those remaining formed a House Corps, drilling with rifles on the roof. Rifle practice was offered to all female staff and they were encouraged to enrol in self-defence classes. The whole store hummed with patriotic activity. The Palm Court Orchestra played 'Rule Britannia' twice a day, and war-work charities were given space and offered discounts on knitting wools for blankets, with free afternoon tea provided for the 'sewing circles'.

Just as elsewhere in the country, the shortfall in staff at Selfridge's was made up by recruiting women. Over half a million in England fled the servants' quarters and sweatshops to work in munitions factories, man buses and drive ambulances. Their newfound freedom put money in their pockets. A young female munitions worker earning

£3 a week (£120 today) and often still living at home had serious spending power.

By the autumn, people flocking to the cinema each week were being informed of what was happening on the Front by newsreels. The newsreels were no more accurate than the 'War Windows' at Selfridge's, in which maps of various campaigns were given pride of place. War reporting quickly fell victim to propaganda, and proud mothers had little or no idea what was actually happening to their young sons. They just kept sending food parcels.

Selfridge's futuristic white marble Food Hall had opened in its own dedicated building opposite the store some months earlier. It looked more like a science laboratory than a grocery supplier and focused heavily on hygiene. Only very limited – albeit artistic – displays of fresh food were on show, the rest being kept in refrigerated cold rooms. Customers ordered from individual booths, marking up printed sheets listing all stocked provisions. Displays of tinned food, as well as the newly popular processed items such as Marmite, Heinz Tomato Ketchup and Fry's Cocoa, were for show purposes only. Customers carried nothing away – all orders were delivered the same day from warehouse space off-site.

The Food Hall had a consulting service to help hostesses plan menus. There were daily demonstrations on the art of laying a table and arranging flowers. While wives were engrossed in etiquette, their husbands could browse in the wine room or the temperature-controlled cigar room. W. W. Astor's *Observer* declared it to be 'yet another achievement of the ceaseless energy and genius which is part of the enterprise of Selfridge's'. But the concept was so ahead of its time as to be frankly terrifying and the place was practically deserted. Reluctantly accepting defeat, Selfridge installed a more familiar, food-friendly layout which thereafter worked commercially.

Like the 'Callisthenes' columns, most of the Chief's speeches were written for him. He would then amend the copy, often to the despair of his writers, who grumbled that he was too ponderous. But when one of his staff, Herbert Morgan, came up with the phrase 'Business as

Usual', nothing was changed. It summed up exactly how Selfridge felt about his business during the war. He used the slogan so often that it became a catchphrase, famously adopted by Winston Churchill who in November 1914 declared: 'The maxim of the British people is business as usual.' Selfridge, a great fan of his fellow Freemason, was delighted.

It might have been expected that Selfridge would have been given a job during the war. Though an American and therefore, until America entered the war in 1917, a neutral, he longed to do something useful. But the British Government never asked him. The French Government were more astute. They invited him to act as their purchasing agent in equipping the army with underwear – a contract said to have been worth over a million pounds – which he did gladly, waiving all commission. In an interview with the *Westminster Gazette* he said: 'War requires two forces; one of men who fight, another to carry on the work of making and providing. The order of the day must also be advertising as usual.' Fleet Street applauded him, none more so than Horace Imber, in charge of advertising at Lord Northcliffe's *Evening News*, when Selfridge signed the biggest order ever placed with a British newspaper to run 150 daily half-page advertisements. Imber, a larger-than-life character who sported white spats and a monocle, was called 'Lord Imber' by Northcliffe because, he said, 'he's better at business than most of us real members of the House of Lords'. Mr Imber already drove a Rolls-Royce, otherwise Northcliffe might have given him one in gratitude for the Selfridge coup. There was a rumour he had won the pages throwing dice with Harry: the deal was certainly a huge gamble and not one in which his store managers had much faith.

They needn't have worried. Business at the store was, in real terms, rather good. A particular effort was made to dress the windows, which dazzled during the day. At night, thanks to the Defence of the Realm Act, they went dark. DORA had been passed in 1914, creating emergency powers for all sorts of measures that the Government felt necessary in a time of war. The Act allowed for the requisition of property, applied censorship, controlled labour, commandeered economic resources 'for the war effort', shut off street lighting, darkened shop windows at night – and closed public houses for all but five and a half hours a day. The working man, reasoned the Prime Minister, if he wasn't already fighting for King and Country, should be working on the factory floor, and preferably be sober at the time.

Selfridge thought all his staff should be on the shop floor, but it wasn't beer that was the problem, it was tea. Walking the floor one afternoon with the store director Percy Best, he noted that a department seemed understaffed. 'Where are they?' he asked. 'At tea,' came the reply. 'No more tea breaks,' said Selfridge firmly, whereupon Mr Best said, 'No more staff.' Reluctantly, Selfridge gave in.

Selfridge himself was often to be found taking tea with Lady Sackville at her bijou house in Green Street. Their friendship had endured, much to the delight of her friends who benefited from Harry's largesse in sending lavish food parcels to her London town house when she was entertaining. 'Mr Selfridge sent me some wonderful ice-cream sodas for dessert,' she wrote in her diary, while another entry recorded, 'At *last* I have got Selfridge's to import peach-fed Virginia hams, there is nothing like them.' The hams in question had made a perilous journey across the Atlantic, part of the huge amount of supplies being sent to war-torn Europe by neutral America.

America's continuing neutrality was intensely debated in Britain. Selfridge wrote to Harry Pratt Judson in Chicago, grumbling furiously that the 'American Government was trying to please the pro-German party and to assist the astute Jews who are largely in charge of the copper business in America, to dispose of their supplies to Germany'. He went on: 'The feeling exists here – unfairly perhaps – that America's first thought is to chase the dollar.' The press was reporting that American merchants were shipping cotton, foodstuffs and copper to Germany, a policy he found distasteful, perhaps forgetting that America, being neutral, was free to ship anything anywhere it wanted – including Virginia hams to his store.

Pratt Judson was quick to retaliate, pointing out that the great majority of Americans sympathized with the Allies 'because they believe that Germany and Austria really aim at the mastery of Europe and ultimately of the world'. However, he also pointed out that 'American citizens have a perfect right to sell contraband of war to either belligerent and will do so unimpeded by the American Government. Of course, they do that subject to the risk of capture and condemnation.' Whether Selfridge liked it or not, there would always be merchants involved in war profiteering. He just hated the thought that anyone might associate him with it.

There were of course many legitimate merchants who just needed to ship their goods, among them the American Frank Woolworth. By the time war broke out, Woolworth was operating over forty branches in Britain. When the Germans invaded France, Woolworth was trapped in Paris and had to scramble to find a ship to get him home safely. For Woolworth, the war presented serious problems of supply. Much of his merchandise was sourced in Europe – particularly Christmas decorations, toys, confectionery, musical instruments, clocks, watches and perfumes, variously made in Germany, Switzerland, Austria, Russia, Belgium and France. Woolworth's had both German and French offices and warehouses, from which goods were sent for consolidation in Liverpool before being shipped to America. Tons of goods were now stranded in the English port, and Woolworth appealed to the First Lord of the Admiralty, Winston Churchill, for permission to take empty hold space in Atlantic convoys. His request was refused: if America wasn't prepared to support the British Empire in the Great War, then Americans would have to forgo such luxuries. They didn't have to go without for long. The enterprising Mr Woolworth simply transferred production of all such things to America, where factory staff were trained to copy the previously imported ranges.

The Selfridge family, holding American passports, were free to travel wherever and whenever they wanted. Harry's wife, mother and children went to Chicago. Harry himself went regularly to Paris and even, on one occasion, to Germany, a trip that caused endless speculation in the media. The visit was made to assess the situation at his

German offices, but also in the interests of design. In March 1915, an exhibition of German goods was staged at the Goldsmiths' Hall, under the banner of 'A Proposal for the Foundation of the Design & Industries Association'. The exhibition focused on the aesthetics of goods, hitherto available from Germany, whose manufacturers had long championed industrial design. Earlier attempts by the Government to encourage British manufacturers to replicate blockaded goods had failed. Examples presented at Board of Trade exhibitions were frankly shoddy. This project was different. It sought to promote excellence in design and to encourage British manufacturers to be more creative. Among the original patrons and instigators of the scheme were St John Hornby of W. H. Smith; Fred Burridge, Principal of the Central School of Art; Frank Warner, the silk manufacturer; H. G. Wells; Frank Pick of the London Underground; and H. Gordon Selfridge, all of them committed to 'a more intelligent demand amongst the public for what is best and soundest in design'. Even *The Times* approved. 'Entirely practical,' they reported, 'not vaguely artistic.'

In 1915, Gaby Deslys moved to London to prepare for her new show, a revue called *Rosy Rapture*. The besotted Selfridge bought her the lease of a house in Kensington Gore, filling it with expensive ephemera from the store. Hampers packed with delicacies were delivered daily by a Selfridge's motor van, along with vast baskets of flowers. At Easter that year, he instructed the store florist to make up an Easter Egg made from fresh violets – with the added twist that a live chick be put inside. Used to his eccentric requests, on this occasion the florist flatly refused, fearing the chick would die. Selfridge, who loathed confrontation, apparently backed down. Alongside flowers and furniture, Gaby got jewellery – including a sensational necklace of black pearls. When *Tatler* ran a feature on the star 'at home', they swooned over her 'chinchilla fur bed rugs and rooms that were scented with Rigaud'.

London suited Gaby like no other city, and Londoners adored her. As *Rosy Rapture* went into rehearsal, it became the talk of the town. It wasn't just Gaby who attracted attention. The revue had been written for her by J. M. Barrie. The distinguished author of *Peter Pan* and *The Admirable Crichton* was fêted wherever he went, but he was shy and lonely. A year earlier he had become entranced by the petite, fluffy, feminine Deslys. To him, she was like a living doll – a blonde, beautiful child-woman. Fascinated by the music hall, Barrie offered to write something special just for her. London's chattering classes were agog.

That Barrie wanted to experiment with the music hall was not surprising. In the aristocratic venues of the West End such as the Alhambra, the Empire, the Palace Theatre and the Hippodrome; in the huge bourgeois music halls of the less fashionable boroughs such as the Hackney Empire; even in a rickety venue down a murky alleyway in the East End, the public in their thousands gathered to sing, clap and laugh at the curious mix of comedy sketches, dancers and chorus girls who supported the legendary leading ladies – whether Lottie Collins belting out 'Ta-ra-ra-boom-de-ay' or Marie Lloyd's brilliant *double entendre* that 'she'd never had her ticket punched before'. The music halls were not licensed by the Lord Chamberlain's Office and could therefore get away with risqué performances not possible in the regular theatre. At the time Barrie was writing *Rosy Rapture*, they were also acting as recruitment centres for the Army. Young lads hearing Marie Lloyd singing 'I didn't like you much before you joined the army, John, but I do like you, cockie, now you've got yer khaki on!' enlisted the next morning.

Barrie's hopes for his show were dashed. It wasn't cheerful enough for an audience that craved humour. Despite a couple of songs from Jerome Kern and some innovative use of cinematography by Barrie, the show was a flop. Barrie didn't attend the opening night, having just heard of his close friend Guy du Maurier's death in action and the loss of his adopted son, George Llewelyn Davies. But Arnold Bennett was there. He wrote to Hugh Walpole: 'Went to the 1st night of Barrie's eccentricity. It was a frost & most of it extremely poor. Selfridge, the official *amant* of Gaby Deslys, was in a box with his family.'

Selfridge's family may or may not have known about the affair, but his staff most certainly did. Gaby toured the store like the diva she was, helping herself to anything she wanted, the bills, as always, being charged to 'the Chief's private account'. On one memorable day she lost her tiny pet dog and sat sobbing hysterically in Harry's office until he sent her home and set about masterminding what his secretary called 'Operation Dog'. Missing notices were posted up, the police were informed and a substantial reward was offered. The pampered pooch was eventually found.

Barrie meanwhile, rattled by the poor reviews, had cabled his friend and mentor Charles Frohman in New York, asking him for help in putting *Rosy Rapture* to rights. Frohman obligingly booked a passage on the *Lusitania*. The ship sailed from New York on 1 May, loaded with munitions for the war effort. Just off the coast of Ireland, it was torpedoed and sunk with the loss of 1,200 lives – including that of Charles Frohman. *Rosy Rapture* closed at the end of the month.

Somerset Maugham meanwhile had high hopes that his new play, completed while he was living in Rome in 1915, would be a success. He had crafted his story about an amoral, lascivious and depraved group of rich Americans and decadent British aristocrats very carefully, dipping his pen in acid to excellent effect. In *Our Betters*, Pearl Grayston, a rich American woman married to a British peer, has manipulated herself into becoming London's leading hostess. Her lover Arthur Fenwick – who conveniently provides the money for the lavish entertaining – is a snobbish, elderly American war profiteer. Pearl's girlfriends are drawn from a motley bunch of rich Americans who have acquired themselves British titles and gigolo boyfriends. Maugham's character Pearl was based on a combination of the society hostess Emerald Cunard and Victoria Sackville, while Arthur Fenwick was very obviously Harry Gordon Selfridge – right down to his soft voice and distinctive mannerisms.

The Lord Chamberlain was so concerned at the anti-American thrust of the play that he sent it over to the Foreign Office for Sir Edward Grey to read. The response was to ban it, the material being considered so offensive it would be detrimental to the efforts being made to persuade America to join the war. If Selfridge was unaware of the plot then, he certainly heard of it in 1917, when *Our Betters* opened to rave reviews in New York. When the play finally opened in London in 1923, it was a sell-out. Selfridge's humiliation lasted for months. Maugham had exacted his revenge.

The business of shopping continued apace, as did the business of publicity. A writer from a distinguished arts and literary magazine, *The Academy*, was given the store's 'VIP tour' by the Chief himself, who proudly pasted the resulting editorial into one of the huge press-cuttings books that he always maintained personally, right down to writing the captions and dating the pages. The *Academy*'s report was full of admiration: 'Outside all is war sensationalism, stress and danger. Inside the store all is beauty and order ... [there is] a pervading sense of well-being and efficiency. It made an impression that lingers ... of piles of dainty fabrics, of colour ... of capable young women who have replaced our soldiers at the door and in the lift.'

In fact, the lifts at the store had always been operated by uniformed girls who were as good-looking as those in the best chorus line. The 'Selfridge's Red Cross Corps' were also particularly well kitted out, their uniforms being specially tailored to fit. Women were now driving the motorized delivery vans – many of which had been transformed into ambulances – and, in an effort to save petrol, holding the reins of the store's horse-drawn carts. Women were on guard as commission-aires, in green woollen great-coats, braided caps and huge gauntlet gloves. Wherever there was a job in the store that had been done by a man who had enlisted, a woman took it over – some even stoking the boilers. The shortage of men was affecting most households. Servants – especially footmen – were in short supply, much to the annoyance of Winston Churchill's mother, who so disliked parlour-maids that she transformed her two into 'foot-maids'. The girls wore black skirts with smart swallow-tail coats and evening waistcoats, white shirt-fronts, winged collars and black ties.

Selfridge's was always putting on a show of one sort or another. Phil

Mead, Hampshire's star county cricketer, was hired to lead 'Cricket Fortnight', while less cheeringly, a few days after the Germans had used chlorine gas at Ypres, the store's pharmacist demonstrated its stinking toxicity by mixing spirits of salts with chlorate of potassium in front of a fascinated crowd on the roof terrace. Anxious mothers flocked to the pharmacy to buy supplies of bleached cotton gauze, elastic and extra-absorbent cotton wool to send out to their sons, along with packets of morphine that were readily sold and always used. The Duchess of Rutland – seemingly a constant presence in the store – opened an Art Exhibition in aid of the War Seal Foundation, one of the endless charities that kept upper-class women busy. The Duchess had hoped to open a hospital in France – her daughter Diana had solicited a donation of £2,000 from 'dear Mr Selfridge' – but the plan fell through. Diana instead became a nurse, while the Duchess confined herself to two rooms of their Arlington Street house, turning the rest into a hospital.

By 1916, Asquith's Government was in disarray. Having resigned over the disaster at Gallipoli, Churchill had gone to the Western Front. The war was escalating. Zeppelin raids had begun and the U-boat campaign was edging Britain towards the brink of starvation. The country yearned for dynamic leadership. They got it in December when David Lloyd George became Prime Minister, in part thanks to the machinations of Sir Max Aitken whose reward was a peerage. Ennobled as Lord Beaverbrook – and by now the owner of the *Daily Express* – he would soon become Minister of Information, but even his own newspaper couldn't print the truth about what was really happening. There was still no job for Selfridge, despite his friend Sir Albert Stanley being appointed as head of the Board of Trade. Late that year, Selfridge moved his family to the country, taking a lease on Highcliffe Castle in Christchurch on the Hampshire coast. Officially, their move was due to the threat of the Zeppelin raids. Unofficially, it was due to Harry's heightening affair with Gaby Deslys.

~

CASTLES IN THE AIR

'Business carried on as usual during alterations on the map of Europe.'
Winston Churchill

The store published record year-end figures for 1917, with profits of £258,000 (over £10 million today) mainly achieved, said Selfridge on announcing the results, 'by an increase in household goods and cheaper clothing while luxury goods and expensive women's wear has fallen off'. A year earlier, Condé Nast, the owner of American *Vogue*, had taken the view that even if women weren't buying luxuries, they would still enjoy looking at them. He launched a British edition at the price of 1 shilling a copy, perhaps not understanding that the women with the most disposable income were working in munitions and reading *Tit-Bits*. With the upper classes showing their customary thrift and the middle classes strapped for cash, launching the glossy magazine hadn't been easy. *Vogue*'s fashion editors responded with features explaining 'how it is possible to have a smart wardrobe even with the handicap of a limited income'. Shortages meant higher prices everywhere – the cost of food had risen by 65 per cent and clothing by 55 per cent. The Government Food Controller had imposed fixed prices on basics such as bread and jam which Selfridge delighted in undercutting, using his 'Callisthenes' column to hammer the point home. There were, however, no discernible cuts in his own household budget – he was living in customary style at 30 Portman Square and spending prodigiously on renovating Highcliffe Castle.

The Highcliffe estate had originally been acquired by King George III's young Prime Minister, the Earl of Bute, who, having the advantage of a very rich wife and a taste for beautiful buildings, commissioned Robert Adam to design several for him. These included Luton Hoo, Lansdowne House and Kenwood in London, and a seaside mansion, then called High Cliff, where in 1773 he laid out exotic botanical gardens. High Cliff was left to Lord Bute's youngest and favourite son, General Sir Charles Stuart, but sadly for Sir Charles, without the money to maintain it. He demolished the property, sold the contents and also parted with most of the land.

His son in turn, also called Charles and a distinguished diplomat, vigorously set about restoring his inheritance, gradually reacquiring the land his father had sold. While *en poste* in St Petersburg he ordered timber; in Spain he commissioned bricks; as British Minister in Lisbon during the Peninsular War he sent instructions about the purchase of the remnants of the original mansion, by now a notorious smuggler's den. When he was dispatched to Paris to choose a house for Lord Wellington's anticipated sojourn as Ambassador, his unerring eye settled on Princess Pauline Borghese's *hôtel* in the rue du Faubourg St Honoré – still the British Embassy today. On his own subsequent appointment as Ambassador, he delighted in attending the auctions taking place in the capital after the fall of Napoleon's regime. Among other treasures, he bought furniture and carpets from the estate of the gallant Marshal Ney, stonework from the Norman Benedictine abbey of St Peter at Jumièges, and a complete window of sixteenth-century stained glass from the church of St Vigor in Rouen. His pièce de résistance was a gloriously carved oriel window from the Grande Maison des Andelys, where Henri IV had sat with his dying father. Twelve huge barges were needed to ship his acquisitions back to England, and it took him another five years to build the impossibly romantic Highcliffe Castle, completed in 1830. Now ennobled as Lord Stuart de Rothesay, he divided his life between Highcliffe and his London town house in Carlton House Terrace, where he installed the bed on which allegedly the Empress Josephine had died.

At the time Harry Selfridge took the lease, Highcliffe had passed to a Rothesay cousin, Major-General Edward Stuart Wortley, who had fought with distinction in Sudan, Egypt and Afghanistan. Major-General Wortley had been sent back to England after the first day of the Somme for the simple reason that his regiment hadn't lost enough men, the inference being that he had shown 'a lack of offensive spirit' in somehow keeping his men back. Eddy Wortley subsequently spent the rest of the war training troops in an Irish backwater.

Harry Selfridge found Highcliffe's history irresistible, but for the Stuart Wortleys the castle was an expensive headache. Never rich, they were delighted with the offer of £5,000 a year in rent, and even more pleased when Selfridge set about fitting modern bathrooms, installing steam central heating, and building and equipping a decent kitchen. Rosa Lewis, the eccentric owner of the Cavendish Hotel and one of London's most sought-after private caterers, wouldn't have recognized the place. When she was in charge of catering for the Kaiser's three-week stay with the Stuart Wortleys in 1907, she had had to bring in portable cookers.

All in all, it is thought that Harry spent £25,000 (£1 million today) on improvements at Highcliffe in the six years he rented the property, during which time the Stuart Wortleys decamped to a modern Edwardian villa they owned nearby called Cliff House. The Selfridges adored living at Highcliffe where, poignantly for Harry, Mary Leiter Curzon had recuperated from a bout of pneumonia before making her last trip to India. Rose and her elder daughters Rosalie and Violette joined the Red Cross, working initially at Christchurch Hospital. When America joined the war in the spring of 1917, Rose opened a tented retreat, the 'Mrs Gordon Selfridge Convalescent Camp for American Soldiers', in the castle grounds. Beatrice meanwhile was sent to St Mary's Wantage, and Gordon Jr, now in his final year at Winchester, applied to read Economics at Cambridge. When the family travelled to Highcliffe, they did so by train from Waterloo, alighting at Hinton Admiral, a tiny station nearby built on the wealthy landowner Sir George Meyrick's estate, from which he had the right to flag down any passing train to board or disembark his guests. Selfridge usually motored down on Friday evenings, his chauffeur Arthur Gardener drawing increasingly scarce petrol from the store supplies before loading the car with provisions.

The bracing sea air was a tonic for Rose, who herself was subject to bouts of pneumonia. But while she grew her favourite Liberty roses at Highcliffe, her husband was seen squiring Gaby Deslys around town, where it was rumoured that he intended to fund the lease of her own theatre. Gaby was helping to raise money for the French Relief Fund and inviting wounded soldiers to tea at her Kensington Gore house, with Fleet Street in attendance. True to form, Gaby wasn't Harry's sole companion. Teddy Gerard was wowing audiences at the Vaudeville Theatre in a show called *Cheep*, in which she sang a little ditty that went:

Everybody calls me Teddy
T, E, double-D, Y
Yankee, Swanky, full of hanky-panky,
With the RSVP eye.
All day long my telephone keeps repeating hard,
'Are you there? Little Teddy Bear?'
Naughty, naughty, One Gerard!

The use of the store's famous telephone number was not lost on some of the audience, who were aware she was being seen arm-in-arm with Selfridge. Not that Miss Gerard herself came cheap – she had a great fondness for furs and, regrettably, an even greater one for opium, which ultimately played havoc with her career. One scene in the show was called 'Goodbye Madame Fashion', with the chorus kitted out in wartime work-wear. Ironically, the shortage of textiles helped launch the career of the woman who would come to dominate fashion for decades to come, when Coco Chanel introduced her simple dresses made up in jersey material sourced from Rodier at her shop in Biarritz in 1915.

Events in Russia, where the Tsar had abdicated, were much in the news and watched by the Selfridge family more keenly than most. Rosalie had become close to a Russian called Serge de Bolotoff, whose family had moved to Paris before the war. Calling himself an 'aviation engineer', Bolotoff had been something of a pioneer when in 1908 he designed a large triplane, built at the Les Frères Voisin factory. Serge knew all the players in aviation's tight-knit world, being advised by Blériot and backed by a consortium of rich individuals, including Admiral Lord Charles Beresford. Before the war, the de Bolotoffs had moved to England, where Serge's mother (there being no mention of a Mr de Bolotoff) now called herself Princess Marie Wiasemsky and set up home in a series of grand, rented houses, first Kingswood House in Dulwich and later Kippington Court in Sevenoaks. Serge continued with efforts to get his plane off the ground. Trials were held at Brooklands, but the monumental triplane collapsed when the undercarriage disintegrated on take-off. Bolotoff's machine was moved to a nearby shed where it languished until the start of the war, subsequently vanishing when the army commandeered Brooklands.

Serge went on to advise the German Albatross Biplane Company and in 1912 became their British sales agent, struggling to make headway against the home-grown De Havillands. On the outbreak of war, he hastily resigned, offering his services to Russia instead. The Albatross meanwhile became the aeroplane beloved by Baron von Richthofen and his famous travelling circus. The Red Baron's planes, manned by his star pilots, were sent to fly across various parts of the line to boost the morale of German troops, who watched in awe from the trenches as their heroes looped the loop in fragile 'birds' made of canvas and wood that could barely fly at 100 miles per hour. It was a breathtakingly exciting time to be working in aviation. Developments seemed to happen daily. Initially, planes were only used for observation, but when the French pilot Roland Garros bolted steel deflectors to his propellers, enabling guns to be fired, and the German-employed Dutchman Tony Fokker improved the interrupter gear which made firing even more reliable, the aeroplane became an offensive weapon, with dashing pilots delighting in notching up aerial 'kills'.

By the time Serge met Rosalie, the Imperial Russian Government that he had signed up to serve no longer existed. Whether he actually still drew a salary from his desk job at the Russian Government's Naval Aviation Department in London is impossible to say, but it seems unlikely. Rosalie, a rich man's daughter, did not worry about the future prospects of the man she loved, but her father was more pragmatic. Clearly keen to put some distance between the young couple and thinking his family would benefit from some travel, in 1917 Selfridge planned an extraordinary journey for them in the middle of a world war. Their intended escort was to be the equally extraordinary man, Joseph Emile Dillon.

Dillon, by now a regular weekend visitor to Highcliffe, was a highly regarded foreign correspondent of the *Daily Telegraph*. He spoke over a dozen languages fluently, had witnessed epic events from the 1900 Boxer Rebellion in China to the 1905 Russo-Japanese War, and was consulted by Allied governments around the world. His particular speciality was Russia, where at one point he had been confidential adviser to the Tsar's Prime Minister, Count Witte.

By 1917, Selfridge was pushing Dillon to accept payment to take his family travelling: 'I am extremely anxious if possible to complete plans – a trip to America, say anywhere from the 15th of August. A fortnight or more spent in that country, then sailing from San Francisco for the Hawaiian Islands, a day or two at Honolulu and further sailing to Japan, then to China, then perhaps Singapore and arrival at Calcutta about the 1st January would be roughly what I would like to see done.' Dillon politely declined the offer, explaining that the situation in Russia made it impossible for him to be out of touch for long. Selfridge tried again. 'I very much hope that in a week or so you will see your way clear to changing your mind. We are most anxious that you and Mrs Dillon should be the leaders of the party.' In the event, the trip never materialized. Rose busied herself with her hospital, Rosalie continued her courtship, and Selfridge himself went shopping.

A lover of sculpture, he was an eager bidder against the American newspaper magnate William Randolph Hearst at Christie's 'sale of the century' when artefacts, jewels and books belonging to the impoverished aristocrat Lord Francis Pelham Clinton Hope were sold. Lord Hope, the Duke of Newcastle's brother, had become a bankrupt in 1894 and had steadily been selling off his possessions ever since. First to go was a clutch of Dutch old masters, then in 1902 the famous – and famously cursed – blue Hope diamond, which netted him £120,000. Finally, in July 1917, the contents of his property, Deepdene in Surrey, were put up for sale. They included items from the family's extensive collection of porcelain and books, and quantities of ancient Greek and Egyptian sculpture and pottery.

All the notable collectors attended the sale. Lord Cowdray acquired a prized statue of Athena for 7,140 guineas. The international dealer Joseph Duveen bought anything he could get his hands on. Sir Alfred Mond, Chairman of Imperial Chemicals, bought four pieces, while Lord Leverhulme bought in bulk, picking up no less than fourteen pieces. Selfridge bid energetically against Henry Wellcome for a Roman statue of Asclepius that was said (probably erroneously) to have come from Hadrian's Villa at Tivoli. Wellcome's agent withdrew at 1,400 guineas and Selfridge got his prize for 1,700 guineas. In a pleasing tussle against the obsessive collector Mr Hearst (via his London agent), he also bought a statue of Zeus for 650 guineas, while a statue of Apollo Hyacinthus, long thought a favourite of the sculptor Canova, rounded off his shopping list at a cost of £1,000.

At the store, there was an ambitious event to mount a sale of War Bonds, with cash prizes offered to winners whose tickets were entered into a special draw. Selfridge's 'Bonds' were printed, permission from the Postmaster-General obtained, posters designed, advertisements booked and Mrs Lloyd George herself invited to pick the winning tickets. By the day of the draw, 20 December 1917, the response had been so overwhelming that the store had to hire an extra forty cashiers to cope. The promotion, which cost Selfridge around £11,000 to mount, raised the astonishing sum of £3.5 million pounds for the war effort.

Next came a book launch. Craving gravitas for 'trade and traders', Selfridge had long planned a book of his own on the topic. Ghost-written by his old friend Edward Price Bell and published by John Lane, it was entitled *The Romance of Commerce* and covered the history of trading giants from the Fuggers of Augsburg to the Mitsuis of Japan. The book was launched in December at a dinner hosted by John Lane, but it presented Fleet Street with a dilemma. Newspapers were anxious not to offend the country's most valuable retail adver-tiser, but it was clear that the book was both wordy and worthy, and getting reviews was going to be tricky. Ralph Blumenfeld, Selfridge's old friend and ally at the *Daily Express*, having opted out of the dinner on the grounds of ill-health, solved the problem by cleverly inviting Sir Woodman Burbidge, the Chairman of Harrods, to review Harry's beloved book.

Burbidge had recently inherited both his title and his job on the death of his father, the equally highly regarded Sir Richard, about whom Selfridge had written a glowing obituary. He reviewed the book cautiously, tactfully saying that in it he found 'something of the vision splendid'. Meanwhile Selfridge's press office worked overtime organizing interviews with 'the Chief', which he gave in his office surrounded by no less than seventy-seven leather-bound ledgers and accounts books from the Medici family archives in Florence, some of which dated back to Cosimo de' Medici himself and which he had bought at Christie's. Those on the store 'gift list' were usually sent food hampers, perfume or cigars at Christmas, but in 1917, whether they liked it or not, they received a copy of *The Romance of Commerce* painstakingly inscribed by Selfridge.

Early in 1918, at the behest of Lord Northcliffe, head of the British War Mission to the United States, Selfridge crossed the Atlantic. Northcliffe announced that 'Mr Selfridge has gone, at the urgent request of American business leaders, to explain our problems of supply.' Northcliffe's reward for his role was a viscountcy. Selfridge, who had to pay his own expenses, received no reward other than the realization that, as he rather sadly observed on his return, 'in

America, the captains of business constitute a greater factor in the life of the nation than is the case here'. Still, he continued to do his best for his newly adopted country, offering to pay 'for all war shrines erected within a mile of us' and putting up £500 in prize money for a competition run by the store for 'ploughmen showing the best results using the new farming technology'. The top prizes were won by Titan tractors, made by his old friend Deering's International Harvester Company, who obligingly lent models to display in the store.

The war was going badly and desperation was in the air. By now there was hardly a family in Britain who had not lost someone they knew or loved, and in May, tragedy struck at Highcliffe. Rose Selfridge contracted pneumonia and died just one week later. Grief-stricken, Harry sought comfort in organizing her funeral at the simple parish church of St Mark's with military precision. The store's seamstresses travelled to Highcliffe to sew a blanket of fresh red roses to cover the simple oak coffin, while American soldiers from the convalescent camp formed a guard of honour, their leader carrying a Stars and Stripes flag woven from red carnations, white narcissi and bluebells from the Highcliffe woods.

Less than three months later, Rosalie quietly married Serge de Bolotoff in the chapel of the Russian Embassy in Welbeck Street. Since the family were still in mourning, the wedding was a small affair. The bridegroom however, showing his own flair for publicity, ensured that he and his mother were given ample coverage by handing a note out to the press explaining that they were 'direct descendants of Prince Rurik, who had founded Russia in the ninth century'. Not that anyone had actually *heard* of Rurik, but a Prince – any Prince – had tangible glamour in the wake of the Russian Revolution.

Serge's mother attracted more attention than the bride. Madame Marie de Bolotoff – to call her correctly by her married name – was a petite, blonde bombshell with extravagant tastes. Already a beneficiary of the legendary Selfridge generosity, she was delighted by the marriage. She had separated from her husband some years earlier and, with four children to support, had decided that life would be much easier if she had a title. She hadn't entirely made it up. Instead, in about 1908, she persuaded the Tsar to allow her to use the title Princess Wiasemsky, claiming descent through maternal relatives.

Serge and Rosalie's grandson, the guardian of a mass of family documents, tactfully admits that 'there was a substantial argument about her claim to the title' but points out that Marie had some powerful friends ready to back her claim, among them Lady Tyrrell, the wife of the Foreign Office Under-Secretary, who took an oath that she had seen the Tsar's decree. Another supporter was Marie's friend Sofia, the estranged wife of Admiral Kolchak, whose evidence also played a part. Harry, satisfied that his beloved eldest daughter would ultimately inherit a title, gave his blessing along with a lavish thirty-six setting Crown Derby dinner service for their use while living with him at Portman Square. A flat of their own might have been more useful. But he liked his family around him and, given he paid, that's where they stayed.

In October 1918, Joseph Dillon finally went to America, without the Selfridge family but armed with letters of introduction to several of Harry's powerful Chicago friends. 'Over here,' wrote Selfridge, 'we feel he is the best informed man in the world of European politics.' Selfridge himself went to France, making a tour of the battlefields at the invitation of General 'Black Jack' Pershing. As the year drew to its end, the huge job of clearing the battlefields began and soldiers started to return home. At Selfridge's, the store kept its promise to take back its own serving men. By the time the Armistice was signed, nearly a thousand had returned.

In the wake of Rose's death, Selfridge kept himself busy. As early as 1915, he had announced that a new extension would be designed by the architect Sir John Burnet, whose brief was to incorporate a majestic tower. The concept of a tower had always formed part of Harry's grand plan for Oxford Street. After five years or so of lobbying, the Portman Estates and St Marylebone Council finally consented, at the same time agreeing to a plan drawn up by the engineer Sir Harley Dalrymple-Hay for a tunnel running under Oxford Street.

Sir John Burnet, who had designed the King Edward VII Galleries at the British Museum (completed just before the war), found that he and his team were part of an extended group. Selfridge's policy was always to hire several people to do the same job in the hope that one of them would get it right. Among the architects was Albert Miller, who at this point moved to London from Chicago to work full-time at the store.

Selfridge relished the new project, giving a mischievous speech to the London Society in which he declared that 'All around us in Oxford Street are numerous little shops that should be burned because they are so ugly.' Warming to his theme, he went on to tell the *Evening Standard*, 'I shall try to build something that is good. A store used every day should be as ennobling a thing as a church or a museum. I love to look at a beautiful building.'

He bought on board yet another architect, the fashionable Philip Tilden, who was putting the finishing touches to Port Lympne, Philip Sassoon's house overlooking Romney Marsh. Tilden executed various drawings for the Oxford Street tower, none of which came to fruition. No more did Sir John Burnet's elegant efforts. 'Forget it. Forget it,' snapped Selfridge when a journalist asked him about the future of the much-publicized 450-foot tower. The difficulty of bringing his scheme to fruition was clearly irking him.

At the same time, however, Tilden was set to work on a project dear to Harry's heart. Having acquired Hengistbury Head, a tract of land of outstanding beauty with a glorious view of the Isle of Wight, from his Highcliffe neighbour Sir George Meyrick, Harry planned to build his own castle. The project created unease in the local community. Hengistbury Head was recognized as one of the most important Bronze Age archaeological sites in Europe, and any plan to build on it was bound to be controversial, especially since Selfridge grandly announced that it was going to be 'the largest castle in the world'.

Over the next five years, Tilden lovingly – and expensively – set about drawing Harry's dream. The two men formed a close friendship, and Tilden later recorded how impressed he had been by 'the magnitude of [Selfridge's] imaginative thoughts'.

The plan involved a huge castle, with a smaller, private house below. Drawings were made for cloistered gardens, a winter garden, a Galerie des Glaces as at Versailles, dining-halls capable of seating hundreds, 250 bedroom suites and a domed central hall that would be seen from far out at sea. It was intended that artists from all fields would be able rent space at Hengistbury Head and work there surrounded by beauty. It was a strangely noble idea, but the locals hated it. Some said Selfridge was building a factory on the site, others that he intended to create a theme park with a Wild West show. Selfridge assured Christchurch Town Council that 'he would work with archaeologists during construction and he would take steps to prevent erosion of the Head and always allow the public access'. Tilden meanwhile executed hundreds of drawings, admitting that the only way he could cope with the design was to develop it section by section. Whenever Selfridge was asked how, or when, the plan would be executed or what it would cost, he refused to be drawn. Tilden later recalled that he would simply look at his interrogator 'with a cold, clear, blue and calculating eye, thrusting out his chin with never a glimmer of a smile'.

In March 1919 Selfridge's celebrated its tenth birthday and Harry went on a spending spree. A swathe of impressive advertisements marked the anniversary. Lord Northcliffe in particular took note, writing to his managers: 'I feel we all owe a great deal to Selfridge for the way in which he woke up the drapers. He should be helped in every possible way.'

Flush with funds from a new issue of 500,000 preference shares, and with post-war building restrictions curtailing the Oxford Street development programme, Selfridge expanded into the provinces. He was convinced that the drapery stores presented a unique development opportunity and he bought businesses in Liverpool, Leeds, Sheffield, Gloucester, Peterborough, Reading and Northampton.

Selfridge was a man in a hurry. When he went to Dublin on 25 June to negotiate a deal to buy the city's old-established draper's Brown Thomas, he reasoned that the journey by train and ferry would take too long. So he flew. The chartered plane, a De Havilland Airco 9 piloted by Captain Gathergood, winner of the Aerial Derby, took off from Hendon just after lunch, touched down in Chester for refuelling and tea, and arrived in Dublin in time for dinner. It was the world's first commercial flight. Back at Hendon the next afternoon Selfridge told the press: 'This only shows what possibilities there are now in high speed aerial transport to the businessman in a hurry.' Reading about it in a rival paper, Lord Northcliffe was furious, shooting a note off to his staff: 'Why no reference to Selfridge's air journey to Dublin? It was the first business flight.' He might also have asked why Selfridge was proposing to buy a business in Dublin at a time when the city was under curfew and Michael Collins and his IRA men were battling it out on the streets with the brutal Black and Tans. Selfridge, however, felt that the city presented a 'wonderful opportunity'.

From that point on, Selfridge became addicted to aviation, and the pioneering commercial airline Aircraft Transport & Travel flew him not just to Highcliffe but also around the country to visit his growing empire. As always, he milked the press potential for all it was worth, putting a Handley Page seventeen-seater passenger plane fuselage on show in the store as the back-drop for a fashion show of the latest leather 'flying clothes'. At a time when flying was still a dangerous business and uninsurable, his bankers and his board members might have queried the wisdom of 'the Chief' – at the age of 63 – gallivanting around the skies. But such exploits were part of the Selfridge magic. He was on a roll, and no one could stop him.

At home, the loss of Rose had been a crushing blow. At work, the loss of his genial mentor Sir Edward Holden, who died in the summer of 1919, was another. Sir Edward's portrait joined that of Marshall Field in Harry's imposing office, where he had a new lady in his life. It had taken two years to find a suitable replacement for the inimitable Cissie Chapman who, having been his personal secretary since 1914, had been promoted to launch the store's Information Bureau. Indeed, Selfridge – who had got through an entire battalion of temporary staff since her promotion – was beginning to think she was irreplaceable. Then he found Miss Mepham. Calm, organized, efficient, tactful, loyal and discreet, Hilda Mepham was exactly the right woman to look after Harry Selfridge – and she did so until the day he left the store. She shared the outer office with an urbane young man called Eric Dunstan, who had joined the staff as his Social Secretary. The well-connected Dunstan had spent two years in Fiji working for a Colonial Governor and a period in the Conservative Party's headquarters. He was also discreet, which, given some of the requirements of his job, was probably just as well.

With commercial construction curtailed, Selfridge turned his hand to residential development. Encouraged by his friend Sir Harry Brittain, the newly appointed Conservative MP for Acton, Harry made his own public-spirited contribution by forming the non-profit-making Victory Construction Company. His plan was to build 300 inexpensive brick and concrete dwellings. Admitting that 'they were not very lovely', they would, he said, 'be easy to run and would serve as a temporary resting place for those whose lives have been disrupted until they see better days'. Each of the five-roomed, semi-detached houses on Lowfield and Westfield Roads was priced at £310 and offered initially to Acton residents. In the end, only seventy were built before the scheme went awry due to escalating costs, but it was a fine gesture.

Allied victory, meanwhile, was being discussed at the Paris Peace Conference, held at Versailles. As the protracted negotiations neared completion, Selfridge planned a special celebration. His creative director, Edward Goldsman, was dispatched to Paris where he was given special access to sketch and photograph the famous Hall of Mirrors, using Louis XIV's marvel as the theme for the store's 'budget no option' décor planned to coincide with the signing of the Treaty of Versailles. It wasn't just about window displays. The store took the decoration right out into the street, laying out a 'Court of Honour' in front of the main building, with imposing plaster columns and bas-relief figures holding shields and flags. Even the lamp-posts were decorated. Selfridge's was no longer just a part of Oxford Street. To the thousands of people who flocked to see the decorations, it had *become* Oxford Street.

~

VICES AND VIRTUES

'A store should be like a song of which one never tires.'
H. G. Selfridge

As the new decade arrived, the band in the store's Palm Court played all the latest hits at the daily *thés dansants* and the place was packed. To some observers, it was astonishing how many people had so much time in the day to dance. Why weren't they at work? But at a time when jobs were proving increasingly difficult to find, very often dancing *was* a job. A lot of unemployed ex-officers danced for a living. There was many a 'gentleman escort' available to take a turn on the floor with a war widow, while the impresario Albert de Courville used to boast that several of the more talented chorus boys in his revues at the London Hippodrome held either the MC or the DSO. Honours, however, didn't pay the rent.

At Selfridge's there was no cover charge in the Palm Court – Harry reasoned that those who came to dance might do a little shopping in between numbers. At the Piccadilly Hotel or the Café de Paris, the charge was 4 shillings for 'afternoon tea and dancing', while at the swankier Savoy, it was 5 shillings. For the lonely, a mere 2 shillings bought tea and sympathy at the Regent Palace or the Astoria Dance Hall, where girls were rumoured to offer more to those who wanted it. The lost and the louche went to Kate 'Ma' Meyrick's Dalton's Club in Leicester Square, which really was a pick-up place and where for the price of £2, 'Ma's' girls would offer a lot more than sympathy. When Mrs Meyrick subsequently appeared in court on vice charges, part of her defence was that 'the West End was a regular hotbed of lawlessness' and that 'her girls' were just 'bringing cheer to some of the terribly disfigured boys home from the war'.

The big musical hit of the moment was 'Ain't We Got Fun?' but as Mrs Meyrick had so aptly put it, for a lot of people, life wasn't much fun. Most young men, regardless of their social background, were struggling to rebuild their shattered lives after the horrors of the war. Demobbed with brutal haste and little if any government support, many of them faced a bleak future. Some were so shell-shocked that nothing but prescribed morphine, cocaine or the illicit but widely used opium could numb the pain. Others, haunted by the blood and gore of the trenches, simply drank their memories away. Large numbers of young men, without much education other than being trained to kill, joined gangs in London, where there were rich pickings to be had from protection rackets. Petty crime – pick-pocketing and bag-snatching in Oxford Street, shoplifting in the stores – was on the increase. At Selfridge's, where the open-plan floors were particularly vulnerable, dozens of extra store superintendents were hired to keep a watchful eye.

The media took to blaming all the woes facing society on 'drink, dancing and drugs', especially the latter which made for better copy. When the young and rather pretty dancer Billie Carleton died in late 1918 of a cocaine overdose, her companion, the fashion designer Reggie de Veulle, was charged with her manslaughter and viciously attacked in the press. In the end, the rather pathetic Mr de Veulle was found innocent of anything except 'having an effeminate face and a mincing little smile', whereupon he disappeared into obscurity. Meanwhile, the real culprit was found to be a Chinese immigrant, Lau Ping You, a drug dealer who worked for Britain's biggest supplier, Brilliant Chang. The tabloid press whipped itself into a frenzy over the 'yellow peril in Limehouse', while mothers were warned not to let their daughters 'go anywhere near a Chinese laundry or other places where the yellow men congregate'. In 1920, only six years after the Army had first handed out tablets containing cocaine to its troops, the Dangerous Drugs Act banned the drug altogether.

The clergy ranted from the pulpit about the licentiousness of the dancing youth (though Victor Sylvester, the undisputed king of the Black Bottom, was a vicar's son); organizations such as the London Council for the Promotion of Public Morality warned of the growing influence of the uncensored cinema; and the influential Temperance Movement urged even stricter licensing laws. Most of the young people in question took absolutely no notice. All they wanted to do was dance. But as far as officialdom was concerned, dancing went hand in hand with drinking. While Lloyd George and Nancy Astor, the country's first woman MP, who both loathed 'the demon drink', would have been delighted to see alcohol banned in Great Britain – as it had been in America to disastrous effect – they had to rely on DORA instead. The wartime law was dusted off and made more stringent still. It became illegal to get a drink anywhere after 10 p.m. without food, and anywhere at all after midnight. Such absurdities only succeeded in driving dozens of flourishing nightclubs underground – quite literally, as most of them were in dank cellars.

Such attempts to enforce a new morality had little effect. Everyone converged on club-land. Rich war profiteers, the *jeunesse dorée* up from Oxford and Cambridge, the young British royal princes, a clutch of their dispossessed European royal cousins – all sat side by side with newly rich provincials up from the suburbs, dancing and drinking till dawn, their night out all the more thrilling because it might end in a police raid.

Before the war, apart from the odd glass of sherry or a celebratory glass of champagne, pre-dinner drinking had hardly existed. Wine was drunk with food, never on its own, women would rarely drink spirits and men passed round the port. Then cocktails arrived. 'Cocktail time' seemed to begin anywhere from 12 noon to 5 p.m., with people giving cocktail parties, eagerly exchanging recipes for the perfect Martini, and praising barmen who made a great White Lady.

Not everyone approved. The distinguished restaurateur Monsieur Boulestin said: 'Cocktails are the most romantic expression of modern life, but the cocktail habit as practised in England is now a vice.' It was a vice to which even the otherwise fairly abstemious Harry Selfridge took. Pre-war he would nurse a glass of champagne for an entire evening. During the war, he joined the King who declared Buckingham Palace a 'dry zone' and gave up drinking altogether. But post-war, Harry took to having 'a cocktail or two' before dinner. He also took to eating a prodigious amount of food while dining which resulted – as was noticed by one of his inner-sanctum office staff – in him taking to wearing a corset. Selfridge's meanwhile joined in the craze for cocktails by selling shakers, fancy ice trays, cocktail napkins, recipe books, martini glasses, gold swizzle sticks, olives and all the paraphernalia of the drinker – right down to the white mess jackets that the barmen wore.

It wasn't just the fashion in drink that changed. Clothes were changing too. The influence of the once great Paul Poiret was waning. He was still making sumptuous clothes and was still surrounded by an eccentric coterie – the poet Max Jacob, a gifted amateur astrologer, liked to advise his friend on the colours he should wear so as to be in conjunction with the planets – but his style was about to be eclipsed. When fashion revived in Paris after the war, the look was distinctly less dramatic. Coco Chanel, poised to become the defining leader of style, declared: 'I make fashions women can live in, breathe in and look younger in.' The latter effect made her clothes irresistible. Everyone wanted to look younger, including Harry Selfridge. Now 64, he seemed utterly determined to push back time, travelling to Vienna for treatments with Serge Voronoff, whose anti-ageing experiments with monkey glands were exciting other youth-conscious luminaries such as George Bernard Shaw, Helena Rubinstein, Augustus John and Winston Churchill.

Thousands of women had found war work and the utility clothing that went with it a liberating experience. The watchwords in fashion were 'simplicity', 'modernity' and 'freedom'. Many women now widowed or without much prospect of marriage were having to become self-supporting through need as much as choice. They wanted clothes for work rather than for leisure, but above all they needed clothes that worked for them – less ornate, less contrived and certainly less expensive. Mechanical methods originally devised to cut material for military uniforms were quickly adapted to produce ready-to-wear clothing – chiefly coats and suits – which transformed not just the clothing industry but also the jobs of many women working in it, as unskilled and semi-skilled machinists took over what had previously been made by hand.

The lean, short shift dress of the quintessential Twenties flapper was actually a mid-decade innovation. Its precursor was a low-waisted combination of droop and drape in soft fabrics such as lamé, panne velvet and crêpe de Chine, often tied with a deep sash at the hip. All those lush, Edwardian curves were now out, and as corset sales slumped by two-thirds, the underpinnings industry had hastily to reinvent itself. Although Dorothy Parker famously quipped 'that brevity is the soul of lingerie', there was still quite a lot going on underneath. To flatten the bosom, women bought Symington's side-lacer camisole-style bra, wore a straight-cut camisole or, in an emergency, simply taped their bosom down with a crêpe bandage. The more mature, used to some support and still priding themselves in standing up straight, wore the longer-line corset pioneered for the pre-war straighter skirts, while the young and more athletic favoured a lighter-weight 'corselette' and even took to wearing garter belts. The cotton industry was in disarray as layers of servant-starched petticoats were discarded in favour of a simple petticoat shift – usually in satin or silk. Then, in 1924, there arrived the working girl's greatest saviour, rayon.

At the beginning of the Twenties hemlines moved up by about eight inches, revealing gleaming silk stockings, coloured kid-leather shoes, the hitherto unseen shape of a lady's leg and, in the case of Lady Londonderry, the grand political hostess of the day, the surprising fact that she had a snake tattoo from her ankle to her knee.

Stockings were no longer just black or white. With the introduction of synthetics, artificial silk stockings also came in skin-tones of flesh and beige. They weren't as nice to wear as silk, but they were less than half the price and very practical. Selfridge's was actually prosecuted for falsely selling synthetic stockings as 'real silk'. The store vigorously protested that it was the fault of the supplier but agreed to refund disgruntled customers nevertheless. This incident was one of the rare occasions when anyone in the office saw 'the Chief' lose his temper. He loathed confrontation and hated arguments, thinking them a waste of energy, but any misrepresentation of goods ran against his entire business philosophy. He prided himself on accuracy and his copywriters were never allowed to put a false spin on store promotions or use misleading price promotion tricks.

Selfridge himself may have been an early adopter of ethical advertising in respect of price and value, but his creative team was part of the swelling army of copywriters and image engineers who helped to build an ideology of consumerism. The seductive hum of shopping was in the air. Women were wearing make-up (no more lipsticks under the counter), flashing their powder compacts in public, using moisturizer and worrying about wrinkles, smoking cigarettes and gargling with Listerine, listening to all the latest records at home instead of playing the piano, and going out unchaperoned. They still wore hats – *everyone* still wore hats – but the hats were getting much, much smaller, and the hair underneath them was changing.

Long hair was out. Short waved hair, as pioneered by the film star Gloria Swanson, was in. At Selfridge's, the hairdressing department (now seating fifty clients at a time) was busy all day using the latest waving machines – price 3 guineas for shingled hair, 4 guineas for long. Hairdressing had by now become big business. Most of the original stylists from Selfridge's early, innovative department had left to open their own salons, 'colour, cut and curl' then as now being a profitable business. But even in a smaller salon, marcel waving cost at least 2 guineas, so anyone who couldn't afford a week's wages to wave their hair did it at home with tongs heated on a tiny spirit stove.

Women's magazines were settling into their stride. *Harper's Bazaar*,

Good Housekeeping, *Vogue*, *Queen*, *The Lady*, *Tatler* and *Woman Magazine* – the latter edited at one stage by Arnold Bennett – were essential reading and always available at the best hairdressers. Who ever was making or selling something fashionable was starting to advertise it seriously, although full stand-alone pages were still rare. Most stores ran quarter-pages, crammed with copy and cluttered with a multitude of different typefaces, usually accompanied by a deadly dull sketch produced by an art-agency draughtsman struggling to show the projected bestseller at Arding & Hobbs or Pontings.

High-style fashion illustration on the other hand had become recognized as an art in its own right – at its peak exemplified by the Russian émigré Erte's glorious work for *Harper's Bazaar*. Erte, Tamara de Lempicka and George Barbier, whose inspired work for the pre-war *Journal des Dames et des Modes* had helped establish the trend, were at the height of their powers. It didn't last. The illustrators would soon be eclipsed by photographers, with Baron de Meyer, Edward Steichen and George Hoyningen-Huene dominating the field.

Selfridge's advertising was aimed at the high-circulation daily newspapers, but when the store did place advertisements in magazines, Harry Selfridge made sure the pages were uncluttered and the message was clear. One early page in *Vogue* typifies the style:

Vogue is a beautifully-printed Journal and this typographical beauty lies in the excellence of its type and composition ... its paper, *its every detail*. Selfridge's endeavours to be an admirable Store by striving for excellence in its many departments, by insisting on variety and newness and novelty in its merchandise ... on charming courtesy and delightful service ... by studying every one of the thousands of details which go to produce the great 20th Century Store.

The establishment, on the other hand, was rather wary about all this newness. Old habits and grand manners died hard, and the old guard were disconcerted to find their racy daughters borrowing their motor-cars, footmen whistling in the corridors and their maids 'dressed to the nines' rushing off to Selfridge's or Swan & Edgar's on their afternoon off. That the latter did so was hardly surprising. Maids could now afford to go shopping, for their wages had more than doubled since the war and a good maid could earn £2 10s. a week plus her keep. Chauffeurs, much in demand as the rich changed their carriages for cars, earned £4 10s. a week, their accommodation provided in the stable mews above what were now garages.

The great landed families were feeling the pinch as death duties and taxation on unearned income took their toll. The profligate Duke of Manchester was declared bankrupt; the Duke of Portland threatened to close up his huge Nottinghamshire mansion, Welbeck Abbey; and even the fabulously rich Duke of Westminster was realizing assets, selling Gainsborough's exquisite *Blue Boy* and several other important pieces to Joseph Duveen. The sale, which caused an outcry among art experts and the public alike, netted 'Bendor' a useful £200,000 to go towards maintaining his yachts, horses, houses, wives and Coco Chanel, one of his more famous mistresses. Duveen stated firmly that the painting was not going to America: 'I have bought it for myself. It is my wish the picture should remain in this country.' He had in fact pre-sold it to the American railway magnate Henry E. Huntington and his wife Arabella for $620,000, reassuring her that the picture would clean up well when she expressed concern that the subject of the painting 'wasn't *quite* as blue as she had thought'. The Duke of Devonshire moved from his vast London palace, Devonshire House on Piccadilly – where developers were planning a 'super-cinema-restaurant' complex – to a mere mansion in Carlton Gardens, while his father-in-law the fifth Marquis of Lansdowne rented out his magnificent London house which came with twenty servants, including a nightwatchman who guarded the private passage that ran through to Berkeley Square. News that Lord Lansdowne's tenant was none other than Harry Selfridge raised eyebrows among London's élite. 'Think of it,' said Sir Gilbert Parker, 'Selfridge in Lansdowne House. It's *appalling*.'

It was certainly intriguing. The cost of renting and maintaining one of London's largest houses was phenomenal. At a time when an average family could live reasonably well on £500 a year, Selfridge was paying £5,000 to rent his new London home, plus £5,000 a year for his lease on Highcliffe. On top of that there were servants' wages and his high living expenses, covering everything from food to flowers, travel and, last but not least, generous entertaining. All this supposedly came out of the £40,000 that Harry earned each year, but in reality, the store provided a lot more. What wasn't charged to 'the Chief's' personal account was set against 'public relations and entertainment', which neatly covered food, wines and the dozens of boxes of Corona cigars, specially imported from Havana for Selfridge and distributed to grateful friends such as Ralph Blumenfeld. Selfridge enjoyed living like a lord. Now he lived in a lord's mansion.

Like the estate at Highcliffe, Lansdowne House had originally been owned by the Marquis of Bute, though he never actually lived there. In 1765 he sold the partly finished Robert Adam property to the Foreign Secretary, Lord Shelburne. Shelburne – later the first Marquis of Lansdowne – had battled valiantly to conciliate the American colonists during the War of Independence. Having failed in the task, he resigned from government and consoled himself in the time-honoured way by travelling through Italy and, advised by the antiquities dealer Gavin Hamilton, acquiring beautiful things. By 1782, he was back in power as Prime Minister, and the second Treaty of Paris, which conceded America's independence, was drawn up for signature by Benjamin Franklin in Robert Adam's exquisite Round Room at Lansdowne House.

Thus the Selfridge family, formerly of Ripon, Wisconsin, and Chicago, Illinois, settled into one of the most famous and historically important houses in Great Britain, living surrounded by ceilings and panels painted by John Francis Rigaud and Giovanni Cipriani, entertaining in rooms where Dr Johnson had dined and where the country of their birth had ceded from Great Britain. Max Beerbohm drew a cartoon of the Marquis obsequiously showing Selfridge around Lansdowne House: 'Statuary, sir? Majolica, all the latest eighteenth-century books – this way.'

A highly valued client of the Midland Bank, Selfridge now had the undivided attention of no less than three of their senior general managers. Sometimes collectively, sometimes individually, Mr Frederick Hyde, Mr S. B. Murray and Sir Clarence Sadd would lunch with Selfridge in the store or motor down for meetings at Highcliffe, where in 1920 the quiet little town of Christchurch had acquired an imposing new pillared and porticoed branch building. That same year, the Midland managed a new issue of 1 million 10 per cent preferred ordinary shares of £1, which was subscribed seven times over and which brought the company's share capital to £3.55 million. When Eric Dunstan prepared the Chief's entry for *Who's Who*, he listed him as Managing Director. Furious, Selfridge scratched it out, shouting: 'Damn it, man, I own the place!' The trouble was, he didn't.

What impressed the bankers was the breadth of his ideas and the speed with which he put them into action. They liked his expansion into the provinces. They admired his diversification, such as the move into food via the launch of the John Quality grocery chain, with branches in, among other boroughs, Westminster, Kensington, Ealing and Acton. Above all, they liked his catch phrase, 'Best Value in London: Always', and the fact that he was unafraid to make markdowns. As if foreseeing the financial slump of May 1920, Selfridge had pre-empted disaster by reducing the store's stock by 10 per cent, advertising price cuts aggressively and adding 'spot offers' and 'an additional 10 per cent off prices on selected items'. This sort of mid-season sale was unheard of, and it rattled his competitors. For the first time, Selfridge used the 'fear factor' in his copywriting, talking of global trading difficulties and increases in the price of raw materials. Such comments, said his critics, were decidedly 'un-public-spirited' and 'deliberately designed to encourage stockpiling'. Ignoring them all and determined to clear dead stock, Selfridge relentlessly ran the promotion for five months.

He also instructed his buyers to cancel anything and everything that was late, and to cut purchasing budgets for the autumn season. 'Never talk to suppliers about discounts,' Selfridge told his buyers, 'till you have secured rock bottom price – then go for best discounts and dates. Keep a poker face and always preserve freedom to trade hard.' Manufacturers who had enjoyed the store's bulk-buying policies were distraught as orders were slashed to the bone. Defending his actions in the trade press, Selfridge said: 'Retailers cannot be expected to assume the risks of production – all business is more or less speculative.' Arguments raged about 'Selfridge's war on prices' as the local Chamber of Commerce – even the Board of Trade – waded in to complain. Selfridge, who was always impervious to criticism, didn't care. He has judged the economic situation accurately. The Mutual Communications Society – the retailers' own forum for monitoring credit and debt – was now meeting weekly, not monthly. The post-war economic boom had been short-lived. By 1921 unemployment had risen to over 2 million. The only shop a lot of families were visiting was their local pawn shop.

Meanwhile, Selfridge's staff continued to receive bonus payments if they met targets and to enjoy 'benefits in kind' that were the envy of their friends. The store director Percy Best escorted fifty personnel on an eight-day junket to Paris; 5,000 employees danced the night away at what the press called 'A Selfridge Revel' at the Albert Hall; and over 45,000 shares were set aside for an employee purchase scheme. If some noticed an increase in the Chief's yellow envelopes hitting their desks, they didn't mind, though some of the messages in them were becoming a little odd – one blouse buyer was asked: 'What great thought have you had today?' Selfridge was a great believer in the value of surprise and was quick to defend his shock tactics: 'It's important to give people new angles, it jerks them out of a rut.' They didn't always work. When he sent a tin of spinach to senior buyers before the spring sale, with a note saying 'Let us see if the result is as beneficial as it always is to Popeye', very few appreciated the gesture.

To those who knew him well, Selfridge seemed to be becoming markedly more frenetic. Like the 'mile-a-minute' Harry of earlier years, he was bursting with ideas but would set staff on to a project only to drop it at the last minute. His insomnia was becoming worse and he took up 'yoga breathing', extolling the virtues of deep inhaling and exhaling as being 'completely invigorating especially when tired'. Not that Harry ever seemed tired. His mid-afternoon cat-nap seemed to set him up for the rest of the day, and he partied late into the night as though he dreaded the thought of sleep or of being alone. How he missed Rose. Plans for Hengistbury Head were a diversion and visitors to his office would be shown drawings of the proposed castle, which jostled for space with schemes for the new store extension.

Friends were bemused by his grand plans for the castle. Lord Beaverbrook, on being given the 'virtual tour', said: 'No one has yet discovered this castle, for it exists only on paper. When Selfridge requires mental relaxation, he may be found poring over the plans which are to be the basis of this fairy edifice – moat and parapet, tower, dungeon and drawbridge, are all there, only awaiting the Mason of the future to translate them into actuality.' Ralph Blumenfeld was worried. 'He plans to build a wonderful castellated palace which shall be the most beautiful architectural effort of modern history,' he wrote in his diary, 'yet I feel it will remain in the region of dreams.'

When at Highcliffe for the weekend, Harry would write letters at the study table that had once belonged to Napoleon, paste up his scrapbooks and put flowers on Rose's grave. Dinners were hosted by his mother, who at the age of 86 still enjoyed a party. Philip Tilden later wrote: 'Old Madam Selfridge was an ideal for us all. A hostess of the rare old school of American propriety, all lavender, lace and an exquisite link with bygone standards. It was a privilege to know her. She was the soul in all the world that her son loved best.' Although mother and son were very close, shared literary pastimes and talked about business and investments, she wasn't privy to his innermost thoughts. He was an intensely private and inhibited man and would never have had the courage to open up to her about the extent of his gambling or his escalating expenses. She would have known of his strange sex life – mothers and wives almost always know when the men they love are behaving badly. But he was a grown man – indeed almost an old man. She couldn't change him. So she continued to do what she did best. She dined with him at Lansdowne House, putting a shawl round Canova's *Venus* not because the bare breasts offended her but because 'it made her feel chilly'. She was at his side at the High-cliffe fête at which a revelling crowd of 5,000 people enjoyed brass bands, a jazz dance competition, fortunes told by an Indian mystic and even a beauty contest – won by Miss Phyllis Palmer of Bournemouth who proudly collected her prize of £10 from Mr Selfridge. He himself impressed guests with his unerring eye in judging the weight of a giant cheese to the nearest ounce. Mother and son went to Wimbledon each season, never missing the matches of the French tennis star Suzanne Lenglen who had won the ladies' singles championship every year since 1919. She astounded the audience with her athleticism and, with her short hair, short *plissé* jersey tennis dresses, short white ermine warm-up coat and, most exciting of all, her glorious suntan, she had an equally electric effect on fashion.

In June 1921 the family celebrated the marriage of Violette to the French Vicomte Jacques de Sibour in a ceremony at the Brompton Oratory attended by 1,200 guests. In truth, Harry wasn't keen on his daughter's choice of husband. De Sibour had caught Violette's eye a year earlier in the store, where he was working rather than doing his shopping. De Sibour's father and step-mother lived on the Isle of Wight, where they had met Sir Thomas Lipton and had thereby moved into the Selfridge family orbit. Jacques was dashing, attrac-tive and brave – during the war he had flown with the French Air Force. He was also unemployed. His father, perhaps hoping retail management was a career with prospects, asked Selfridge to give him a job. Less than three months later, when Jacques got engaged to the boss's daughter, he promptly resigned, saying he preferred to pursue 'prospects in aviation'. Violette and Jacques rented a flat in London and another in Paris. They also invested heavily in a coffee farm in the White Highlands of Kenya, later notorious as 'Happy Valley'. Selfridge, of course, paid for it all.

When Harry was interviewed, he was always happy to talk about his work, the store, his son, his eldest daughter, even his mother, but he rarely discussed his two younger daughters. In the extensive archives there are dozens of photographs of him with Rosalie, her husband Serge and their daughter Tatiana. There are a handful of him with Violette, mainly taken when she and her husband set off to fly round the world in their Gipsy Moth plane called 'Safari'. There are few photographs of Gordon Jr and even fewer of his youngest daughter Beatrice who later married Jacques de Sibour's elder brother Louis, a man even more attractive than his brother, also beautifully dressed – and also with little visible means of support.

In truth, Harry was not close to his children. He gave them money of course – he was always more than generous – and he gave their husbands money too. He also gave Rosalie and Serge a home, albeit not one of their own. Serge, always experimenting in the hope of patenting some potentially profitable piece of motoring gadgetry but never quite succeeding, gladly accepted the hospitality. In reality, he and his mother Marie happily sponged off Selfridge. Serge and Rosalie's grandson Simon Wheaton-Smith is also convinced that 'the entire family, certainly my Uncle Gordon, and almost anyone else, would have been afraid of him. He always got things his way – and he paid all their bills.'

The entire family lived a curious life partying together, and often travelling together – but seemingly not talking much. Certainly Gordon Jr's affair with a very pretty girl from the toy department was never discussed. Not even when she had their first child in 1925, and then a second, third *and* fourth. Gordon Jr continued to live the high life as a bachelor in a Mayfair apartment with cowhide-covered banquettes and soft lighting, while Charlotte Dennis, the mother of his children, looked after them in a house in Hampstead. Selfridge refused to acknowledge the relationship. As far as he was concerned, it simply didn't exist. Whatever hopes and dreams he had cherished for his only son, they hadn't included marriage to a girl who worked in the toy department.

Having left Trinity College, Cambridge, with a third-class degree in Economics, Gordon Jr had joined the store in 1921. Working there was always his destiny. Arnold Bennett vividly recalled an early visit to the inner sanctum during the war:

> There is a small closed roll-top desk in his room. It is his son's aged 16. Boy now home for holidays from Winchester. He was upstairs learning accountancy. He takes a boxing lesson every day at 12.30. His father showed us photos of him at his desk in various attitudes, including the attitude of dictating to a girl-clerk. I continue to like Selfridge.

Gordon was moved through the business at break-neck speed. He spent a few months learning the ropes in packing and delivery, then a year working for the highly regarded Merchandise Manager, Thomas Anthony. By 1923, he was managing the menswear department and by 1924, at the age of just 23, he had a seat on the main board. By the time he was 25 he was Managing Director. Mr Anthony meanwhile had moved to Harrods.

Whatever his son's responsibilities, Harry still controlled promotion, advertising and publicity. No one ever came between Selfridge and the media. His zeal for booking space continued unabated – although to some observers it seemed he was more concerned with the number of pages appearing rather than what he put in them. In 1922, he went a step further, seriously considering becoming a newspaper owner himself, when he apparently attempted to buy *The Times*. Lord Northcliffe had died in extraordinary circumstances in August that year, with even his foes showing discretion about his sad final weeks. Northcliffe had lost his mind. Convinced he was in danger of being poisoned by a German gang, he had taken refuge in a hut on the roof of the Duke of Devonshire's house in Carlton Gardens, where he kept a gun under his pillow.

Selfridge's friend Edward Price Bell, at the time the London correspondent of the Chicago *Daily News*, described Harry's attempt to acquire a newspaper in letters to his editor in America. 'All his peculiar vanity and ambition are enlisted in trying to get it,' wrote Bell, explaining that the funds would come from 'what one might call international-amity or world-friendship money from those who want to bring about a closer union of Great Britain and the United States. He [Selfridge] seems to be able to get as much money as he wants for any purpose.'

Harry's dream wasn't quite as wide of the mark as might be imagined. He had influential friends, among them Sir Harry Brittain, the MP for Acton, founder of the Empire Press Union and President of the British International Association of Journalists. He also knew Brittain's colleague, Evelyn Wrench, founder of the Over-Seas League and the English-Speaking Union, who would go on to edit *The Spectator*. Another connection linked both Brittain and Wrench. The former had, in 1902, founded the Pilgrims' Society, a dining club whose 'strictly invitation only' membership was exclusively formed from an élite group of wealthy British and American businessmen, bankers and politicians. Their aim was then (and remains today) 'to foster good-will, good-fellowship and everlasting peace between the US and Great Britain'. The super-rich, power-broking Pilgrims would have had unimaginable resources readily available to back the right sort of people. The trouble was that while Harry had strengths, he also had one weakness. It wasn't women that worried these men, rather the fact he was a profoundly addicted gambler. Such a vice made him vulnerable. *The Times* passed into the capable hands of one of the leading Americans in Britain, Colonel J. J. Astor (later Lord Astor of Hever), and Harry's Hearstian visions of a newspaper empire remained a dream.

Unlike William Randolph Hearst, who was devoted to only one mistress, Marion Davies, Harry scattered his largesse, evidence of which came up for auction in Paris when, following her death, Gaby Deslys's jewels – including her sensational black pearls – were sold. She was only 39 when she died from the after-effects of traumatic surgery for a throat tumour, and her estate was wound up in a blaze of publicity. The contents of the house that Harry had acquired for her raised an astonishing £50,000 as dealers and collectors scrambled to bid for Gaby's belongings. Harry's generosity proved a good investment for his girlfriends. In 1922, Syrie Maugham put his gifts on the block, selling the expensive furniture bought for the Regent's Park house to finance her new interior design business and decorative antiques shop in Baker Street.

As a rich, eligible widower, Harry Selfridge could have wined and dined any number of equally eligible and elegant women. But for the man who was at heart a showman, seemingly only showgirls would do. In 1922, his affection was focused on another French *danseuse*, Alice Delysia, the highly paid star of Charles B. Cochran's London review *Mayfair and Montmartre*. Unfortunately for Mr Cochran, Alice caught a throat infection and had to withdraw from the show, a debacle which cost C. B. over £20,000. What she cost Harry Selfridge, we will never know.

C. B. Cochran and his stage director Frank Collins were part of the innermost Selfridge circle. The store promoted theatrical productions through its window displays, invited stage stars to make presentations at events in the Palm Court, and was happy to loan furs and jewels for photographic sessions. When Selfridge wanted new uniforms for his beautiful bevy of lift girls, Cochran's office was asked about 'new design talent' in town. Recalling a polite, albeit nervous young designer who had visited recently, Mr Collins thought his work might suit Selfridge. The appointment arranged, the young man anxiously presented twenty carefully prepared sketches, looking hopefully in Harry's direction. 'Go away, my boy, and learn to draw,' Selfridge told Norman Hartnell. Sir Norman, who would become Britain's most famous fashion designer, recalled the incident in his memoirs, adding: 'Later I grew to admire and like him. He would send lovely ladies to be dressed by me, and his guineas well recompensed me for that early humiliation.'

The lift girls got their new clothes – designer unknown – while the lifts themselves got new doors, designed by the sculptor Edgar Brandt whose work Selfridge saw at the Paris Salon des Artistes Décorateurs in 1922. Adapted from Brandt's piece in bronze, *Cicognes d'Alsace*, the magnificent doors were not actually cast in bronze but were made from raised and formed sheet steel and wrought iron, mounted on plywood and painted with a mixture of varnish and bronze powder. It was beauty on a budget, but only an expert could tell.

Selfridge loved Paris. Commuting regularly on the boat train, he would visit his great friends Théophile Bader and Alphonse Khan, the owners of Galeries Lafayette. He lunched with his French banker, Benjamin Rosier of Banque Suisse et Française, saw his young grandson Blaise de Sibour and spent his nights playing baccarat for high stakes at François André's exclusive club Le Cercle Haussmann. It has often been said that Harry's gambling only began in earnest when he took up with the Dolly Sisters in the mid-1920s. But he had *always* gambled – and he knew where to go.

At first it was Monte Carlo, where the casinos operated by the Société des Bains de Mer ruled supreme, but Monaco was too far to go for a weekend. Having banned gambling in 1837, the French Government, bowing to pressure, reinstated it in 1907, with the result that Grand Casinos were built in Nice, Deauville, Cannes and Biarritz. For the most part under the aegis of the man known as 'the Casino King' of France, Eugène Cornuché, they offered baccarat and chemin-de-fer – roulette then being the exclusive fiefdom of Monte Carlo. Cornuché, keen to boost his casino in Cannes, hired sixteen glorious girls from Paris, dressed and bejewelled them, and installed them at his tables with enough chips to convince other gamblers that they were genuinely playing the game. Nicknamed the Cornuchettes, his team players became both rich and famous – one married a French duke. In Paris, however, such things weren't allowed. For years, the city banned women from gambling. Playing the tables in Paris was never about fun and flirting, it was about serious money.

In England, where gaming was banned, there were illegal gaming clubs, just as there were speakeasies in America. But outside private weekend house parties, British gambling was controlled by men just as tough as those running liquor in America, and there was little pleasure playing in an uneasy atmosphere of sinister violence. Still, Harry indulged in London. For a compulsive gambler – especially one who liked to hold the bank at baccarat – there wasn't much choice. His private ledger shows the extent of his losses. In 1921, he listed fifteen payments in less than five months, totalling an astonishing £5,000, each made to his private secretary Eric Dunstan. It must have been 'money owing'. Dunstan's job was to deliver it.

Years later, when a journalist was writing a feature about Selfridge, he asked an employee who knew him well what he was *really* like. 'Oh a genius, totally brilliant all week at work – but at the weekend he was someone completely different,' came the reply. At work through the 1920s Harry hardly put a foot wrong. In October 1922 the store hosted the first of its celebrated 'Election Night' parties. Store events are commonplace now, but then it was unheard of to entertain after hours. The black-tie dancing party with supper before the results – a Conservative victory which meant Andrew Bonar Law became Prime Minister – followed by bacon and eggs for breakfast was a wild success. Champagne flowed all night, the barber's shop was kept open to refresh the men with hot towels, while Lady Curzon, the Duchess of Rutland, the Russian Grand Duke Michael and the actresses Gladys Cooper, Alice Delysia and Anna May Wong danced, it was noted in the press, 'with vigour'.

Selfridge adored statistics and busied himself with data collected by his Information Bureau. He knew, for example, that 15.3 million people had shopped in the store in 1922. He also knew that his newly uniformed waitresses – now wearing trousers – could take 'nine steps more per minute to get to the kitchen than they could in a skirt'. Speed didn't cut any ice with critics of women wearing trousers. One cleric raged against Selfridge from his pulpit, quoting Deuteronomy: 'The woman shall not wear that which pertaineth unto a man.' The vicar was wasting his breath: before long women wouldn't be wearing very much at all.

Having put up with three years of delay over his planned store extension, in March 1923, when political change heralded the lifting of commercial building restrictions, an intriguing group of men gathered on the roof of the old Thomas Lloyd building adjacent to the store. Led by Selfridge in his customary morning coat and silk top hat, the team wielding pick-axes for the photographers included Sir Woodman Burbidge (Harrods), Mr John Lawrie (Whiteley's), Colonel Cleaver (Robinson & Cleaver) and Mr Barnard (Thomas Wallis's). That such a group gathered to celebrate the expansion of a supposed rival indicates how popular Selfridge had become. The business of retail had changed radically since Selfridge's arrival in London. Indisputably, he was the accelerator of that change.

On 26 April, the Duke of York and Elizabeth Bowes-Lyon were married at Westminster Abbey in front of 3,000 guests, the women glittering with jewels, the men with decorations. That night, the Marchioness Curzon hosted a Charity Ball ('by kind permission of Mr Gordon Selfridge at Lansdowne House') for Queen Victoria's Jubilee Institute for Nurses. The guest-list resembled the pages of *Debrett's*, with an occasional leaf taken from the *Almanach de Gotha* – it was a wonderful opportunity to entertain a host of visiting royals in town for the wedding who might otherwise have had nowhere to go. For the price of 3 guineas a head they could dance to Paul Whiteman's orchestra, drink champagne all night courtesy of Perrier Jouet and admire each other's court decorations. Patrons of the event included the Duchesses of Sutherland, Somerset, Norfolk, Grafton, Beaufort, Northumberland, Abercorn, Westminster and Portland, as well as the Marchionesses Salisbury, Anglesey, Londonderry, Linlithgow, Carisbrooke and Blandford. Then there were the Countesses (from Bathurst and Beatty to Lonsdale and Shaftesbury), the Ladies (Ribblesdale, Islington, Desborough and Guinness, among others), and finally the mere knights' wives: Lady Lavery, Lady Tree, Lady Cunard. The Prince of Wales was expected, though sadly he failed to arrive, but the Royal Princes Henry and George were there, along with King Alfonso of Spain.

As the royal procession was moving through to dinner, a very drunk, near-naked Isadora Duncan bounced through the crowd and threw her arms round Selfridge, slurring: 'Harry darling, how *are* you?' Selfridge stayed calm, hissing an aside to the omnipresent Eric Dunstan that he should 'get *rid* of her' before moving through to dinner. Isadora however slipped away, disappearing up a back staircase to the ballroom where the band was playing rather romantic waltzes during the supper interval. When Dunstan eventually found her, she was wafting around in the middle of the floor, dress and arms flying, and with them a valuable terracotta knocked off its pedestal. Dunstan dutifully picked her up, carried her to a car and drove to the Cavendish Hotel where, as he later said, 'I believe the resourceful Mrs Rosa Lewis locked her in a room.'

Back at Lansdowne House, the band played on.

MAKING WAVES

'I discovered that men will pay anything to be amused. Pleasure and amusements
are the only things in the world where the buyer rarely counts the cost.'
Kate Meyrick, nightclub owner

Whether it was a teenager spending 7/6d of his savings on a
crystal radio kit, or any one of the legions of enthusiasts
reading *Amateur Wireless* while they fiddled with knobs in the hope of
hearing the Savoy Havana Band live from the hotel ballroom, Britain
had become besotted with radio. It had been hesitantly launched in
1920, when the *Daily Mail* sponsored a recital by Dame Nellie Melba
broadcast live from Marconi's Chelmsford works. While commercial
radio was poised to take America by storm, most of Britain's frustrated
radio fans had to spend the next two years with little service to speak
of, thanks to the Postmaster General's misconception that Marconi's
station 2MT, run out of a hut in Writtle, 'would interfere with air to
ground controls in matters of aviation'. The cheery voice of ex-Royal
Flying Corps Captain P. P. Eckersley, the country's first radio presenter,
was thus strictly rationed to just fifteen minutes a week.

Marconi were soon granted a second licence, setting up a call
sign, 2LO, at the company head office in the Strand where the
transmitter was housed in an attic room and the aerials were strung
between towers on the roof. Then, in the summer of 1922, a hybrid
between commerce and government called the British Broadcasting
Company Ltd was formed. Marconi's 2LO was transferred to the BBC
in November and sales of 'licences to listen' soared from 10,000 to

500,000. By 1924, 2LO's newly updated transmitter was installed on the roof of Selfridge's, where Mr Wragg, the buyer for the new radio department, was kept busy trying to keep pace with customer demand for wireless sets. By 1927, over two and a half million homes would own one. Selfridge's was a launch pad not merely for unstoppable consumer trends but also for employees involved with them. Just three years later, Mr Wragg left to help set up a business called Rent-A-Radio, which ultimately evolved into Radio Rentals, with a shop on virtually every high street in Britain.

Newspaper publishers, many of whom felt threatened by this new way of disseminating news, refused at first to publish programme listings. Seizing an opportunity to highlight the store's 'public service programme', Selfridge rode to the rescue, using the 'Callisthenes' column to inform readers when they could hear their favourite music or listen to the news. It struck a chord. Within the week, national newspapers followed suit and thus their 'radio pages' were born. Although enamoured with the potential of radio, Harry refused to accept a manufacturer's offer of £3,000 in cash to display their latest model. He abhorred the concept of concessions, telling Mr Wragg, 'If we did this sort of thing, we should eventually discover that someone else was running our business. Next, they would demand the right to dress our windows to suit themselves, then where would we be?'

The store meanwhile positively hummed to music. The phonograph department wired up a player to serenade the workmen busy on the Oxford Street extension, who were cheered along while they worked to the big hit of the moment, 'Fascinating Rhythm' by Jelly Roll Morton. When Selfridge himself visited the Palm Court for tea, the band struck up with 'I'm just wild about Harry', which was always guaranteed to raise a smile.

He needed cheering up. Somerset Maugham's play *Our Betters* had opened at the Globe Theatre to rave reviews. For the next twelve months Selfridge was parodied six nights a week and during matinées. He claimed he never saw it – just as William Randolph Hearst said he never saw *Citizen Kane* – but it's hard to believe he didn't slip in one evening. Every mannerism of 'Arthur Fenwick', the character based on Selfridge, was chillingly accurate. Eric Dunstan, a close acquaintance of Maugham's confidant Gerald Haxton, was told that Maugham and Syrie had invited Selfridge out to lunch years earlier 'so Willie could get the detail right'. Selfridge never talked about Syrie, who was herself now bitterly unhappy in her sham of a marriage. Indeed he never talked about any of his mistresses. Those members of staff closest to him – Dunstan, Miss Mepham and Mr Williams, by now the store Sales Manager – were never privy to his innermost thoughts. Williams would later say: 'He wasn't a man who either invited or gave confidences. He had a monumental detachment from all matters of personal concern.'

The Government meanwhile was in disarray. Bonar Law, his health failing, resigned in May 1923 and in December there was another General Election and another party in the store. The 1,200 guests, who included the Asquiths, the Churchills, Jack Buchanan, Gladys Cooper, Lady Headfort, the beautiful Lady Lavery, the Ranee of Sarawak and the Hollywood hero Charlie Chaplin, danced to music from the famous band-leader Ambrose and his Embassy Club Band. Fifty telephone operators manned special lines bringing information in from around the country. As news of one close count was supposedly coming through, the famous music-hall comedian and emergent film actor Leslie Henson took the microphone. 'No change,' he said to cheers from the audience, as he pulled out his empty trouser pockets and shook them. The real results were posted up on a cricket scoreboard by six pretty girls. Those watching outside on the street crowded round the 'electric newspaper' which lit up the results in blazing lights. In fact they caused such a bottleneck in the street that the police insisted the store close it down.

To the consternation of many wining and dining at Selfridge's, the collapsing Conservative vote resulted in a hung parliament, and Britain's first Labour Prime Minister, Ramsay MacDonald, moved into Downing Street. The Selfridge family were also on the move. Their lease on Highcliffe had expired and the castle was discreetly put up for sale by the Stuart Wortleys. Country weekends were now spent in the open environs of Wimbledon Park, where Rosalie, Serge and their daughter Tatiana had moved into the once grand but now rather shabby Wimbledon Park House. The heavily mortgaged mansion – originally built for the 4th Earl Spencer, who owned the Manor of Wimbledon – belonged to Serge's mother, Marie Wiasemsky. Desperately short of money, she had recently been taken to court by an irate servant owed three months' wages of just £12. Rosalie and Serge, clearly hoping Selfridge would fund them, struck out on their own, taking over financial responsibility for the vast property. Serge, already popular in Wimbledon where the family hosted an annual fête and a historical fancy dress gala, had become something of a local hero when locals read press reports about him diving to rescue a mother and child from the sea near Boulogne.

The deeds of the house were in the name of Prince Wiasemsky, Serge having adopted the title. The principal branch of the Wiasemsky family, headed by Prince Vladimir, was not amused. Vladimir, his married sister Princess Lydia Wassiltchikoff and his mother had escaped the turmoil of the Russian Revolution, and settled in the South of France, but his two brothers had not been so lucky: Prince Boris was murdered by his estate workers after having his eyes gouged out, and Prince Dimitri was shot. Memories of these atrocities were still fresh, so it is hardly surprising that Prince Vladimir was less than impressed when the 'self-styled Prince Serge Wiasemsky', as he caustically called him, took it upon himself to form a movement called the Russian National Progressive Party. When Alexis Aladin, leader of the Russian Peasant Union, was in London that year for talks with Ramsay MacDonald, he shared a platform with Serge who told the *Sunday Times*, 'the land of Russia belongs to the people. My party has no connection with, and totally disagrees with and disapproves of the monarchical group.' By this he meant the Romanovs rather than his own supposed ancestors the Rurikids. The exiled Romanov Grand Duke Michael, who had previously enjoyed the Selfridges' hospitality, declined an invitation to their next party.

Whatever Serge thought of the ill-fated Russian monarchy, he relentlessly clung to his own title, hobnobbing with other Russians who had married well, among them Prince Serge Obolensky and his bride, the 20-year-old Alice Astor, who had inherited a trust fund of $5 million when her father went down with the *Titanic*. Young Tatiana Wiasemsky made an angelic bridesmaid when Prince George Imeretinsky married the society beauty Stella Wright.

Meanwhile, Harry Selfridge had also parted with Harrose Hall on Lake Geneva, reportedly selling it for a tidy sum. The sale prompted his elderly mother to make a trip to Chicago to see the house once more, visiting old friends both there and in Washington. Chicago, cheerfully described in the hit song of 1922 as 'That Toddlin' Town', was a city under siege. By the time Lois Selfridge arrived in November 1923, it was reported that over 60 per cent of the city's police were involved in one way or another in the liquor business. Al Capone had established himself as a leading light in organized crime, his own employees running over 160 bars and gambling houses. Capone, having 'seen off' three rival families with an assortment of weapons ranging from bombs to Thompson sub-machine guns, was driven around town in a $30,000 bullet-proof Cadillac flanked by posses of armed hoodlums. Madam Selfridge, a life-long supporter of Prohibition, could now see for herself what it had created – a speakeasy life of violence and crime, swinging along at a fast and furious rate.

Her trip lasted three months. Although she was away for Christmas, Harry sent out a card to store staff, showing mother and son together in the library at Lansdowne House. The card also bore a message: 'What a wonderful privilege it is to live – to see – to hear – to think – to learn!' His mother, however, did not have long to live. In Washington the following February, she contracted pneumonia. Harry rushed over to America and brought her home on the SS *Berengaria*. They landed at Southampton on Saturday, 23 February, but by the Monday she was dead. Her funeral took place at St Mark's in Highcliffe, where she was buried next to her daughter-in-law Rose. The store, draped mournfully, albeit exquisitely, in black, closed for the day, while the tiny Hampshire parish church was filled with flowers sent by, among others, Mr and Mrs Adolph S. Ochs (owners of the *New York Times*), John Lawrie (the Chairman of Whiteley's), the Blumenfelds and Mr and Mrs John Shedd from Chicago. There was also a spectacularly beautiful bouquet bearing an engraved card from 'La Princesse de Monaco'. The 26-year-old Princess Charlotte had sent equally stupendous flowers to Rose's funeral five years earlier and was evidently a close friend of the Selfridge family. Though no trace exists of the origins of this intriguing relationship, Princess Charlotte was certainly in need of friends.

Charlotte had always been sneered at by Monaco society. Her mother, Marie Louvet, had been a cabaret singer in an Algerian nightclub when she first met Prince Louis II of Monaco, then an officer in the French Foreign Legion. Their illegitimate daughter Charlotte Louise was born in Algeria in 1898, and her lonely upbringing was financed by her father. Since Prince Louis never married, young Charlotte became, dynastically speaking, the last chance for the Monaco ruling family. In the absence of an heir, the throne would pass to a German cousin, and with it would go the Grimaldi share of the lucrative profits from the casino. So, by special decree, Charlotte was formally adopted by her father, created a princess, and hastily married off to the 'dandy' Count Pierre de Polignac who, during their uneasy marriage, fathered Prince Rainier and Princess Antoinette. The dynasty now being secure, profits made in what Somerset Maugham wittily described as 'a sunny place for shady people' continued apace. Selfridge himself, although he gambled at Monte Carlo, preferred the vast municipal casino in Nice, where he kept his own apartment and where, for a while, the exotic Princess Charlotte lived until she set up home with René Gigier, France's most infamous jewel thief. She and Harry would remain friends until his death.

An inveterate traveller, Selfridge liked nothing better than rushing to board the boat train at Victoria for the journey to Paris. He was an early passenger on the Calais–Nice–Rome Express, whose clattering wooden sleeping cars took travellers south to the newly fashionable summer playgrounds of the sun-seeking rich; and he was ecstatic when in December 1922 the new First Class-only Calais–Méditerranée Express service – known simply as *le train bleu* – was launched.

Years later, a senior guard on the boat train from Victoria recalled Mr Selfridge fondly: 'He crossed nearly every week, either to Le Touquet or on to Paris ... he once went all the way to Cannes just for six hours' sunshine. He was the most remarkable person – brisk, methodical and so original. He had the gift of getting to sleep immediately but would jump up in the morning, brush his hair and be fully alert – the only passenger to think of bringing his disembarkation card on board pre-prepared and to put his American passport in a coloured silk folder so it could be easily identified.'

In April 1924, the vast extension to the store was officially opened. Much to Harry's annoyance, there was still a gap between the original, eastern building and the new section that was being argued about by builders, bankers and borough councillors, but below ground, the Bargain Basement stretched unbroken from Duke Street to Orchard Street, covering an area of three and a half acres. Most of the upper-floor departments were replicated 'below stairs', where customers enjoyed keen prices, cool white walls, white marble floors and, for the first time in England, cool air, courtesy of the very latest in American mechanical wizardry, a 'comfort cooling' system. Air-conditioning was the quantum leap that created a comfortable environment out of artificial, windowless spaces. To London's shoppers in 1924, it was a revelation.

When King George V opened the vast British Empire Exhibition at Wembley later that month, Selfridge's had nineteen speakers wired around the store so customers could hear the King. One chap taking tea in the Palm Court Restaurant was so awed he stood to attention. 'It's *the King* speaking,' he said. In the days of silent films, people were enchanted by the wonders of radio. Wembley Stadium itself was built as the centrepiece of the BEE, as the vast exhibition was fondly called. Ironically for Selfridge's, part of the enormous plot of land that had been compulsorily purchased had been the original location of the store's staff sports club. With the money from the enforced sale, Selfridge bought a fifteen-acre plot in Preston Road, between Wembley and Harrow, where the staff held teas, supper dances and quiz nights in a handsome pavilion after a hectic Saturday and Sunday afternoon of football, netball, cricket and tennis matches. Over 27 million people poured into Wembley to see the exhibits, travel on experimental railways, inspect a coal mine, visit an amusement park and buy such things as the first ever commemorative stamps issued by the Post Office – which were also on sale in the Selfridge's branch post office on the store's fourth floor.

Selfridge, who had used the concept of a post-war World Fair as the central theme of his many after-dinner talks to various business groups, might justifiably have felt hurt at not being invited to join the Exhibition Organizing Committee. He made up for it with his own displays in the store, where Empire 'flags, emblems and decorations' were on show in a vast department selling ephemera such as printed cotton Union Jacks priced at 1 shilling a dozen and portraits of the King at 1/11d each. Selfridge had long celebrated Empire Day with a staff party on the roof, and to inaugurate the BEE he invited Lord Beaverbrook to entertain the staff with what turned out to be a rousing speech.

Harry Selfridge believed in engaging emotionally with his workforce and he had an innate understanding of the importance of ritual for customers and employees alike. He made a point of observing Armistice Day. Each year since the war, on 11 November, a bugler had stepped out on to the central balcony to sound the Last Post at 11.00 a.m. After a two-minute silence came the Reveille. It was a moving experience for all who heard it, and it continued each year until Selfridge was evicted from the store. Creating 'experience' was central to his beliefs. His critics said it had less to do with shopping and more to do with theatricals. But he knew – as few other retailers did – that emotion and experience formed a huge part of what customers craved. 'The whole art of merchandising,' he said, 'consists of appealing to the imagination. Once the imagination is moved, the hand goes automatically to the purse.' Years later, one of his directors, Frank Chitham, who left to work for D. H. Evans, said, 'He had the closest insight into customer psychology. When he was expressing ideas they came alive in your mind.'

After the morning tour, there was usually an ideas session in the Chief's office where his desk was flanked by the Stars and Stripes and the Union Jack. Reports on new trends in England and France or new gadgetry from America that he might usefully use in Oxford Street were discussed. Sometimes he would just sit for a while, hands clasped behind his head, looking out of the window at the clouds high above Oxford Street. No one ever dared interrupt him. And then the ideas would flow. Some were prosaic. If he saw that it was going to rain he would have someone call to check on the number of raincoats and umbrellas and ask that extra stock be put on to the floor.

In the new men's department, opened in 1924, the ex-world champion Melbourne Inman challenged Tom Carpenter at the billiards table. An ice rink was opened on the roof terrace where the American champion ice skater Howard Nicholson and his partner Freda Whittaker – the Torville and Dean of their day – enthralled the public, helping to establish the trend for skating. Poppy Wingate, England's first female professional golfer, gave demonstrations in the ladies' sportswear department. All these events were supported by linked merchandise displays often marked at 'special prices', which invariably ran for the rest of the week. The events made news because Selfridge's press room was open to all, whether news reporters or sports or women's page writers. Once they had met and photographed whichever sports star or stage star was in the store that week, only one task remained: the celebrity in question had to sign the Chief's autograph window with the diamond-tipped stick before a chauffeured car whisked them back to their hotel. Finally, their visit was reported in the store's own house magazine, *The Key*.

In what the press called the 'Ball of the Season', in the early summer of 1924, Selfridge threw open the doors of Lansdowne House for another Royal Charity Gala, this time to raise funds to endow hospital beds. The guest list included the British royal princes Henry and George, their cousins the Marquis and Marchioness of Milford Haven, Princess Marie Louise and Princess Helena Victoria. The seat of honour, however, was given to Princess Serge Wiasemsky (née Rosalie Selfridge), and her cameo, charmingly drawn by Rex Whistler complete with coronet, adorned the front cover of the programme. Selfridge pulled out all stops to put on a show: Garrard's and Carrington's loaned gold plate; no less than five champagne houses kept supplies flowing freely through the night; a jazz and classical band played; and Ivor Novello's mother – herself a noted musician – put her celebrated Clara Novello Davies Male Choir through their paces for the society audience.

More of a café society crowd poured into the store at the end of October, to celebrate at the third General Election night party when 2,000 guests whooped it up on both the roof-top ice rink and the ballroom roller-skating rink. Fearful of gate-crashers, the store's smarter staff – drawn from the growing band who had attended public school – were on duty at the entrance to vet, and sometimes veto, the arriving guests. Those admitted included Joseph Pulitzer Jr, Freda Dudley Ward, Sir Gerald du Maurier, Ivor Novello, Barbara Cartland, the Asquiths, the Aga Khan, the McAlpines, the very rich Lady Louis Mountbatten, and Marshall Field's equally rich granddaughter Gwendoline and her husband, the Scottish baronet Charlie Edmonstone. The hottest actress in town, Tallulah Bankhead, was there with the best-selling author Michael Arlen, whose book *The Green Hat* was top of the lists in every lending library. 'The whole *world* was at Selfridge's,' enthused *Tatler* breathlessly.

That night the Conservative Party won the General Election and the Bright Young People who would personify the Roaring Twenties came of age. They couldn't have cared less who won the election; they just wanted to have fun. The next five years would be spent battling with the new Home Secretary, Sir William Joynson-Hicks, who tried his best to stop them. Called 'Jix' by the cartoonists, who mercilessly lampooned him, Sir William was a High Victorian disciplinarian who represented everything about the establishment that the young loathed.

Jix loathed a lot of things, particularly 'non-registered aliens'. When he discovered there were 272,000 of them in Britain, he instigated a visa system so strict that merely travelling without the precious document meant a spell in prison before being shipped straight back home. He didn't care much for sex either – especially any forms of affection in public, which to his eye were 'gross indecencies'. He viewed most modern authors, artists and sculptors with grave suspicion, unilaterally censoring their work. A life-long teetotaller who had yearned to see alcohol prohibited, he also had an absolute fixation about nightclubs, calling them 'drug-filled sewers of society', while contemporary dancing was a 'disease against civilization'.

When an overseas visitor, awed by the scale of the Home Secretary's impressive office and vast staff, asked Sir William what he did there, Sir William replied: 'It is I who am the ruler of England.' To a certain extent he was, at least as far as law, order and licensing were concerned. In all these things, he was ably assisted by his treasured friend DORA. Many who yearned for the Defence of the Realm Act to be modified to suit the times, waited in vain. Jix took it out, dusted it down and applied its regulatory powers with relish. The police were instructed to take a stern view of public morality and an even sterner view of nightclubs. Naturally, they made mistakes. A girl arrested in Liverpool and charged with being a prostitute turned out to be *virgo intacta*. When the former Liberal MP Sir Leo Money was arrested and charged for merely sitting next to a young woman on a bench in Hyde Park, his case was dismissed. Sir Basil Home Thomson, ex-Chief of London's CID and one-time head of British Intelligence, was less fortunate. Found in a compromising situation with an actress called Thelma de Lava, he declared in his defence that he was researching material for a book on vice in the West End. The magistrates were unimpressed and fined him £5 with costs.

Harry never needed to risk a romp in the park – his children were now grown-up and had an insouciant attitude towards his affairs – but the matter of a visa was pressing. To obtain one he enlisted the help of friends in high places – Sir Reginald McKenna, Chairman of the Midland Bank, various members of the Masonic Lodge frequented by the Home Secretary, and Ralph Blumenfeld, editor of the *Daily Express*. The latter was popular with Sir William, not just because his newspaper adopted a strict view of morality, but also because he had founded the Anti-Socialist Union, a group heartily approved of by Jix. Thus Selfridge acquired a letter on Home Office stationery allowing him residential status. Things weren't as easy for his son-in-law Serge, whose Russian National Progressive Party was thought rather dubious. Conveniently, however, Alexander Onou, head of the Russian Refugees Permit Office in London, came to the rescue, issuing 'Serge de Bolotoff, Prince Wiasemsky' with the necessary photographic identity card confirming his refugee status.

In many ways, the jazz decade suited Selfridge. He had the ability to enter into the mood of the moment and was always enchanted by youth, which kept him if not literally, then certainly figuratively, on his toes. 'Let me see, Mr Selfridge,' said a reporter from the Manchester *Daily Dispatch* in 1924, 'you're sixty I believe?' The answer was merely an agreeable smile. He was 68. Had he coupled the dignity of age and experience with youthful zest, his life might have taken a different turn. As it was, surrounded by a circle of sycophants and an eager press, he believed he was invincible. With no one to restrain him, his hedonistic cravings raged unchecked. By 1925, he had crossed the line.

Fuelled by the unrelenting fashion for everything new, business was booming. Since it had first been seen in the Broadway show *Runnin' Wild*, the charleston had quite literally swept everyone off their feet. In London there were charleston competitions and charleston clothes. Flimsy underwear, especially Directoire knickers and silk chemises, beaded headbands, feathered fans and the essential 'flappers'' footwear – shoes with a powder compact in the jewelled buckle, whether for cheeks or cocaine – flew out of Selfridge's. Skirts were short and nights were long. Dance halls and nightclubs were crowded, and parents of all classes despaired of their offspring's passion for dancing. Even the King was alarmed, writing to his wife, 'I see David [the Prince of Wales] continues to dance every night and most of the night. People who don't know will begin to think that either he is mad or the biggest rake in Europe. Such a pity.' Young people didn't think anything of the sort. They loved the informality, the energy and the gaiety of the Prince; they loved him *because* he danced. Such things, however, are not founded on substance. As the Prince of Wales became famous for his clothes, his lifestyle, his girl-friends and his aura of celebrity, he too was heading for disaster.

London was awash with nightclubs, much to the anguish of the Home Secretary who did his best to close them down, but the clubs – particularly those patronized by the Prince of Wales – reigned supreme. The list was endless. On Thursday nights, the Prince himself could usually be found at the Embassy, essentially a dining club with a tiny cheek-to-cheek dance floor, where he smooched with Freda Dudley Ward to music played by Bert Ambrose and his orchestra. A more bohemian, theatrical crowd hung out at Wardour Street's Fifty Fifty, the Hambone or the rakish Uncle's in Albemarle Street. Arnold Bennett, a keen nightclub aficionado, was a fan of the Gargoyle and Kate Meyrick's Silver Slipper, with its glass dance floor and twinkling mirror globes, while those who really wanted kicks headed to another of Mrs Meyrick's clubs, the infamous 43 in Gerrard Street. The 43 also had a distinguished clientele: even the Prince of Wales went from time to time, but it was really the haunt of European royalty – all those lost souls who had also lost their crowns – along with racing drivers, pilots and sportsmen like Steve Donoghue the jockey and 'Gorgeous George' Carpentier, the achingly handsome boxer. The 43 was frequented by people who lived on the edge – the serious gambler Major Jack Coats, the international financier Ivar Kreuger (who had been involved with Selfridge's construction all those years ago), the theatrical and property entrepreneur Jimmy White and London's richest asset stripper, Clarence Hatry. Michael Arlen, Avery

Hopwood, Jessie Mathews and Tallulah Bankhead were regulars – and a young Evelyn Waugh would sit quietly at a side table observing the sights, later immortalized in his novels.

Everyone in town went to the 43. When Rudolph Valentino paid a visit, wearing, in the very latest fashion, a short, fitted tuxedo jacket, he was mistaken for a waiter. He took it well apparently, picking up a bottle with a flourish to pour drinks for several delighted guests. The house champagne sold at £2 a bottle and the dance hostesses cost considerably more. Ma Meyrick presided over the door, taking 10 shillings a time from patrons eager to hear Sophie Tucker belt out a song or Paul Whiteman's star musicians jam late into the night.

All this fun came at a cost, however, especially to Mrs Meyrick. Since she had launched her first club after the war, she had been arrested several times, fined thousands of pounds and served two six-month sentences in Holloway. She was the bane of the Home Secretary's life and the target of the leading light in London's Police Vice Squad, Station Sergeant George Goddard. Fortunately for Ma, Sergeant Goddard proved to be a man of extravagant tastes, which he found hard to meet on his police pay of £6 a week. His weekly wage was supplemented with a brown envelope containing £50 in crisp £1 pound notes courtesy of Ma, with the same amount paid by her friend Mr Ribuffi, the owner of Uncle's. Every Friday afternoon, Sergeant Goddard would head to Selfridge's where he carefully placed the envelope in his personal safety deposit box. It couldn't last of course. Shopped by an envious colleague, Goddard was eventually caught in 1929. He tried to explain away a large house in Streatham, an extremely comfortable car and £12,000 in cash in his Selfridge's deposit box by saying he had made the money 'selling confectionery on the side at the British Empire Exhibition', but he was laughed out of court. Goddard, Mr Ribuffi and Ma Meyrick were all sent to jail – Ma herself getting fifteen months' hard labour.

Selfridge himself was more of a Kit Cat Club man. The expensive premises had opened on the Haymarket early in 1925, complete with the requisite big band but also with a line-up of gorgeous girls in a showy cabaret. The Kit Cat too was raided and then closed down. In an attempt to circumvent the law, it subsequently reopened as a 'cabaret restaurant'. To celebrate the event, the club's Chairman, Sir Charles Rothen JP, engaged a dazzling dancing duo called the Dolly Sisters to perform on the opening night – and among the guests was Harry Gordon Selfridge. It wasn't the first time he had seen the girls in action. They had been on the London stage in a C. B. Cochran show called *The League of Notions* in 1921, when Harry had carefully noted in his ledger that he had spent 17/6d on a ticket. After seeing them again four years later at the Kit Cat, he began an affair with Jenny – some say with both sisters – which, by the time it fizzled out in 1933, had cost him quite literally millions of pounds.

Jenny and her sister Rosie were identical twins. Hungarian by birth – their real names were Jansei and Rosika Deutsch – they were born in 1892. They moved with their family to America where the girls trained as dancers, going 'on the road' as entertainers when they were just 14. The Dollies got their first big break when Flo Ziegfeld signed them up in 1911. By the time they hit London they were 29 – rather old to be playing ingénues, but they did it well.

The twins specialized in synchronized 'tandem' dancing, their movements 'mirroring' each other so they blended into one – as indeed did the girls. The only way to identify one from the other was to listen to them – Jenny giggled more. She had been briefly married to the creator of the foxtrot, Harry Fox, and in post-war Paris she performed various outré dance numbers with a professional partner, Clifton Webb, while Rosie specialized in a particularly erotic form of flamenco. On the whole, though, the girls danced – as they did most other things – *à deux*. With their penchant for jewels, a passion for gambling and a fondness for rich men, they were quickly nicknamed 'the Million Dollar Dollies'.

Their act was especially popular with the gay crowd (both happy and homosexual) and with the sex tourists who frequented the club world of Paris, where nightlife was more lavish and louche than in London. In the French capital Elsa Maxwell, the supreme party-organizer of the period, ran a club called the Acacia in partnership with the fashion designer Captain Edward Molyneux. There Jenny would dance, making her entrance each night in a cloak of fresh gardenias. The sisters apparently regarded London as stuffy, preferring to perform in Paris and throughout France. In reality, their déclassé behaviour meant they weren't accepted socially in a city that still regarded public performers which a shiver of unease. To call them uninhibited would be an understatement. As a cub reporter on the *Sunday Times* Charles Graves recalled interviewing them after a performance of *The League of Notions*: 'I knocked on the door and they said in chorus, "Wait a minute." I did so. "Now you can come in," they called. I entered. Both were stark naked.'

During their first foray on to the London stage, the Dollies had been squired around town by Sir Thomas Lipton. In reality, the genial Sir Thomas, although keen on promoting a reputation as a ladies' man, was uninterested in women and happily returned home each night to his live-in companion, his loyal secretary John Westwood. During their Kit Cat season, when the Dollies found escorts who were more interested in their charms, it was share and share alike. Lord Beaverbrook's daughter, Janet Aitken Kidd, recalled in her memoirs that 'my father and his friend Harry Selfridge were batting Jenny and Rosie back and forth between them like a couple of ping-pong balls'. The Dollies were a *succès fou*. They were painted by the artist Kees Van Dongen; Edouard Baudoin hired them to promote the opening of his divinely chic Casino Sea Bathing Club created out of a tattered wooden shack in Juan-les-Pins; and Cecil Beaton drew them for *Vogue* while playing chemin-de-fer at Le Touquet. The Dollies, in short, were the first celebrities to be famous merely for being famous.

While fame meant a lot to Selfridge, fashion hardly touched him. He wasn't part of the 'designer world' nor was he on Condé Nast's lunch list. He spent a fortune on entertaining, but had become frugal when it came to his own clothes. Arnold Bennett, killing time between appointments one day in the store's basement, met Selfridge 'wearing a rather old morning suit and silk hat. He at once seized hold of me and showed me over a lot of the new part – cold-storage for furs – finest in the world. Then up in his private lift to the offices and his room, where I had to scratch my name with a diamond on the window.'

The signature window, the Chief's pride and joy, was by now a *Who's Who* of fame and included Charlie Chaplin, Fred Astaire, Douglas Fairbanks Jr, Suzanne Lenglen and Michael Arlen. During his working day, Selfridge was still orderly and in control, working longer hours than men half his age. But he was playing hard too, delighting in showing off his conquests. He would walk the store with Suzanne, or Jenny, or Fanny Ward – just as he had done with Gaby – helping them to chose various things and telling the staff to 'send the bill upstairs'. One wonders what the sales girls, earning a few pounds a week, thought about their ageing, albeit much-revered boss blithely signing off shopping worth hundreds – sometimes thousands – of pounds for his famous lady friends. Were they impressed by contact with celebrity? Absolutely. Did they talk about it when they got home? Definitely. Did it sadden them to see a doting old man fussing over rather greedy women? Almost certainly.

The life of the store continued apace. During the week of Selfridge's sixteenth birthday celebrations in 1925, it is estimated that over a million people came through the doors. To mark the occasion, Selfridge sponsored an innovative fifteen-minute radio broadcast by the actress Yvonne Georges from the Eiffel Tower on the couture collections in Paris. This early attempt at commercial radio was the brainchild of an ex-Flying Corps radio wizard, Captain Leonard Plugge. Sadly for Selfridge, when the research survey notes were completed, only three people admitted to having heard the broadcast. Captain Plugge, cheerful in adversity, went on to launch the radio station Radio Normandy as well as making a fortune perfecting the first motor-car radio.

Meanwhile, some shoppers in the store stumbled across history in the making as they watched the young Scottish inventor John Logie

Baird demonstrate his 'televisor'. Baird had struggled long and hard to get recognition for his work. Calling in at the *Daily Express* in the hope of explaining the principles of television to the science editor, he was met with the response: 'For God's sake go down to Reception and get rid of a lunatic who's down there. He says he's got a machine for seeing by wireless. Watch him – he may have a knife!' At Selfridge's, where they were more enlightened, Baird was paid £25 to demonstrate his apparatus, for one week, three times daily. Since he was penniless, the money was a godsend.

It was a time of change not just outside the business but inside it too. Staff were leaving. Well-trained and experienced, they were able to command high salaries elsewhere. Percy Best went to the traditional drapers Schoolbred's, while the three Americans went home, the display chief Edward Goldsman rejoining Marshall Field, although he returned at vast expense once a year to mastermind Selfridge's Christmas windows. Crossing the Atlantic in the other direction, young Ralph Isidor Straus of the then family-owned Macy's in New York, who was studying for an MBA at Harvard, joined the store as a hard-working summer intern. Eric Dunstan left to work for Syrie Maugham, who had by now moved to Grosvenor Street. It wasn't a happy experience. Dunstan soon moved out, saying: 'I cared little for her décor and less for her.' His replacement in the Selfridge inner sanctum was Captain Leslie Winterbottom, late of the Hussars, who stayed with the Chief until 1939.

In 1925 the Chancellor of the Exchequer Winston Churchill presided over a return to the gold standard. The aristocracy were being hit hard by death duties – on the Duke of Rutland's death, the Duchess had to put their Arlington Street mansion up for sale – while the newly rich were awash with money. For those with an eye for acquisitions, mergers and debt reconstruction, there were fortunes to be made. Selfridge himself would soon become part of that trend, making him rich beyond even his dreams. But what would he do with the money?

Meanwhile, Mr Asquith had finally accepted a peerage, becoming the Earl of Oxford. From the stage of a hugely successful revue called *The Punch Bowl,* Norah Blaney sang to an applauding audience:

Mr Asquith now is an Earl
Oxford is his seat:
But Mr Selfridge still remains
The Earl of Oxford Street.

13

~

TOUT VA

'The chains of habit are generally too small to be felt
until they are too strong to be broken.'
Samuel Johnson

In the mid-1920s, a leading business magazine, *Expressions*, wrote:
'To the best of our knowledge, no one has ever dared to refer to
Mr H. Gordon Selfridge as a shopkeeper. He must be given credit
for teaching London and the rest of the country that serving the
public is business of the highest order.' As the growth in consumerism continued, the Drapers' Chamber of Commerce inaugurated
a summer school in Cambridge, offering courses in 'new methods
of merchandising, display and window dressing'. Their star speaker
was Selfridge himself, whose talk centred on his favourite themes of
in-store entertainment, customer service and value for money. 'The
first,' he said 'will get them in, while the second and third will keep
them there.' He concluded by giving the students the same mantra
he always gave his own staff: 'There are six useful things for notable
success in business – judgement, energy, ambition, imagination, deter-
mination and nerve. But the greatest of these is judgement.'

In the context of business decisions and planning, his own
judgement appeared to be as sound as ever, his critical faculties
seemingly unimpaired by the frivolity of his after-hours escapades.
At 69, he still arrived at work early. He still walked the store. He
still controlled board meetings with a brisk 'Any business? No? Well
then, let's move on, shall we?' leaving his directors more often than

not merely nodding their agreement. The much more lively monthly meetings with buyers and senior sales staff continued as they had always done, with the Chief singling out individuals whose departments had exceeded their targets and making them blush with pleasure at his praise.

The potential of television had excited him. 'This is not a toy,' he said, 'it is going to be a link between all peoples of the world.' He was also convinced of the long-term future of the motor-car, commissioning the civil engineer Sir Harley Dalrymple-Hay to prepare a feasibility study on the logistics of building an underground car park in Portman Square and enlarging the store's fleet of motorized delivery vans. Cars were beginning to clutter the streets. By the mid-1920s as many as 51,000 motor vehicles and 3,300 horse-drawn carriages were passing round Hyde Park Corner each day and one-way traffic systems were introduced to help traffic flow. Nothing was too much trouble for Selfridge. When an American friend complained about the quality of the coffee in the Palm Court Restaurant, Selfridge had the brand changed. Walking in St Marylebone, he observed the local fire brigade practising on a piece of waste land. He wrote to offer them practice facilities in the store, and in return got the smog-soiled façade cleaned for free. Of course, there were those who knew things were getting out of hand, not least A. J. Hensey, head of the Bought Ledger Department, whose job it was to draw up cheques to cover the Chief's costs. The ever-discreet Mr Hensey who, in his own words, witnessed Selfridge 'going gaga' over various women, wasn't merely in charge of payments: he drew up cheques for generous pay-offs when the affairs ended.

Selfridge excelled in blurring the lines between professional and personal entertainment, ensuring his guest lists included influential businessmen and, unusually for the era, businesswomen such as his friend Elizabeth Arden, whose range was by now the top selling line in the store. Since moving into Lansdowne House, he had already hosted some glamorous soirées, but during 1925 he upped the pace, dispensing largesse on a spectacular scale. The media were always invited to cover such events, though they were allocated special tables rather than seated with the VIPs. Selfridge also shrewdly included the American media correspondents based in London, thereby guaranteeing coverage not just in New York and Chicago but coast to coast, courtesy of *Time* magazine who found his lifestyle irresistible. The store display department took charge of flowers and décor, the food halls delivered provisions, and restaurant staff were on hand to supplement his own domestic staff. The Stars and Stripes flew at an American-themed Rodeo Night where, after a supper of char-grilled hamburgers, fries and ketchup, washed down with a dozen different beers had been served in the Sculpture Court, enthusiastic guests were taught square dancing and watched Red Indians doing lasso demonstrations.

At another party, to honour the newly arrived Japanese Ambassador, the display team created a Japanese water-garden which ran down the centre of the vast dining-table. Checking the area in the afternoon, Selfridge noticed there were no goldfish. A series of frantic forays by taxi to the store's pet department soon ensured that fifty fish were happily swimming among the water-lilies. Satisfied with the result, Selfridge went upstairs to change into his customary white tie. Then disaster struck. The paint on the sides of the artificial pond had poisoned the water and the fish started to die. Selfridge immediately sent to the store for a dozen bicycle pumps and ordered his staff to pump oxygen into the water to revive the survivors. It was a good idea, but it didn't work. Happily, the Ambassador remained blissfully unaware of the drama and spent a delightful evening in the company of, among other dignitaries, the Home Secretary Sir William Joynson-Hicks, enjoying arias performed by an Italian soprano and watching Hawaiian 'hula-hula' dancers shimmy to a native band.

Whatever happened at home was usually a spin-off from an event that had taken place in the store. A dinner hosted to honour the tennis player Suzanne Lenglen followed the launch of her book, *Lawn Tennis: The Game of Nations*. Suzanne was still playing at her usual fast and furious pace, fortified by her customary brandy rather than barley water between sets, and Selfridge and his daughter Rosalie had been in their Centre Court seats to watch her win the Wimbledon Women's Singles for the fifth time. Suzanne's teaching manual had been eagerly awaited by her fans who swamped both the store's book department and the sports department, where the very latest in short tennis skirts and her signature salmon-coloured jersey *sportif* turbans flew off the rails.

Personal appearances by sports stars were promoted in the London newspapers, and Selfridge continued to advertise heavily in the national press, though not in *Vogue* – the store's regular pages having been cancelled after a tiff with the management. Harry Yoxall, *Vogue*'s business manager, recalled the incident in his memoirs. Towards the end of 1924, when the magazine's page rate was increased from £36 to £40, he was summoned to Oxford Street. Yoxall, finding Selfridge 'wearing his hat in the afternoon, always a bad sign', braced himself for battle. 'I am an old man now,' said Selfridge, 'and have few pleasures left in my life, other than that of buying space at a lower price than anyone else enjoys. Now, if you will let me have my advertisements at £37 10 shillings, I'll give you an order for twenty-six pages.' Rather courageously, given that the magazine was losing around £25,000 a year, Yoxall refused to compromise, with the result that *Vogue* lost a client. They pretty soon lost an editor too when Dorothy Todd, the sapphic 'thinking woman's heroine', was fired for her overly artistic and intellectual approach. Her replacement was the much more fashion-orientated Mrs Alison Settle of *Eve* magazine, who, along with her senior fashion editor, Dorothy Todd's most intimate friend Madge Garland, between them secured British *Vogue*'s role as the arbiter of fashion.

Selfridge was uninterested in the comings and goings of the growing band of influential women who wrote about fashion, leaving such things to his public relations department. What Mrs Wish of the *Daily Express* thought of the store's latest season's dresses was of little concern to him – he felt more at ease in conversation with the paper's editor Ralph Blumenfeld or its owner Lord Beaverbrook. In any event, fashion editors in those days did as they were told, and one way or the other, the store was constantly making news. The press were never short of a story. Sophie Tucker sang at a Dance Week which featured the young and beautiful Jacob Epstein model, Oriel Ross, who melted hearts playing the piano. Ivor Novello, the actress Evelyn Laye and the diva Marie Tempest launched the spring sale. An electronic scoreboard delivered the results of that year's Test Match at the front of the store, once again bringing Oxford Street to a standstill, while the American golf professional Walter Hagen gave advice to fans on their swing, and the pilot Alan Cobham's plane – in which he had flown to Africa and back – was put on display.

Returning from an adventurous trip to Russia with Rosalie and Serge, Selfridge demanded that Mr Yoxall pay him another visit. Selfridge had scoured the station bookstalls in Constantinople before boarding the Orient Express and discovered only one English title. 'Which one do you think it was?' he asked Yoxall. Magazine circulation *circa* 1925 being a haphazard affair, Yoxall hadn't the faintest idea but replied hopefully, '*Vogue*?' 'You're right,' said Selfridge, 'and I don't think my great store should be out of such a magazine.' He promptly reinstated his order for twenty-six pages, failing to notice that in the meantime *Vogue* had upped the price per page to £48. Mrs Settle and Miss Garland were soon commissioning the young and struggling photographer Cecil Beaton to take celebrity pictures. Beaton took his film to the patient Mr Barnes in the store's photographic department, noting in his diary: 'I've been giving Selfridge's nearly all the developing. This morning I traipsed for the fifty millionth time to get the results of Edith Sitwell.'

Vogue also commissioned illustrations and text from Beaton, who quickly turned his attention to the most glamorous pastime of the period – gambling. Before long, Beaton's witty little drawings of the chic set who frequented Deauville, Le Touquet, Biarritz and Cannes were a regular feature in *Vogue*, with titles such as 'The Season at Le Touquet – An Exotic World of Sophisticated Elegance'. Anyone who was anyone relentlessly played the tables. Being seen playing the right game at the right casino was as important as being seen in the right nightclubs. In the French casinos throughout the 1920s, no one yearned to show off and be seen more than Jenny and Rosie Dolly, and their passion for gaming infected Selfridge. He had spent decades hiding the extent of his habit, but when his mother died, the final restraint was lifted. In Jenny and Rosie he found his soul mates. With them he crossed the line between habit and addiction. It wasn't just about sex. It was about dealing a six and a three – or any other numbers that made the magic nine of the winning hand at baccarat.

In the post-war era, the heady combination of sun, sea and gambling in France was all the rage. And even if you didn't play, you could pay to watch those who did. All you needed were some evening clothes and the sum of £3, for which, on presentation of your passport, you could enter a casino. A further few pounds would buy dinner and a bottle of wine, and the opportunity to dance to the band which played until the small hours of the morning. For another payment of £4 10 shillings, those who cared to watch fortunes being won and lost were allowed to step beyond the ropes and stanchions and enter the *salles privées* where those for whom gambling was a way of life spent their evenings. There, the powerful players showed they could afford to lose as well as win.

Among those who could well afford to lose were the Aga Khan, Major Jack Coats, the Duke of Westminster, a clutch of Rothschilds, the Belgian financier Jacques Wittouck, Marshall Field III, the Kimberley diamond mining millionaire Solly Joel, King Alfonso of Spain, the Kings of Sweden and Denmark, Indian maharajas and their various wives, the automobile magnate André Citroën, the cognac producer James Hennessy, the Canadian tobacco tycoon Sir Mortimer Davis and various super-rich war profiteers. Millionaires from Chile, Argentina and America flocked to the tables, although after the revolution the impoverished Russian grand dukes weren't able to play unless they had hooked a rich lover to foot the bills. When Coco Chanel finished her affair with Grand Duke Dmitri Pavlovich, who had been earning a precarious living as a champagne salesman,

Above and on the facing page: The Dolly Sisters at the tables in Le Touquet, 1928, by Cecil Beaton (Cecil Beaton/Vogue © The Condé Nast Publications Ltd)

she passed him on to a wealthy girlfriend, saying: 'You can have him. These Grand Dukes are too expensive to keep.' In fact Dmitri had introduced Coco to Ernest Beaux, who created Chanel No. 5 for her, so the poor man had more than earned his keep.

Each season, the gambling group migrated *en masse* to their chosen habitat. In the summer it was always Deauville, Le Touquet or Biarritz, in the winter, Monte Carlo, Cannes or occasionally Nice. The casinos of France were run by Eugène Cornuché – who had made his fortune through Maxim's restaurant in Paris – and his protégé and ultimate successor, François André. Between them, these men instigated the concept of the luxury resort hotel, with its sumptuous seaside casino, its elaborate floor show and its six-course foie gras and caviar dinner. They also shrewdly invited women into the casinos and bars, and for over three decades they watched people lose their money. For the truth is that gamblers always lose. Monsieur Cornuché and Monsieur André, however, couldn't lose. Although during their era Monte Carlo held the monopoly on roulette, the French casinos offered both baccarat and *chemin de fer* – and the baccarat bank was run not by the casinos themselves but by a syndicate of Greeks headed by the fearless Nicolas Zographos, who paid the casinos for the privilege of controlling the cards. When Zographos died in 1953 he left a fortune of £5 million, every penny of it made from baccarat. When Harry Gordon Selfridge died in 1947, he left just £10,000, having ploughed his way through a fortune estimated by some to be as much as £3 million.

Nicolas Zographos changed the face of twentieth-century gambling when he sat down at the baccarat table in Deauville in 1922 and quietly said: '*Tout va.*' For those playing against him, the sky was, quite literally, the limit. He and his colleagues had put together a pool of 50 million old francs (£16 million today), which was more than enough to get them started. Although they had some alarming moments over the next few years as the richest of the rich played furiously against them, they kept their cool and ultimately their money. Someone once asked Zographos why he did it. His answer was 'It's like morphine.'

For the Dolly Sisters, gambling was indeed a drug, one on which they had become hooked as teenagers in America. There they had been squired by the legendary sugar-daddy 'Diamond Jim' Brady, who took them to the private members' Canfield Casino at Saratoga in upstate New York and out to Coney Island. By the mid-1920s, having each discarded a husband, they were commuting effortlessly between Paris, New York and the French casino resorts where they regularly took bookings to appear in cabaret. When they had finished on stage, the twins, known variously as 'the Pep Sisters' or 'the Gold Diggers', continued the show at the tables.

The girls had expensive tastes. When they were flush, they bought jewels, but what they liked most was gifts, and they perfected the art of acquiring them. Apparently, one of their favourite tricks was to strip

off all their jewels, passing them to a friend, and sit looking discon-
solate at the tables. When a wealthy duke, maharaja or banker asked
why they were so downcast, they would say they had 'lost everything,
right down to their last bracelet'. Not for nothing did every important
jeweller have a boutique in the casino resorts. Following their display
of crocodile tears, the Dollies could expect deliveries from various
admirers by morning. They didn't invest sensibly like their actress
friend Pearl White, who on her retirement bought property and
opened a bar in Paris and a hotel and casino in Biarritz, where she
wisely ignored the tables. Nor were the Dollies as indulgent with
money as their gambling contemporary, the French actress Maude
Loti, who used to light her cigarettes with 1,000-franc notes and relax
each day by shooting off blank cartridges in her bathroom. However,
the girls variously earned, won, spent and lost a fortune. As a result,
they were always in need of a rich companion.

When Jenny and Rosie met Selfridge, he wasn't actually that rich.
He lived like a lord and spent prodigiously, but it was really all show.
So when the opportunity came for him to make some serious money
– apparently at no risk to himself or his beloved store – he grabbed
it with both hands. In early 1926, the idea of forming the Gordon
Selfridge Trust was put to him by James 'Jimmy' White, a man who
had made a fortune from property (among other deals he had bought
and rapidly sold Wembley Stadium after the British Empire Exhibition), boxing promotion and share speculation. White was a bluff and
tough Lancashire man, an ex-bricklayer with a thick accent, profane
language and a bad temper. Yet somehow the softly spoken, mild-
mannered Harry Selfridge – whose strongest expletive was 'My stars'
and whose pet phrase was 'As sure as God made little green apples'
– became very taken with him. White and he had been nodding
acquaintances for years, having first met at National Sporting Club
boxing events at the Café Royal. Their paths continued to cross at
various nightclubs such as the Kit Cat and the Silver Slipper, and
at Daly's Theatre, the much-loved musical comedy venue recently
acquired by White as part of his burgeoning 'leisure' portfolio. Jimmy

White's great hobby, apart from making money, was racehorses, which were kept at his flourishing Foxhill stables in Surrey.

White had a friend whose family owned two London stores – John Barnes of Finchley and Jones Brothers of Holloway. Strapped for cash and scrapping amongst themselves, the family wanted out. White's Charterhouse Investment Trust brokered a deal whereby both stores were bought by Selfridge's as part of the existing 'Provincial Stores' group. From this evolved White's grand scheme to make his friend a rich man and earn himself a sizeable cut. The retail sector was in favour with the City. Many of London's leading stores had posted good profits – Harrods, Barkers, D. H. Evans, Dickens & Jones and Liberty's all claimed a record year. Only Whiteley's seemed to be suffering. Pre-tax profits at Selfridge's for 1925 stood at £500,000. Selfridge, with his unerring grasp of statistics, was able to tell the media that the store had been dealing with up to 200,000 transactions a day; that it had handled its largest amount of cash sales ever, and that stock had turned over a record number of times.

The department making the most money was perfumery and cosmetics. Pulling out a powder compact to strike a pose had by now become the epitome of sophisticated chic, just as shingled hair, cloche hats, ever-shortening skirts and shiny stockings were now the height of fashion. An astonishing 800 films a year were now coming out of Hollywood, and there was hardly a young woman in the country who didn't follow the fashions set by film star heroines such as Clara Bow, Louise Brooks and Greta Garbo. Elinor Glyn, herself now working in Hollywood, had famously coined the phrase 'The It Girls', which perfectly summed up the brittle mood of the moment. Manufacturers were quick to use the latest synthetic fabrics, now available in a whole range of colours thanks to better-quality industrial dyes, to produce affordable ready-to-wear clothes. Fashion, with all its essential accessories, was no longer merely a perquisite of the rich. It was finally on the move among the masses.

Investors were learning to like the business of fashion and beauty, representing as it did so much spending of disposable income. In

December 1925, an impressive prospectus outlining the formation of the Drapery and General Investment Trust had resulted in over £2 million being raised by its creator, the smooth-talking, high-living businessman Clarence Hatry. Regarded in the City as a 'boy wonder', Hatry had started his career as an insurance broker. He made a fortune in war profiteering and by the 1920s was living in a Mayfair mansion with a swimming-pool in the basement and spending weekends on board the *Westward*, then one of the largest yachts in the country. Clarence Hatry ran a complex clutch of companies under his umbrella vehicle, the Austin Friar Trust, with a peer of the realm – the Marquis of Winchester – on the board to add the requisite cachet.

Hatry's Drapery Trust scheme was centred on family-owned department stores, which were mostly now run by the second or third generation and mainly operated in provincial towns. Though rich in property assets, they often lacked capital for modernization. Such stores represented ripe pickings for Hatry. He took dozens of them into his Trust, promising not just investment but also central buying services, product information and trend reports, management expertise and promotional packages. Within a matter of weeks, Hatry had taken out £1.8 million in charges in a bewildering series of sub-deals and costly service contracts, leaving dozens of stores in limbo and wondering whether it had all been worth it. It would take another four years before Clarence Hatry's world crashed around him but his money-making scheme was the model for Jimmy White in his deal with Selfridge, which they launched in the autumn of 1926.

Selfridge saw in the New Year escorting Fred and Adele Astaire's mother to the ball at the Royal Albert Hall. Busy with plans for his daughter Beatrice's wedding, he eschewed his normal week skating in St Moritz for a quick dash to Cannes where, side by side with Jenny and Rosie Dolly, he watched the epic tennis tournament between Suzanne Lenglen and the American champion Helen Wills. Later that night, despite being ill, Jenny and Rosie took their customary seats at the Winter Casino baccarat table, flanked by a pair of nurses in mufti to pass medicine and brandy. Back in London a day later,

Selfridge walked his daughter up the aisle at the Catholic church in Spanish Place where she married Count Louis Blaise de Sibour.

In May, when the TUC voted to back the depressed and disgruntled miners, the first general strike in British history began. For the miners, already struggling to survive on a few pounds a week, being asked to work longer hours for reduced wages was the last straw. For the public, led by the tabloid press to believe there would be anarchy, the whole event seemed to pass in a haze of anticipation of violence that never materialized. King George V took exception to suggestions that the strikers were 'revolutionaries', saying, 'Try living on their wages before you judge them.' As it turned out, he was right. The strike somehow seemed rather civilized. Enthusiastic volunteers drove the trains. Society ladies like Lady Diana Cooper folded copies of *The Times*, while Lady Louis Mountbatten manned the telephones at the *Daily Express*. At one point, a group of miners were seen playing football with the police. Through it all, the group the *Daily Mail* had dubbed 'The Bright Young People' danced the night away, filling their days and nights with endless fun. When treasure hunts became all the rage, they stormed through Selfridge's, leaping over counters and rushing up and down in the lifts. Selfridge didn't mind. It was good publicity and anyway, the treasure hunters all came from 'good' families.

Selfridge loved hiring people from 'good' or famous families, at one point trying to persuade Arnold Bennett's young nephew to join the firm. 'I don't know about your going to Selfridge's,' Bennett wrote to his nephew, 'it doesn't seem to me a very good idea.' Count Anthony di Bosdari, an old Wykehamist friend of Gordon Jr, was hired to work in the advertising department. Bosdari's claim to fame – other than being a distant cousin of the King of Italy – was that he was the best dancer in London. At a time when dancing really mattered, this was a useful qualification. Count Bosdari's snappy suits and fleet footwork caught the eye of Tallulah Bankhead. Within weeks, the two were engaged, and Bosdari bought his famous bride-to-be an expensive diamond necklace. Not being the kind of girl to keep a man with no money, when the invoice arrived marked for her own attention, she wisely called the wedding off. Despite the publicity – or maybe because of it – her ex-fiancé kept his job. Harrods had recently booked a series of bus posters saying 'Look in at Harrods'. Bosdari suggested booking a series to be pasted alongside them, saying: 'I'd rather look in at Selfridge's' but the Chief reluctantly turned the idea down as being too bold. The Count soon solved his own financial problems when he left to get married, having hooked a rich young Chicago heiress called Josephine Fish.

Anthony di Bosdari was a regular at the Café de Paris, the Embassy, the 43 and the Silver Slipper. By now there were literally dozens of such clubs, all doing a roaring trade. The faster the Home Secretary tried to shut them down, the quicker they reopened. Selfridge's commissioned the BBC 'disc jockey', Christopher Stone, to supervise the selection of top dance hits of the day recorded under the store's own 'Key' record label and pressed by Decca, while within the store, music played as though it would never stop. The young élite adored the ditty written in their honour:

We mean to spread the Primrose Path
In spite of Mr Joynson Hicks
We're People of the Aftermath,
We're girls of 1926
In greedy haste, on pleasure bent
We have no time to think or feel,
What need is there for sentiment,
Now we've invented Sex-Appeal?
We're young and hungry, wild and free,
Our skirts are well above the knee,
Come drink your gin, or sniff your snow,
Since Youth is brief and Love has wings,
And time will tarnish, 'ere we know
The brightness of the Bright Young Things.

Before the General Strike, Selfridge's had mobilized a hand-picked team to protect the roof-top radio masts and made plans to transport staff to work in their delivery vans. Even so, Selfridge himself saw no reason to cancel a planned trip for fifty of his buyers to visit top American stores and examine merchandising techniques, generously including W. R. Adams, the store's wines and beverages buyer, in the junket. Quite what Mr Adams hoped to learn in Prohibition America is hard to fathom, but he was graciously received by, among other senior store owners, Bernard Gimbel of Gimbel Brothers, who hosted a jocular 'dry' lunch for the touring group.

By the summer, the Selfridge family were in Deauville, where their father was *à trois* with the Dollies. The two girls were seen in violet wigs and matching violet chiffon and net frocks, and photographed taking a much-publicized dip in swimsuits trimmed with waterproof ostrich feathers. The besotted Selfridge bought each twin a pair of four-carat fine blue diamonds, instructing Cartier to set them on the back of a pair of matched tortoises. The ballet dancer Anton Dolin, dining with the Dollies at Deauville, recalled that after a particularly heavy session at the tables, at which both sisters had 'lost a lot', a beribboned box of pearls for Rosie and a diamond bracelet for Jenny arrived from Selfridge with a note saying: 'I hope these will make up for your losses, darling girls.' Dolin was speechless. '*Your* losses indeed!' he exclaimed to Elsa Maxwell. 'It was *all* Selfridge money!'

By now, the Dollies' stage career had peaked. The previous autumn they had suffered a run-in with the celebrated Parisian 'Queen of the Night' Mistinguett, arguing over their scene in her big revue at the Moulin Rouge. Realizing during rehearsals that they were being parodied in a particular sketch, they pulled out of the show and promptly filed a law suit for 500,000 francs, claiming damages for loss of work and saying that the script wasn't 'worthy of their status' and was demeaning to their reputation. The court case dragged on for a year, with the Dollies ultimately winning a settlement, but it left a bad taste in the theatre world. Just as Selfridge had always said 'never cross a newspaper', so the Dollies should have realized that it was unwise to cross Mistinguett. She got her own back two years later when she discovered a pair of divinely handsome Norwegian drag artists called the Rocky Twins and trained them to perform as the 'Dolly Sisters' to utter perfection. No one, it's said, could tell the difference.

Throughout the spring and summer, Jimmy White had been breezing in and out of the fourth floor inner sanctum at Selfridge's as he, Harry and his son plotted their deal. 'Hello Pop,' White would bawl out on arriving for another cigar-filled, whisky-drinking session. Harry's staff had never, ever heard anyone be that familiar with the Chief and worried at the influence the rash, brash White appeared to have over their boss.

By September 1926, the Gordon Selfridge Trust, in the name of Selfridge and his son, was established. Formed to acquire the ordinary share capital of £750,000 in Selfridge & Co. Ltd, the Trust was capitalized at £2 million, with one million 6 per cent preference shares of £1 each and one million ordinary shares of £1 each. Father and son retained 900,000 of the ordinary shares. The issue was launched in a blaze of the publicity, with the store hosting a fashion show for city investors who watched appreciatively as gorgeous models burst out of giant hat boxes on a flower-decked stage. Selfridge himself chaired the press conference, saying: 'A modern business should aim at building an edifice that will last for ever.' When one reporter had the temerity to ask him how old he was, Selfridge sidestepped the question: 'I retired once at 40. I don't intend to do it again. I've been told by my very conservative business adviser this Trust is the right thing to do.' To believe Jimmy White was a conservative adviser was extraordinarily naïve, but when Selfridge was on a roll, nothing could stop him.

Later that year, the Selfridge dynasty's domain grew still larger when Selfridge Provincial Stores Ltd was launched with capital of £3.3 million. Once again the deal had been put together by Jimmy White and once again, it was over-subscribed. The new company swiftly went on a spending spree, buying the charming and long-established, albeit now run-down store Bon Marché in Brixton, together with

Brixton's second store, Quin & Axten, Holdrons of Peckham, Barrats of Clapham and Pratts of Streatham. The financial press were bemused at the high prices paid to acquire these suburban stores and equally concerned at the guarantee of a 7 per cent dividend on the ordinary shares for ten years. Father and son ignored it all, delighting in the fact they were now rich. At the age of 26, H. Gordon Jr became Managing Director of the Provincial Stores Group, while his father celebrated by installing Otis escalators in the Oxford Street store. He also gave Jenny Dolly a thousand shares in his newly formed business and bought a horse called Misconduct, the first of several steeple-chasers he would acquire from White's Foxhill stables, which raced under the store's distinctive dark green colours. Not to be outdone, Gordon Jr ordered a custom-made teak-decked speed boat he called *The Miss Conduct* and took to piloting his own Gipsy Moth plane when visiting his regional empire.

Early in 1927, the Dollies' much-publicized Paris show *A vol d'oiseau* closed after a run of only eight weeks. In future, their fame would derive from their appearances at the gaming tables where Selfridge was spending more and more time with the dazzling duo, and spending more and more money on them. Jenny's jewels became legendary. Thelma, Lady Furness, a future mistress of the Prince of Wales and no stranger to good jewellery herself, observed Jenny playing the tables at Cannes: 'I have never seen so many jewels on any one person in my life. Her bracelets reached almost to her elbows. The necklace she wore must have cost a king's ransom, and the ring on her right hand was the size of an ice cube.' Cecil Beaton also saw Jenny at work, this time at Le Touquet:

> The greatest thrill in this sensational playground is the vision of Jenny Dolly playing baccarat at the high table. Here is a sight which will go down in history, for in years to come old doddering bores will weary their grandchildren saying I am old enough to remember Jenny Dolly looking rather like a guttersnipe as well as a regal queen, my dears, literally *harnessed* with colossal jewels of incalculable worth, sitting

sphinx-like as she won or lost the most vast of fortunes. Her coolness. Her grimaces, the movements of her arms and her diamond-smothered hands. Her hundreds of cigarettes, cups of tea, coughing and shoulder-shrugging are all part of her 'tableside' manner which has been brought to a pitch of technical perfection. Every other woman pales before her and is silenced in awe of envy!

After the Dollies had effectively retired from show business, Rosie was briefly married to Sir Mortimer Davis's son Morty Jr (who regrettably turned out to be less rich than she had thought), while Jenny divided her time between Jacques Wittouck, the Belgian financier with a bulging wallet, and Harry Selfridge. Between them, they indulged her every whim. She acquired a tumble-down house in Paris which was expensively rebuilt and decorated, and a château at Fontainebleau, where the long hall was lined with softly lit glass jewel cases exhibiting her trophies. Most weekends, Selfridge would take the boat train to France, carrying a two-quart thermos jug filled with Jenny's favourite chocolate ice-cream. He also bought a luxuriously fitted steam yacht called the *Conqueror* which was moored in Southampton Water, permanently crewed and ready for sailing instructions. The trappings of success rested easily on his shoulders. He basked in the adulation of his staff and was lionized by the press as chairman of England's largest retailing business.

When Jimmy White came calling again in 1927, Selfridge welcomed him with open arms. It was a fatal mistake. White's big plan was that Selfridge should buy Whiteley's of Bayswater, which had been ailing for some time. Selfridge knew the property well. It was the store he had most admired on his first trip to London decades earlier. Indeed, he was close to John Lawrie, who had been chairman since old Mr Whiteley had been murdered by his supposed illegitimate son in 1907. Whiteley's two legitimate sons, however, found the prospect of a wealthy retirement alluring. Having invested in a brand-new building, they had spent the last fifteen years presiding over a declining store in a declining area. Bayswater had become dismally run-down, its once elegant properties subdivided into crowded boarding-houses, or lived in by the elderly shabby-genteel. The best-known addresses were those used as drug dens. This was no place to run a smart store.

John Lawrie was close to Jimmy White. Both men knew that Selfridge, for all his apparent self-confidence and his heartfelt passion for retailing, was no hard-nosed businessman. Telling Selfridge that if he bought Whiteley's he would own 'a whole mile of windows' and would, as 'the youngest store-owner in London', have acquired the city's oldest store, White moved in for the kill. Whiteley's was not the oldest store in London (Swan & Edgar had opened in 1812), and Selfridge was no longer young, having just passed his seventieth birthday. But the prospect was irresistible and the deal – reported to have cost £10 million – was done. An official announcement of the takeover was made on April Fool's Day. At the shareholders' meeting a little old lady stood up and asked querulously if Whiteley's annual dividends would remain at 25 per cent. Selfridge assured her that they would and that he would guarantee them for fifteen years. 'She reminded me,' he said rather mournfully some years later, when the real cost of his rash promise had made itself felt, 'of my dear mother.'

By June, Jimmy White was dead. His cut from the Whiteley's deal, however big, hadn't been enough to save his crumbling empire. Having made a desperate gamble on oil shares bought on margin, he lost the last of his money. He ended his life by swallowing prussic acid and left behind a curious suicide note: 'The world is nothing but a human cauldron of greed. My soul is sickened by the homage paid to wealth.' Selfridge, who took his death hard, was one of the few mourners at White's funeral. Another suicide reported in the press just a few weeks later may also have caught his attention. William Jones, whose family business, Jones Brothers of Holloway, was sold to Selfridge in the first deal brokered by Jimmy White, had shot himself, his death attributed to depression.

Leaving his management team with the task of turning round Whiteley's, Selfridge took off for several weeks on a triumphant public relations tour of America. Meanwhile, the company laid on free shuttle buses between Selfridge's and Whiteley's, with singing conductors to cheer up the passengers. But they remained worryingly empty. At Selfridge's Mr Miller, the store's resident architect, was busy with plans to fill in the centre of the main façade, paving the way for the formation of a further eleven acres of floor space. Footfall was up – people had clamoured to see Sir Alan Seagrave's record-breaking Mystery Sunbeam car – but profits were down.

In the autumn of that year, Selfridge was back in America, this time to give a speech at Harvard Business School in celebration of his gift to the Baker Library of his priceless Medici manuscripts. The loss of the beautiful documents didn't seem to worry Selfridge. Much as he had loved them, he enjoyed recognition as an élite donor to Harvard's library more.

That autumn, Isadora Duncan died at the age of 50. She had spent her last pathetically drunken years in Paris and Nice, always hoping she would at last break into films by writing scripts. Certainly, her death was as dramatic as anything on screen – she was strangled by her own chiffon scarf in a car driven at speed by the young, handsome Italian mechanic Benoît Falchetto. She had danced beautifully, and Selfridge loved beauty. At a talk he gave to students at Liverpool University's School of Architecture, he said: 'I will tell you the five most beautiful things in creation. First a beautiful woman. Then a beautiful child. A beautiful flower, a beautiful sunset and … a beautiful building.'

His own beautiful building in Oxford Street was completed in 1928, when the huge cantilevered canopy of bronze and glass, supported by two free-standing Ionic columns set in a vast canopy of Portland stone, was unveiled to an admiring public. An enormous three-ton bell, cast by Gillett & Johnston, was installed high above the parapet, while Sir William Reid's impressive bronze frieze of sculptured panels bordering the rear wall of the loggia won him a silver medal from the Royal Society of British Sculptors. *Architectural Design & Construction* called it 'the most imperial building in London'. For Selfridge, it represented a lifetime's achievement.

Adding to his racing stable, Harry bought the much-fancied Ruddyman (Misconduct, having fallen badly in the Grand National, had had to be destroyed), placing him with Captain Powell's stables at Aldbourne in Wiltshire. Powell also trained Rex Cohen's horses. Cohen, the owner of Lewis's of Liverpool, would meet up with Selfridge at the races and exchange friendly nods and tips. There was always a camaraderie amongst the drapers, although Selfridge was virtually alone in attending John Lewis's funeral in June. The reclusive, miserly old retailer was 93 when he died and left strict instructions that he was to be buried in his wife's unmarked grave, that his staff should not mourn him and that the store should stay open as usual.

John Lewis's death marked the passing of the last of the original London store owners. The men now in charge were younger, more ambitious, more in tune with the rise of consumer society. Most of them took business seriously, and many of them had learned their craft working for Harry Gordon Selfridge. The trouble was, Harry himself was now spending his time playing.

FLIGHTS OF FANCY

'There is nothing so enthralling as the conduct of a great business. It is the most
fascinating game in the world – and it brings no sorrow with it.'
Harry Gordon Selfridge

Harry Selfridge's favourite time of day was the quiet hour or
so spent with Mr Miller, the store's resident architect, poring
over plans and elevations. Since the early 1920s, bit by bit he had
begun to acquire parcels of land fronting on to both Orchard Street
and Duke Street. The latter area was used as warehousing and
workshop space and was connected to the main store by a tunnel
running under Somerset Street. By 1928, with enough property in
place to create an enormous rear extension, Mr Miller was preparing
detailed applications for planning permission. Wherever possible,
Selfridge bought plots stretching back to Wigmore Street, always
believing that one day he would realize his dream of an entire
'double island' site. By 1930, as his jigsaw puzzle of prime property
pieces increased – finally taking in St Thomas's Church and the old
Somerset Hotel for £100,000 – the Marylebone Works Committee
recommended that the Council accept Selfridge's application for an
initial £3 million scheme to extend fully on the Duke Street side.
As ever with Harry's hopes and dreams, however, there were strange
anomalies. Sometimes he let valuable options lapse. Quite often,
he invested thousands in buying a plot, despite knowing that it was
useless unless he could get space to the left or right and that such
an acquisition might be problematic – one grumpy hairdresser held

out for over twenty years. At other times, he seemed content simply to gaze at the drawings.

It might have been expected that, having become rich, Harry would finally build the castle on Hengistbury Head. Philip Tilden, who by now had completed hundreds of drawings, waited for the call. It never came. Distracted by the Dollies, his yacht, his horses – and his dreams of a triumphant palace in Oxford Street – he let the plans gather dust, leaving seabirds to circle undisturbed over the peaceful cliff top. Each week, flowers were placed on Rose and Lois's graves in the equally peaceful churchyard at St Mark's, and each quarter, the costs of the sexton who tended the plots were paid from the Selfridge family account.

In bustling Oxford Street, where the magnificent front entrance was now installed, Selfridge turned his attention to developing the roof-top space, already used as an exhibition ground and containing the ice-rink. Now it was announced that Selfridge's was creating 'the biggest roof garden in the world', its construction to be masterminded by the urban garden expert Richard Suddell. When it opened over Whitsun in 1929, the beautiful displays stretched the entire length of the roof on Oxford Street, and the heady scent of roses, lavender, thyme and hyacinths filled the air. For the next decade, 30,000 bulbs would be planted each autumn, ensuring a spring flowering of snowdrops, crocuses, tulips and daffodils. The roof housed ornamental ponds, a water garden, a winter garden, a paved vine walk, a cherry tree walk and clematis-covered gazebos. The technical achievement in constructing such beauty was impressive: the earth, rock, stone, turf, fountains and plants required together weighed over 1,800 tons. Plants and bulbs came from the company nursery, installed at the Preston Road staff sports ground, where greenhouses and flower beds were lovingly cultivated by eight gardeners. The roof-top oasis was crowded all day, with restaurant service available for morning coffee, lunch and afternoon tea.

Flowers were an important part of the Chief's persona. He loved giving them and he loved receiving them. Each year, on his birthday in January, the staff would contribute towards vast floral baskets and bouquets, presented with full ceremony to their beaming boss. Not everyone enthused about the whip-round for the ritual, one irate member scrawling 'Balls to Gordon Selfridge' across the message on the staff notice board. Lord Woolton, the Chairman of Lewis's of Liverpool, was not impressed by such excess: 'His room was filled with flowers, as though they had been placed on an altar. He asked me whether my staff in Lewis's paid such testimony to me, and when I said "never a daisy", he said "you ought to give them a hint".' Lord Woolton, whose firm would subsequently acquire Selfridge's in the 1950s, wrote presciently about Selfridge: 'He had commercial vision and courage of a high order, combined alas with personal vanity and pride in being a public figure, which has ruined so many men who have lost a sense of proportion in the exaltation that comes from surrounding themselves with yes-men.'

He was right of course. Tucked away in an archive file is a record of a conversation between Selfridge and a close business friend, John Robertson, the advertising manager of the *Daily Express*. The two men were long-time poker partners, and Robertson had become used to watching Selfridge settle a business deal by flipping a coin. Soon after the group's acquisition of Whiteley's, the normally ebullient Selfridge seemed particularly low, admitting to Robertson that they had uncovered some serious problems ranging from missing inventory to merchandise too old or damaged to sell. Asked if he had made the deal 'subject to contract following a valuer's survey', Selfridge admitted he hadn't done any due diligence: the deal had gone through at speed and on trust. When Robertson suggested Selfridge sue Whiteley's bankers for misrepresentation, the response was: 'No. I cannot do that. It would not make me look very smart to have bought a business without safeguards.' He tackled the problem by asking his old colleague Alfred Cowper – the store's first systems manager – to run Whiteley's and he set up a new joint supply company. But the cracks in the empire were beginning to show.

Early in 1929, Selfridge staged an exhibition of 'English Decorative

Art' at Lansdowne House, opening the event with a charity viewing attended by Queen Mary. A month later the property was sold. One by one, the stately homes of London were being turned into apartment blocks or hotels – the Duke of Westminster's Grosvenor House, the Duke of Devonshire's Devonshire House, the Duchess of Rutland's Arlington House and, most recently, the Earl of Morley's beautiful Dorchester House on Park Lane, which was sold to the McAlpine family for £500,000. It was, as the press remarked, the end of an era. Lord Lansdowne had already sold a vast tract of the garden to the developers of the Mayfair Hotel. Now, tempted by escalating property prices, he sold the house to American developers for £750,000. Selfridge had to move. Addicted to grandeur, he leased the Earl of Caledon's residence, 9 Carlton House Terrace, taking it fully furnished, along with the Earl's staff of fourteen. The society hostess Emerald Cunard had recently moved on to Grosvenor Square, but illustrious neighbours still included the young Prince Aly Khan, the Earl of Lonsdale, the Duke of Marlborough, Lady Curzon and Loel Guinness MP. Selfridge was also treading the hallowed turf of the late Mrs Potter Palmer, who had once lived in the street.

In Carlton House Terrace, Selfridge hosted large post-theatre suppers, served in the newly fashionable buffet style. Each week, a horse-drawn van would arrive from the store with prodigious quantities of food and drink. Store porter Fred Birss was 14 when he was on the Carlton House run, and he later recalled a typical delivery: 'six cases of champagne, a dozen cases of whisky, six turkeys, four hams, 24 lbs of butter, a dozen loaves of bread, two boxes of cigars and several soda siphons'. This was the Monday order. The larder was replenished on Thursday, with smaller deliveries often made daily. Motorized vans also drove down to the Hampshire coast to provision the *Conqueror*. The cost of maintaining the yacht was enormous. In 1928 Selfridge spent nearly £17,000 on her (wages and victualling alone cost £8,264 3s 6d). The yacht was used to ferry the family to Deauville and Le Touquet in the spring and summer, calling in at the Isle of Wight en route, where Selfridge once famously annoyed the

Royal Yacht Squadron by tying up at the Royal buoy. But when he was going to Cannes or Nice, he continued to use *le train bleu*, only occasionally taking a Mediterranean cruise.

Harry's addiction to the Dollies continued. It has been said that he wanted to marry Jenny, although his daughter Rosalie always denied it. But whatever his intentions, he lost his head, possibly his heart and certainly his wallet. They played at Le Touquet, a resort long favoured by the British smart set where by 1929 the casino was reported to be the most profitable in the world. They played at Deauville, a more international, café society sort of place, where Selfridge rented a 'cottage', as the large houses were always called, furnishing it beautifully and indulging the twins' whims by throwing raucous parties which even he sometimes found overwhelming. One guest, present at what he described as 'a pretty riotous affair', later recalled that 'The only restful thing in the place was the furniture and that white-haired old man, sitting all alone on the sofa.'

Above all, the trio gambled at Cannes, where stories of their gaming became the stuff of legend. *Time* reported Rosie winning £32,000 in a single afternoon. On the same day, however, Jenny lost. Down by £4,000, she stayed at the table until she hit a winning streak and finished £45,000 up. But two hours later she apparently lost the lot. The Dollies attracted attention wherever they went. From Cannes, *Vogue* reported: 'When one is tired of dancing, there is the gambling: in the baccarat rooms the Dolly sisters cause the greatest stir, with crowds six deep standing to watch them play. They wear the most *wonderful* diamonds, both with their little jumper suits by day and their sequin capes and feathered helmet hats by night. The sisters shout over the table, inhale a hundred cigarettes and win or lose hundreds of thousands of pounds ... spectators stand dumb with admiration.'

Jenny adored being known for her gambling almost as much as she had enjoyed being known for her dancing. 'If I don't know anything else,' she said gaily to a reporter, having pocketed £5,000 at Biarritz, 'I know *huit* and *neuf*.' The arrangement she had with Selfridge was simple. If she won, she kept the money. If she lost, he covered her debts. The film producer Victor Saville recalled boarding *le train bleu* at Cannes when the Dollies were on the platform waiting to greet Harry, who had boarded at San Remo. Selfridge alighted, hugged the girls, handed them a diamond necklace each, and got back on board. In the dining-car later that evening, he overheard a fellow passenger exclaiming: 'You should have *seen* the Dolly sisters last night. They lost £25,000 in two sessions. I wonder who the silly old fool is who's protecting them? There must be someone, mustn't there?' Saville and Selfridge, heads down, quietly immersed themselves in their dinner.

Very little of this activity ever hit the British press. Given that Selfridge was chairman of a public company, the famous and fashionable chronicler Lord Castlerosse could – maybe even should – have covered the story in his *Sunday Express* gossip column 'Londoner's Log'. But Castlerosse was astute enough never to expose Lord Beaverbrook's friends, who included the Prince of Wales. Not that the Prince wasn't in the press. He was probably the most photographed person in the world at the time, and his every move made news. The British media, however, were loyally discreet about his penchant for married women. By now the Prince's affair with Freda Dudley Ward had ended and he was deeply involved with Thelma Furness.

Frighteningly sophisticated at just 24, the American Thelma and her sisters Gloria (married to Reggie Vanderbilt) and Consuelo (married to Benjamin Thaw, First Secretary at the American Embassy in London) were just the sort of women the Prince of Wales liked – funny, fearless, just a touch fast and charmingly devoid of deference. The Prince liked to dance, to sing along to the latest records, to talk about fashion – a topic that absorbed him almost as much as collecting stamps absorbed his father – but by now he had become disenchanted with touring the world and being on show. While the brusque shipping magnate Viscount 'Duke' Furness spent his days hunting and shooting in Melton Mowbray, his wife Thelma and the Prince of Wales spent their nights out on the town. They dined at the Ritz and danced at the newly fashionable hot-spot, the Café de Paris, where to avoid any hint of scandal they were rarely alone, their innermost circle of friends including the Duff Coopers, the Mountbattens, Prince George, and Major 'Fruity' Metcalfe and his wife, Mary Leiter Curzon's daughter Alexandra.

Weekends were spent at the Prince's newly acquired bolt-hole, Fort Belvedere in Great Windsor Park, where for the first time in his life, he felt truly at home. The Fort was *his* house, not a royal house, and he later admitted to 'loving it like no other material thing'. Thelma Furness loved it too, helping him decorate and working with her lover in the gardens, hacking down overgrown laurels. She claimed to have 'introduced him to the proper delights of Christmas', finding a twelve-foot Christmas tree and shopping at Selfridge's for the baubles: 'Being American they had absolutely the best decorations.' Christmas at Selfridge's was an opulent and emotional affair. The store was decorated throughout and smelt of cinnamon and spices, choirs sang carols, and the staff usually received a bonus along with an ornate card from the Chief.

Thelma also took charge of the Prince's Christmas shopping, buying dozens of presents for his servants and senior staff. Many of them were bought at Selfridge's where the store superintendent, the ever-patient Mr Peters, would escort her around the departments. The ritual went on for several years, the only change being that in due course Lady Furness was replaced by Mrs Simpson. Mr Peters liked Wallis Simpson – 'I found her a very charming lady' – and admitted that they became quite friendly. As the efficient and apparently thrifty Wallis spent three days tackling the task, pen in hand, ticking off items from her lists, he certainly had time to get to know her. Since she lived for a time in Bryanston Square, and later in Cumberland Terrace, Selfridge's was her local shop and Selfridge himself issued instructions that she was to be well looked after.

There was very little the store didn't sell. If something wasn't in stock, someone went out that day to source it. Selfridge's blended tobacco, allocating a special number for repeat orders. In the cloakrooms, attendants polished shoes, changed laces and sewed on buttons – all free of charge. There was a philatelic department so fine it would have impressed even the King. The travel bureau booked journeys by train, boat and plane, organized hotels and even arranged for luggage to be sent on ahead to await its owner's arrival. The information centre answered the most obscure of queries. The store stored, shipped, dry-cleaned and mended customer's clothes, shoes and soft furnishings. Virtually anything could still be made to measure. The switchboard dealt with 40,000 calls a day, and delivery vans covered a million miles a year.

In 1929, invitations went out for the 30 May General Election night party. For the first time, women under 30 were able to vote. Ironically, it was the hated Home Secretary William Joynson-Hicks who had made that possible when, a year or so earlier, in a sparsely attended evening session, he had agreed to a Private Member's Bill that committed the Conservative Party to enfranchising 'men and women on the same terms'. His deed came back to haunt him when, through what came to be known as 'the flapper vote', the Conservatives lost the election. In fairness to the Home Secretary, bigger political issues than his fixation with nightclubs influenced the public. With high unemployment, recriminations about the General Strike, rising prices and, for the first time, a genuine three-party fight between Lloyd George's Liberals, Ramsay MacDonald's Socialists and Stanley Baldwin's Conservatives, it was a tough election.

The election-night party at the store was a wonderful affair. Arnold Bennett arrived early, stayed late and described it all in a letter to his nephew:

> There must have been 2,000 people at that show. There was plenty of room for them, plenty of loudspeakers, two bands and as much Cordon Rouge as the entire 2,000 could drink, besides solid sit-down suppers for all who wanted it. I wanted it. The whole affair was magnificently organised.

Bennett, a socialist, had real cause to celebrate that night. The cartoonist David Low, however, caught glum faces with his pen, and one observer, watching the huge crowds dancing and drinking, reflected as much on the decline in manners as on the loss of Tory seats when he said: 'It is the end of an age. Our World is going out.' Propped up by the Liberals, Ramsay MacDonald returned to No. 10, little realizing what he would soon have to face.

Times were changing fast. What had been modern was suddenly becoming obsolete. As always, film and fashion led the way. Hollywood studios fitted sound stages and dozens of panicking movie stars were sent for voice tests. Many failed. You could take a beauty out of Brooklyn, but even MGM's magic couldn't take Brooklyn out of her voice. Household names vanished overnight and a whole new generation of mellow-toned movie stars filled the screen. In Paris, women wearing short skirts fidgeted in their seats at Patou's show when the designer – who among other celebrities dressed the Dollies and Suzanne Lenglen – launched his longer lengths. Madelaine Vionnet had already introduced her stunning, bias-cut evening gowns – deceptively simple slivers of charmeuse – which, eagerly adopted by Hollywood costume designers, became the quintessential look of the decade to come. For the first time ever, couture collections featured *sportif* daywear. Hermès launched its signature headscarf, and along every smart coastal promenade – to the confusion of many a maître d'hôtel struggling to uphold a dress code – women took to wearing beach pyjamas. As the androgynous, cropped-haired girl of the 1920s evolved into the soignée, sophisticated woman of the 1930s, many mourned her passing. The flapper had, after all, been great fun.

As if signalling the financial catastrophe to come, in September 1929 the police arrested Clarence Hatry, whose business empire – reported to have been worth over £10 million – turned out to have been built on shifting sands. News of the financier's disgrace echoed across the Atlantic, where the Dow Jones – having hit an all-time high – shuddered and fell back. Hatry had been massaging the company books for some time, but now he was caught issuing forged stock certificates. Remanded in Brixton and refused bail, he was sentenced to fourteen years' imprisonment. Some financial analysts predicted the end of the great bull market. Others ignored the warnings at their peril. In October 1929, Wall Street was swimming in debt. By the 29th, it had collapsed and $9 billion dollars was wiped off the stock market in a matter of hours. The impact in America and Europe was not felt by consumers for some months, but major retailers and manufacturers, already jittery about reduced spending patterns, were worried, and with reason. Recession would soon turn into the Great Depression.

In London, the hedonistic lifestyle of the young and carelessly rich came to an end. As if a portent of the misery to come, the winter of 1929 was one of the coldest in history. Hundreds of people died and Kate 'Ma' Meyrick, incarcerated in a freezing Holloway prison cell, developed chronic pneumonia. Selfridge himself refused to panic. He'd lived through enough recessions in America to know what people wanted in time of crisis – on the one hand a bargain and, on the other, a little luxury. The display manager Leslie le Voi was briefed to make the window themes ever more exotic and exciting, featuring everything from newly installed city traffic lights to the world's first television set, Baird's 'televisor'. In February 1930, the store announced record figures, with pre-tax profits of £480,000. Eternally optimistic, Selfridge told *Business* magazine, 'Business is still largely what you make it. By reiterating that business is bad, people hypnotize themselves into a state of apathy. We broke all our past records in fifty-nine departments during October, and almost as many in November. New methods of selling, new channels of distribution, new ways of advertising are transforming our performance.'

By now, mark-downs weren't just on offer in the Bargain Basement but were promoted throughout the store on separate eye-catching 'Bargain Tables'. The tables – tidied by the hour – were never allowed to get tatty. Goods purchased from them were wrapped and tied with the exclusive 'Selfridge knot' just as though they had been bought at full price: those who bought for less were never made to feel cheap. One manager exclusively controlled the reduced stock offerings, coping with what Selfridge himself called 'the peculiar problems of merchandising bargains in every department outside of the traditional sale-time'. The store came of age in March with twenty-first birthday celebrations. Decca records pressed a souvenir disc of massed bands playing 'The March of the Gladiators', while the Chief's gift from his loyal troops was an impressive bronze plaque in his honour, set into the pavement in the main entrance loggia. Worn thin by the footfall, rarely noticed by people pushing to enter the great doors, the plaque is still there, its quasi-religious inscription echoing that of Zola's 'great cathedrals':

Laid by members of this store in admiration of him
who conceived and gave it being
1909–1930

The store might be 21, but no one, not even his children, really knew how old Harry Selfridge was. 'I don't want to rest,' he said when asked about retirement, 'I want to go on – and on – and on!'

Showing a younger man's enthusiasm for technology – especially aviation – he applauded Amy Johnson at the dinner hosted in her honour by the Hon. Esmond Harmsworth of the *Daily Mail* to celebrate her epic flight to Australia. Selfridge's was by now inexorably linked with aviation, swiftly negotiating rights to display Amy's green De Havilland Moth first in Oxford Street and then at their key provincial outpost, Cole Brothers in Sheffield. The store even launched its own aviation department, where keen customers could not merely order a bespoke aeroplane – not to mention the wardrobe to wear when flying it – but take lessons on a flight simulator operated by trained pilots. Studying the feasibility of an autogyro landing-space on the roof, Selfridge commented: 'This is the way the rich will want to come shopping.' For sheer glamour, flying was hard to beat. Lady Heath flew from the Cape to Croydon, as did Lady Bailey, while the redoubtable 64-year-old Duchess of Bedford set off for the Cape in her tiny Spider, saying it 'helped her tinnitus'.

Flight, whether solo or piloted, wasn't without very real danger. In July 1930, an air taxi carrying the Marquis of Dufferin and Ava, the society hostess Lady Ednam and three others returning from a weekend at Le Touquet, crashed. Broken bits of fuselage – not to mention broken bodies – scattered over a Kent cherry orchard. Reporting the accident, the media showed especial interest in jewels worth £65,000 that were lost in the crash. In October, the giant R101 airship came down, killing Lord Thomson, the Government's Minister for Air, along with forty-five other passengers. Four years later, the by then seasoned pilot, the 'Flying Duchess' of Bedford, took off from Norfolk and was lost at sea.

Harry's daughter Violette and her air-ace husband had flown from Stag Lane aerodrome in 1928 on an adventure to hunt big game, circumnavigating the world in their Moth, *Safari II*. Ignoring the challenges of such an epic journey, the *Daily Mail* excitedly reported that 'Violette Selfridge will fly wearing trousers'. She also packed a lace evening gown and twelve pairs of silk stockings in her luggage – hunting guns and fishing tackle being conveniently shipped ahead by the store.

Violette and her husband returned safely, but her brother Gordon Jr was less fortunate, crashing his Moth into a tree. Apart from a few bruises, only his pride was hurt, but his father insisted he get rid of the plane, putting it up for sale in the store aviation department where it was snapped up for £450 by a young man called Oscar Garden. After just twenty hours of tuition, Mr Garden headed for home – in New Zealand. Selfridge devoted a 'Callisthenes' column to the very modest Mr Garden's amazing achievement, telling awed readers that after a hair-raising journey via Syria and India, he landed safely in Western Australia before crossing to Sydney, thereafter shipping his rather bruised and battered Moth home to Christchurch. By the middle of the decade, however, the adventures of the lone aviator were coming to a close. The rickety, reckless charm of the 'string and sticks' light aeroplane had had its day. In 1936, Selfridge's advertised their aviation department was selling: '*The Jubilee Monospar*' – *Britain's first complete aeroplane and priced at £1,750.00.*' This erstwhile rich man's toy was a five-seater, twin-engine aircraft, the model of which would soon be developed to play its part in the war.

Retailing of a different kind was preoccupying Harry Selfridge. Jenny Dolly had opened a lingerie shop on the Champs-Elysées in Paris. This was no ordinary boutique but rather an astonishing blend of boudoir brash, glitz and glamour. Pink-gilt bedroom furniture created by the designer and artist Jean-Gabriel Domergue included a mirrored bed considered glamorous enough even for Jenny who, according to *Variety*, 'knew a thing or two about beds'. Exquisitely embroidered bed-linen was said to have 'kept a couple of convents working for months', while the display of intimate apparel – wispy pieces of black chiffon, silk stockings and a fine selection of jewelled garter belts – was 'enough to make you think sinful thoughts'. Harry was seen beaming broadly at the opening night party, while the guests sipped gin slings and dunked salt crackers in caviar, and Selfridge's star mannequin, Gloria, wafted through in silks, satin and lace, a chinchilla coat casually flung over her shoulders, and Jenny's fabled black pearls, once owned by Gaby Deslys, round her neck.

'Glorious Gloria', as the press called her, had been under contract to Selfridge's for four years. The most successful commercial model of her era and the original catwalk star, she was the first 'Ovaltine Girl', and her image was printed on posters and postcards throughout the country. When Gloria appeared in the Palm Court fashion shows, she caused a sensation, not least because when she posed, smothered in jewels and furs, the press office would hire bodyguards for her photo-calls – as much to protect her as what she was wearing. Among the staff it was rumoured that she had an affair with the Chief. They were certainly close, and as 'the face of the store' she accompanied him at dozens of events, everything from air-shows to premieres. Whatever their earlier relationship, however, in the early 1930s they were simply good friends. Besotted by Jenny Dolly, however cruel, casual or calculating she might be, Harry always came back begging for more.

During the opening week of Jenny's boutique, Gloria stayed at her Paris town house and in a 'girls together' moment shared Jenny's bedroom. Each morning, Selfridge would knock, and come in in his silk dressing-gown, carrying a breakfast tray. He'd then sit on the edge of Jenny's bed, butter her toast, pour coffee and chat about the shop and plans for lunch as though none of them had a care in the world. Sometimes Jenny would smile. At other times she'd violently push away the tray, yelling at him to get out. Mario Gallati, the famous restaurateur who ran the Caprice and the Ivy, was fond of Selfridge, who had dined there for years, 'dominating the table, erect and stern, looking every inch the formidable tycoon'. It was a different story when he was with Jenny, whose tantrums were well known at the Ivy. 'Mr Selfridge would ring me up before bringing her to dine, ordering the most elaborate meals and the finest vintage wines. All Jenny's favourites were prepared for her – then she'd decide to have a hamburger.' According to Mario, 'Selfridge was like a gauche schoolboy with her. When she made a scene, going off in a huff, he would sit there, eyes downcast ...'

As the Depression took hold, Jenny's de luxe lingerie shop haemorrhaged money. At Selfridge's, things were little better. Selfridge, faced with a weekly wages bill of £155,000, refused to cut costs. The staff repaid him by offering to work until 7 p.m. without overtime – a gesture which thrilled Selfridge as much as it annoyed the hierarchy at the National Union of Shop Assistants. Defying the Depression, with his usual sangfroid he urged local and regional investment. 'Let's make Marble Arch the focal point of an avenue as magnificent as the Bois de Boulogne,' he told the *Daily Chronicle*, while suggesting that councillors in Brighton should 'dream a future' for the town by opening cafés and restaurants and making it 'more tourist friendly'. In the meantime, money was tight. Harry sold over 300 acres of Hengistbury Head to Bournemouth Council, with the proviso that they would never build on it, but retained 33 acres – complete with planning permission – for future use himself. Store profits were down. Trade suppliers, already used to slow payments from Selfridge's, now had to wait longer and longer.

In 1931, the store celebrated the installation of 'The Queen of Time', a magnificent eleven-foot-high bronze statue flanked by winged figures symbolizing Progress and surmounted by a stupendous clock. Designed by the sculptor Gilbert Bayes and the store's architect Albert Miller, 'The Queen' was hailed as a 'horological masterpiece'. *Lilliput* magazine thought otherwise, printing a little ditty:

Hickory-dickory-dock, a mouse ran up Selfridges' clock
It didn't expect such a bizarre effect and it never got over the shock.

While the Chief's watch was five minutes fast, it was always said that the store clocks were kept five minutes slow, though the management later denied it. On the wall near the Information Bureau was a row of accurate clocks, each showing the time in a capital city overseas and part of what was described as the store's 'time-honoured tradition of keeping customers informed on all things of interest'. Time had run out for many of Harry's friends, however. Sir Thomas Lipton, the America's Cup challenger who was only granted membership of the Royal Yacht Squadron in his old age, died without ever setting foot in the place. Harry's old flame Anna Pavlova died of pleurisy in January 1931 at the untimely age of 45. Arnold Bennett was also dead. Harry missed him greatly. Ever since Bennett had written his early novel, *Hugo: A Fantasia on Modern Themes*, loosely based on a combination of Harrods and Whiteley's, Selfridge had hoped he would write about the store. He wasn't alone. Trevor Fenwick, of Fenwick's of Newcastle, also lobbied Bennett in 1930. The author replied: 'The idea of writing a novel about a department store has suggested itself to me many times during the past ten years. Mr Selfridge has offered to place the whole of his establishment at my disposal, and has urged me to do such a novel. But I do not think I shall ever write it … I have had enough of these vast subjects.' There may not have been a book, but there would be a film, when the producer Victor Saville used the store as the live background for his film *Love on Wheels*, made in 1932.

Time had also run out for Ramsay MacDonald. Faced with a tidal wave of unemployment – two and a half million by the end of 1930 – and having reached a deadlock over the financial crisis engulfing Britain, MacDonald was persuaded to form a National Government. With the Conservatives pressing for a public mandate and MacDonald himself being expelled from the Labour Party, the only solution was a General Election. In October 1931, the country headed for the polls again, and Selfridge's, true to form, put on a party. Jenny Dolly flew in to be at Harry's side when he received over 3,000 guests in the store. The store's Sales Director Mr Williams recalled that 'Jenny wore bracelets on both arms from wrist to elbow. As she moved, they flashed prismatic lights from emeralds, rubies, sapphires and diamonds.' Winston Churchill, C. B. Cochran, Emerald Cunard, Prince and Princess Galitzine, the Rajah of Sarawak, Noël Coward, Prince and Princess von Bismarck and a rather sozzled Rosa Lewis escorted by Charlie Cavendish were among the crowd who danced to Jack Hylton's orchestra and were entertained by Cossack dancers, Jimmy Nervo and Teddy Knox of the Crazy Gang, and the Australian jugglers and gymnasts, the Rigoletto Brothers.

When the votes were counted, the Conservatives had 470 seats, Labour 52 and the Liberals 33. As the National Government's Prime Minister, MacDonald spent the next four years isolated from his colleagues and at the beck and call of the Conservatives. Among a rash of new, independent political parties that had put up candidates at the election, Sir Oswald Mosley's New Party failed to win a single seat. Undeterred, the Mosleys were among the guests at the election-night party, where Lady Cynthia – as with all Levi Leiter's granddaughters – was always assured of a warm welcome. Sir Oswald seemed to have an unerring attraction for the Curzon women, marrying one, sleeping with both her sisters and rumoured to have had an affair with their step-mother. In troubled times, Sir Oswald attracted support from some who responded to his rabble-rousing speeches. Selfridge himself, grumbling at an American Chamber of Commerce luncheon about trade tariffs, government intervention and red tape, declared: 'What the country needs is a strong leader, an inspirer.'

Puzzling contradictions were a Selfridge trait. In support of a massive 'Buy British' campaign launched by the Prince of Wales, he invited the Mayor and Master Cutler of Sheffield to exhibit in London, giving them 6,000 square feet to display the city's steel products. At the same time, however, he filled the store's front windows with a million pounds' worth of diamonds, presented in burglar-proof showcases. Quite what prompted Selfridge to promote himself as the 'King of Bling' when unemployment was rife is hard to fathom. People were looking – 27,000 crowded into the store to watch the American Bridge champion Ely Culbertson's team play the British champion 'Pops' Beasley in a sound-proofed room and nearly as many watched the 'Miss England' contest staged at Selfridge's – but they weren't buying much. Figures were down. There were murmurings in the City as well as rumours of Selfridge's excessive losses at the gaming tables in France.

By now Jenny Dolly's foray into fashion had failed. The closure of her shop also marked the end of her relationship with Harry Selfridge. On a misty morning in March 1933, she crashed her car near Bordeaux, fracturing her skull and badly disfiguring her face. Her career as a femme fatale was finished and her famous jewels went up for auction that autumn to raise money for, among things, major plastic surgery. They only fetched $300,000, with Jenny tearfully acknowledging that 'people got beautiful things for next to nothing'. Among the treasures that went were the black pearls once worn by Gaby Deslys and the 'ice cube' 51.75 carat diamond bought for Jenny by Harry Selfridge in 1928.

In London, Harry's own financial affairs made waves when, at a troubled annual general meeting, an irate shareholder asked about the 'Chairman's Account' which owed £154,791 to the company. Selfridge stood up and said: 'I will reduce the matter as soon as possible. I admit I have been wrong.' The trouble was he couldn't reduce it. He also owed money to the Greek Syndicate, where even

Nicolas Zographos wasn't immune to the Depression. A lot of Zographos's high rollers had faded away. Major Jack Coats had committed suicide in his Park Lane apartment and others no longer travelled to gamble. With casino earnings throughout France down 75 per cent, the Syndicate sold on their debts. For Selfridge, this was a situation fraught with danger. Whatever he owed – and it's rumoured to have been over £100,000 – was now being chased by extremely hard men. Liquidating assets, he sold his remaining parcel of land on Hengistbury Head and, in a move that alarmed his Board of Directors, he claimed thousands of pounds in arrears of salary for his titular role as Chairman of Whiteley's, a store he rarely even visited. His daughter Rosalie, who had hoped he would cover their heavy mortgage on Wimbledon Park House, was destined to be disappointed. The bank foreclosed on the Wiasemskys, forcing their return to Carlton House Terrace. Gordon Jr meanwhile continued to live the high life, his photograph appearing in *Tatler* either alongside his plane or alongside a beautiful woman, such as the actress Anne Codrington. Staff would shake their heads, murmuring 'like father, like son'.

Financial catastrophe was claiming more and more victims. Ivar Kreuger, the store's original construction engineer who had subsequently become an industrialist known 'as the richest man in the world', killed himself rather than face accusations of fraud to manipulate the markets. Yet few outsiders observing the apparently seamless operations at Selfridge's would have guessed there was trouble. For the architects and builders who had been working on the new Duke Street extension it was another matter. The extension had originally been planned to have four storeys above ground and two below. Now, because of financial constraints, it stopped at the first floor, albeit reinforced to allow for higher storeys that came later. Work on site being too slow to satisfy Selfridge, he came up with the original idea of using explosives. Half a pound stick of gelignite did the trick nicely, blasting ten tons of clay effortlessly out of the way.

The extension, which used 5,000 tons of Middlesbrough steel to create three and a half acres of extra floor space, finally opened in March 1933. It was nicknamed the SWOD by staff because it encompassed Somerset, Wigmore, Orchard and Duke Streets. The low flat roof was put to good use: Lord Clydesdale's Westland PV-3, which he had triumphantly flown over Mount Everest, went on show, and Suzanne Lenglen arrived in town to demonstrate her skills on the newly fitted *En-Tout-Cas* court. Suzanne and Selfridge's relationship was as tempestuous as her tennis. The Chief's personal store messenger, the teenage Ernest Winn, recalled having to deliver a letter from Selfridge to Miss Lenglen's rented flat nearby. 'She finished reading and started to scream and scream ... I didn't know what to do ... so I just stood there, watching and waiting. I was pleased I was so small the way she was swinging her arms about, I might otherwise have been decapitated.'

Selfridge continued to 'put on a show'. He spent excessively on advertising. He became a financial patron of the new Business School at Harvard University. He chartered an Imperial Airways four-engined plane for an aerial VIP New Year's Eve party with a live in-flight fashion show. He stabled horses that didn't win races and, very charmingly – given he couldn't afford it – he paid Messrs Gillett & Johnston to replace the fabled Great Bell of Bow, which, having rusted beyond repair, had been silent since 1928.

The store celebrated its Silver Jubilee in 1934. *Draper's Record* wrote: 'He has not merely transformed Oxford Street into one of the world's finest shopping centres, he gave a lead to the entire store trade.' At a banquet hosted in his honour by fellow-traders in the borough of St Marylebone, held at the Grosvenor House Hotel, Harry was presented with a beautifully illuminated 'Book of Signatures' containing a heartfelt message: 'From the first you have been a pioneer, and, even in difficult and disheartening times, have had the courage to go forward. Your energy and enterprise have brought fame to your firm, and have added to the prosperity of the community.' Behind his glasses, Harry Selfridge's eyes filled with emotion.

The year 1935 marked another Silver Jubilee, that of King George V and Queen Mary. Selfridge busied himself planning another set of majestic external decorations, much as he had done so for their Coronation. They were utterly magnificent and they cost a fortune. Created by the noted architect and graphic designer William Walcot and the store's own resident design expert, Albert Miller, their theme was 'Empire'. A huge statue of Britannia towered 80 feet above the roof top, attended by two golden lions, flags flew and trumpeters blew.

In one of his many interviews with the *Daily Express* Selfridge had said: 'It isn't the making of money that's the chief motive with me. It's the great game that's the thing. There is nothing so enthralling as the conduct of a great business – it's the most fascinating game in the world – and it brings no sorrow with it.'

Unfortunately, the making of money *was* the chief motive of one of the company's major shareholders – the Prudential Assurance Company. To them, retailing wasn't a game, it was a business. Disturbed not merely by falling profits but by the profligate extravagance of Mr Selfridge, the 'men from the Pru' decided they had to put a man on the Board. They found him in Mr H. A. Holmes, who for many years had laboured diligently at the Midland Bank before becoming the finance director of the India Tyre and Rubber Company. Little did Selfridge know just how much sorrow he would bring.

OVER AND OUT

'Tis better to have loved and lost than never to have loved at all.'
Alfred, Lord Tennyson

In early October 1935, Harry headed for America. His support for Harvard had not gone unnoticed by Dr Silas Evans, the enterprising President of Ripon College, Wisconsin, who had awarded Harry an honorary doctorate. Accompanied by his daughter Violette, Harry was royally fêted in the town of his birth, and at a civic luncheon held in his honour, Mayor Harold Bumby announced the renaming of a special town recreation space as 'Selfridge Park'. Ripon's newspapers made much of the visit and described Harry's successful career in great detail. Being less certain about the status of the pneumatic young blonde accompanying him, they merely described her as 'a family friend'.

A few days later, when Selfridge arrived in Los Angeles, *Time* magazine revealed his companion to be the 'French-Swedish actress Marcelle Rogez, who Harry Gordon Selfridge was intending to bring to the notice of Hollywood'. Miss Rogez, Harry's latest – and last – serious love interest, had great ambitions for a Hollywood career. Observing them lunching together at 20th Century Fox, the film gossip-columnist Louella Parsons wrote: 'The elderly, yet venerable-looking Mr Selfridge had such beautiful manners. He stood when Marcelle got up, pulling back her chair, bowing slightly to her at the end of the meal, walking out behind her – showing old world courtesy rarely seen in this town anymore these days.'

It was reported that Harry was hoping to raise finance on his trip. If that was so, he was destined for disappointment. To American bankers in the midst of the Great Depression, Selfridge represented a bygone era of 'success through excess' in retailing investment. With promotional budgets stripped to the bone, spending money to make money had become unfashionable.

Back in London, and accompanied by the pulchritudinous Miss Rogez, he hosted another election-night party. The eclectic guest list was, as always, a masterful combination of politics, Fleet Street, society and show business. Friends like Lord Beaverbrook, Winston Churchill and Lord Ashfield were joined by Douglas Fairbanks Jr, Noël Coward, Ivor Novello, the actress Madeleine Carroll (fresh from her role in the film of John Buchan's *The Thirty-Nine Steps*), and the Duke and Duchess of Roxburghe. The President of the Royal Aero Club, Sir Philip Sassoon, escorted the rabidly right-wing and very rich Lady Houston, whose enthusiasm for aviation was eclipsed only by her enthusiasm for Benito Mussolini. The fashion designer Elsa Schiaparelli put in an appearance, as did the interior designer Elsie de Wolfe and, surprisingly, Syrie Maugham. The party went on into the small hours. To Lady Londonderry's dismay, her almost inseparable companion Ramsay MacDonald lost his seat, and Stanley Baldwin returned to power as Prime Minister. It was the last election-night party that the store would host.

Missing from his life was Harry's old friend Lord Riddell, Chairman of the *News of the World*, who had died a year earlier. Selfridge had been full of admiration for his boisterous newspaper. In 1933, he had helped broker a deal between the store model Gloria and the *News of the World*, who serialized her racy 'top model memoirs' for an 'undisclosed sum'. It wasn't the first project they had worked on. On one occasion, Selfridge's had sponsored a fashion design competition run by the *World*, offering a cash prize and promising to showcase the winner's outfit in the store. A panel of designers and stage celebrities met in the Palm Court for the judging session and a lunch, at which the actress Sybil Thorndike had agreed to present the prize.

Unfortunately, she hadn't learned her lines. Standing up to make her speech, she gushingly enthused: 'This is the most wonderful event. But then, I have always thought that the *Sunday People* is the most wonderful newspaper ever published.' As the unstoppable Miss Thorndike continued to eulogize the *News of the World*'s bitter rival, Lord Riddell sat frozen faced, quietly decimating his bread roll.

Newspaper editors were allocating an increasing amount of space to reporting on fashion, which in itself was receiving an enormous boost from the cinema as women sought to emulate the glamour they saw on the silver screen. Ready-to-wear clothing was now widely available, and copies of work from designers such as Balenciaga swept into the shops, Madge Garland of *Vogue* observing, 'Coats admired in the February Paris collections can be found this autumn at Jaeger.' Those who couldn't afford to buy what they wanted bought the best-selling paper patterns of all the new silhouettes from Paris. Fortunately for retailers, there was still a clear divide between day and night: women dressed for dinner, wore the ubiquitous 'little black dress' for cocktails, pinned diamanté dress clips to their necklines and wouldn't dream of leaving the house without wearing a hat and gloves. The bias cut, the pyjama suit and cruise-wear were all the rage, while the daring adopted Elsa Schiaparelli's surreal style. Admittedly, not every shopper in Selfridge's took to her cheeky chapeaux with a lobster perched on top, but her influence, in everything from hand-knit swimsuits to ornate embroidery and even fantasy buttons, was undeniable. Intent on outstripping her bitter rival Coco Chanel, 'Scap' was planning her own perfume. Called 'Shocking' and seductively packaged in a bottle based on Mae West's curves, it was launched in 1936 and showcased at Selfridge's.

The 1930s also marked a new era in that profitable department store staple, underwear. Dunlop's chemists had managed to transform latex rubber into a reliable elastic thread, which was in turn transformed into the girdle. With entire new ranges of underpinnings on the market – including Warner's first 'cup-sized' brassiere – manufacturers hastened to claim that corsetry fitting had become a 'scientific' art and trained saleswomen to fit and measure accurately. So seriously did women take to this system that the process of acquiring new underwear could now take an hour or more. Gossard launched their 'Gossard Complete', a boneless foundation garment that could be worn under a backless evening gown, which, since it fastened with side hooks and bars, was promoted with the appealing copy-line 'No maid required.' Only the rich or those lucky enough to have a devoted family retainer still had a personal lady's maid. Meanwhile, thanks to labour-saving devices such as electric cookers, lighter-weight vacuum cleaners and improved washing-machines, domestic tasks could be handled without an army of servants. This was probably just as well, because not only could most people no longer afford to hire them, but young girls no longer wanted to be parlour maids: instead they took jobs as cinema usherettes or waitresses or worked behind the ever-expanding cosmetics counters in department stores.

Selfridge and his store were hardly ever out of the press. In the autumn of 1935 he was profiled in depth by *Reader's Digest* and his 'official' biography, sympathetically written by William Blackwood, was serialized in Chicago's *Saturday Morning Post* and thereafter in England in *The Passing Show*, a once successful but now somewhat ailing society features magazine. Neither the magazine's title nor its diminishing status was lost on the new member of the Board, Mr Holmes, who watched all this self-aggrandizement with unease, later saying: 'Selfridge wanted to go on being king of his own castle, even though it was beginning to tumble.'

There was, in the beginning at least, very little Andrew Holmes could do, other than watch – and wait. He made his own tours of the store, fretted over the payroll of the group's 15,000 employees, queried expenses and sat in on board meetings at which Selfridge would blithely state, 'Minutes agreed unless objected to – business closed,' before ushering everyone out of his office. If Selfridge felt uneasy about Mr Holmes, he didn't show it. Confident that he carried a majority vote, he simply ignored him. By and large Harry's life – within the store at least – continued as before. Staff were summoned to his presence by a twinkling trio of bright blue lights, part of a clever internal security system set up throughout the store. He toured each morning, and again in the afternoon. Miss Rogez continued to shop until she dropped. Most importantly, plans went ahead for the relocation of the food hall from the site on the far side of Oxford Street to custom-designed space in Orchard Street. Just before Christmas 1935, Selfridge went to inspect progress on the new site. Gazing up at workmen painting the ceiling, he took a step forward and toppled twelve feet from the edge of the floor on to scaffolding below. At first, witnesses thought he was dead, but he escaped with little more than concussion and a bruised hip, though he was confined to bed for a week. That Christmas, as the health of the King rapidly deteriorated and he too took to his bed, for the second year running Wallis Simpson arrived at Selfridge's to do the seasonal gift shopping for the Prince of Wales.

King George never recovered, dying at Sandringham on 20 January 1936. His son David, now King Edward VIII, continued to go dancing with Wallis, herself by now a glittering example of Cartier's skill, wearing priceless stones remounted in ultra-modern settings. Their venue of choice was still the Embassy Club, where not much had changed either except the music. Syncopated jazz had been eclipsed by the 'swing time' sound as perfected by Benny Goodman's orchestra and by the show songs of Rogers & Hart, Noël Coward and Cole Porter. The new King-Emperor could still be seen at the Ritz and the Savoy, and he still went to stay with his close-knit circle of friends, but increasingly he spent most of his time at his beloved Fort Belvedere, deluding himself that he could marry Wallis Simpson and keep his throne. The British press continued to be discreet, despite the Court Circular revealing that in June 'Mrs Simpson' was present at a dinner party held at St James's Palace – Mr Simpson being tactfully elsewhere.

That summer, Wallis and the King went on a Mediterranean cruise aboard the luxury steam yacht *Nahlin*, but there was no cruising for the Selfridge family. Harry had had to sell the *Conqueror*. He had also moved house, departing reluctantly from Carlton House Terrace and moving into an apartment in Brook House on Park Lane, where, ironically, Syrie Maugham was busy decorating another sumptuous flat belonging to Mr and Mrs Israel Sieff of Marks & Spencer. Brook House had been built on the site of the mansion owned by Harry's old friend Ernest Cassel, which had subsequently been sold to developers by his granddaughter, Edwina Mountbatten. The Mountbattens themselves had moved into their much-photographed thirty-room penthouse, accessed by a high-speed lift, in June. Making plans to install Marcelle Rogez in an apartment nearby, Harry oversaw the decoration himself, becoming the bane of the builders and exhausting his private secretary Leslie Winterbottom, who struggled to cope with the Chief's demands. Top of his wish-list was a black bath, which proved hard to find. Making daily visits to the flat to check on progress, Selfridge badgered the foreman in charge of the search. 'Now, look here, Sir,' he replied, 'it isn't that easy. But if you want to put a black lady in here, we'll soon find a white bath for her.' The joke was lost on Harry, who returned to the store demanding that Winterbottom change the builders.

Earlier that year, Selfridge's had put on an ornate display to celebrate its twenty-seventh birthday, lighting up the exteriors with an enormous 2-ton rotating globe. Gifts such as silver keys or oak seedlings had always been given out to celebrate special anniversaries (Selfridge himself called them tokens of esteem), but this time customers were merely handed morsels of an enormous birthday cake. In June, shoppers surged into the newly opened food hall. By the time the doors closed, a central display of tinned salmon had been so depleted by shoplifters that only a dozen or so cans remained. The staff dithered about telling the Chief, who loathed the very mention of theft. When in the end they did, Miss Mepham recalled that 'the news rather crushed him. He simply couldn't believe the worst of his fellow man.' Whether due to the endless promotions, the new food hall or the increase in summer holiday shopping as travellers headed to sunnier shores, business that year picked up considerably, resulting in a year-end net profit of £485,000.

Neither Selfridge nor his son was accustomed to restraint. Gordon Jr bought himself a new plane, which *Time* magazine reported as having cost $45,000. He flew his expensive toy to Spain – at that time in the midst of a bitter civil war – taking the de Sibours along for the ride. Lacking his father's finesse in handling the press, his interview with *Time* on his return rather backfired, his escapade being described as 'Sportsman Selfridge having swank fun'. It was also noted that he had stayed safely the other side of the border when Jacques de Sibour courageously returned to rescue thirty stranded American tourists the following day. Whether the trip was wise or foolish, Mr Holmes clearly didn't like it, any more than he liked Gordon Jr flying around the country on business trips. Mr Holmes believed in taking the train.

With the date of Edward VIII's Coronation set for May 1937, and curiously ignoring the gossip about the King and Wallis, Harry started to make plans to deck the façade with the most sumptuous decorations London had ever seen. Exactly as with King George V's Coronation and subsequent Jubilee, he spent hours at the College of Heralds, poring over every detail.

Harry was now 80. He had always believed his mental agility would push back the years, and to an extent it did; but physically he was in decline. At a film premiere at the Regal Cinema in Marble Arch he fainted. When press photographers caught the moment, his embarrassment was made public in the *Daily Sketch*. Just a few weeks later he fell heavily while trying to vault a roped stanchion in the store's restaurant. His own trusted senior staff were also becoming old. Some, like the endlessly discreet Mr Hensey in Accounts and the urbane jewellery buyer Mr Dix, who had recently presided over the opening of England's first store counter selling Mikimoto cultured pearls, retired. Others, like Freddie Day who had spent his career buying trunks and luggage, died. The Chief's trusted confidant, A. H. Williams, left to open his own advertising agency which failed to perform as he had hoped: Williams later ruefully admitted that 'It was Selfridge who made us what we are.' The architect Sir John

Burnet died. Ralph Blumenfeld suffered a bad stroke and spent less and less time in Fleet Street. Lord Ashfield too was ill with a severe eye complaint. Selfridge wrote to Blumenfeld:

> I wish dear fellow you were well enough to come to America with me this autumn. Albert [Lord Ashfield], as you know, seems much improved after treatment in France. So, of the Three Musketeers, when Albert gets in good shape, two of us will pull you around and we will again be ready for the fray. Your friend, Harry.

Selfridge always attended funerals, wrote kindly letters to widows and sent flowers and fruit to the sick. He even visited an incurably ill retiree every week to play a game of cards. The store and its staff meant everything to him. Walking the vast acreage with Williams a few months earlier, the Chief said poignantly: 'This is our life, without it we are nothing.'

Children pouring on to the store roof for the arrival of Father Christmas that year were enchanted when he flew into town in his own aeroplane, triumphantly making a low loop-the-loop above them. Just a few minutes later, as if by magic, he appeared in a vast motor sleigh, riding up Oxford Street waving a star-spangled banner, and bringing the traffic to a standstill. By the time he emerged with his sack from a faux chimney built on the roof, the mesmerized youngsters were beside themselves with excitement. The performance, honed to perfection over the years, ran like a well-oiled machine. It was all very charming – not to mention profitable – and was repeated, albeit less elaborately, in all the Selfridge group stores. Usually, the Chief himself attended many of these performances, but this year he was confined to bed after an accident in which a fire-engine crushed his Rolls-Royce. He therefore missed a visit to Jones Brothers in Holloway. It was probably just as well. That year, Father Christmas ran amok, swinging his fists instead of his sack, and started to beat the children over the head.

The panic in the toy department at Jones Brothers was nothing to that in the display department at Selfridge's where ornate banners, hand-embroidered in gold thread with the insignia of the new King, had been arriving from specialist workshops charged with the task of producing perfection. The trouble was no one knew what to do with them.

On 3 December Wallis Simpson had awoken to find her photograph emblazoned across the front pages of every newspaper in England. People were aghast. Was *this* the woman their King wanted to marry? The press had worked hard to create an image of a blue-eyed Prince Charming. Now, led by the implacable *Times* Editor Geoffrey Dawson, they set about destroying him. They also set about destroying Wallis Simpson. On 10 December, after weeks of speculation and frenzied press reports, the King abdicated. Angry protestors stoned Wallis's house in Cumberland Terrace while she frantically packed her suitcases and trunks. That evening, under the cover of darkness, the trunks were transported to Selfridge's where Ernest Winn supervised their stacking in a corner of the dispatch department. Recalling that curious moment of history in the making, he later said: 'We were told to keep things quiet and not tell anyone what we had in Despatch … some special people were coming to collect it in a few hours. As we were roping it all up, some of the messenger boys were unhappy. It wasn't so hard to understand … we didn't want to lose our King. When we'd finished with Mrs Simpson's luggage we just stared at each other sadly.'

Harry Selfridge spent a miserable Christmas, comforted only by his faithful pug dogs and attended by his dutiful daughter Rosalie who, along with Serge and Tatiana, was also living in Brook House. Mr Priestley, his favoured barber from the store, came over each morning at 9.00 a.m. to shave him, Rosalie slipping him 5 shillings on his way out. He didn't even have Marcelle Rogez for company. She had been cast in the British-made musical *Big Fella* and was now busy filming with Paul Robeson.

At the store, the Coronation decorations had to be changed. Out went the insignia of King Edward VIII and in came those of King

George VI and Queen Elizabeth. Carved panels celebrated England's history since the Roman invasion and the exploits of national heroes such as Drake, Clive and Wolfe. Selfridge believed passionately that the Coronation would be 'the event of all times' to lift London out of its gloom, and the decorations took on an almost mystical meaning for him. Supremely confident that hundreds of thousands of people would flock into town, all of them keen to buy new clothes and souvenirs, he restocked the store and hired extra display staff. The resident architect Albert Miller, the sculptor Sir William Reid Dick and Professor Ernest Stern – a Romanian film production designer with a *tendre* for gilded opulence – created the most extraordinary scheme that Oxford Street had ever seen. Selfridge's became the most decorated building in Britain.

Harry had spent a colossal £50,000 on the pageantry, but not everyone appreciated the result. E. M. Forster wrote scathingly in the *New Statesman*, 'The decorations reminded me of nothing so much as a vulgar old woman, who has trotted out every scrap of her finery for an unaccustomed airing,' while *Punch*, playing on the 'more royal than the royals' décor, ran a cartoon showing a policeman telling an elderly lady: 'No Madam, I understand Mr Selfridge will not be appearing on his balcony tonight.'

Hundreds of thousands did visit London and many of them blocked Oxford Street to gaze in awe at the store. But they didn't spend their money. Takings were nowhere near expectations. Perhaps hurt by the insults hurled at Wallis, the Americans simply didn't come, and the British weren't in the mood to buy – it was almost as if they were grieving at having been rejected by the man they had idolized. For a while at least, his brother was simply second-best. It took six weeks to dismantle the finery, which was packed away and stored in the sub-basement. Selfridge himself remained tight-lipped, while Mr Holmes was infuriated by the cost of it all. The two men were now barely speaking to each other.

That same month, Harry Gordon Selfridge became a naturalized British citizen. Some said it was because he hoped for an honour in the King's Coronation list; others murmured about new, onerous American taxes imposed on Americans living abroad. Those closest to him knew it was simply because he wanted to become British. He wrote proudly to his friend Blumenfeld: 'It is 31 years next Sunday since I came to London. Now I will be a true Briton and now I shall have to try to begin to act like a gentleman. As ever, Gordon.'

He had, of course, always behaved as a gentleman – never more so than in 1927 when he had promised a little old lady that Whiteley's would pay a guaranteed 25 per cent dividend for the next fifteen years. His promise had cost him dear. A decade later, the annual figure had reached £500,000. Profits were down. People were beginning to worry about the prospect of war. As the share price of the Gordon Selfridge Trust and Selfridge Provincial Stores Ltd declined, *The Economist* wrote: 'Selfridge Group prospects have occasioned special concern.' Harry went to America, ostensibly to launch the publication of his now famous 'Callisthenes' column in the *New York Herald Tribune* but also to see bankers. His old friend Jules Bache was uncharacteristically gloomy about trading prospects, and Elizabeth Arden, with whom he lunched, was visibly moved by his dilemma, writing immediately to her London manager, 'It's a shame to see him so worried, we must give him every help possible.'

Back in London, he placed advertisements that declared: 'There will be no slump. Let us kill the whole depressing idea by laughing it off.' Yet he knew, better than anyone, that price was a powerful persuader. Throughout the country, customers were flocking to Marks & Spencer who, since they had registered their St Michael trademark in 1928, had moved rapidly to capture the hearts and minds of middle-market shoppers with their 'quality and value' offerings. The chain now sold food, and some stores even had cafés. In a move that caused some annoyance at Selfridge's, Simon Marks attracted a lot of publicity by launching a swathe of 'staff benefits' which included subsidized canteens, health and dental services, hairdressing, rest rooms and even camping holidays – all of which Selfridge's had been offering since the day the store opened, except perhaps the camping:

Selfridge's staff preferred the company's skiing holidays. One thing the mighty Marks & Spencer did offer, however, was a staff pension scheme. Selfridge had never believed in compulsory pensions, feeling people should save for themselves. Regrettably, he hadn't practised what he'd preached.

In the meantime he raised the bar by opening an even bigger bargain business, located in the store's empty property across the street, calling it 'John Thrifty'. It offered service with a smile, though customers had to carry their own shopping home. Staff still observed the store's rules: no customer was called 'Miss' or 'Dear', and staff themselves were called 'assistants'. They were told to 'walk tall' through the floors, encouraged to attend the long-established courses in 'Voice Culture and Personal Magnetism' and, as always, urged to give 'the utmost attention to the care of hair and hands'. The staff still loved the Chief. While newcomers didn't quite share the evangelical zeal of their older colleagues, their affection for their mentor was tangible.

Harry still gambled, but his days as casino king were over. In the spring of 1938, he went back to Deauville with Marcelle, only to find he wasn't welcome. In refusing him credit, Nicolas Zographos was in fact doing his one-time high-roller a huge favour. Harry could no longer afford to lose. He never went back, confining his gaming to poker, playing with his monogrammed cards and mother-of-pearl chips. He was visibly moved by the news of Suzanne Lenglen's death in July from pernicious anaemia at the age of only 39. That summer, he rented the Duke of Devonshire's seaside villa, Compton Place at Eastbourne, and summoned his children and grandchildren for what would, in effect, be their last luxury holiday spent together. Gordon Jr's four children were not among the house party, and neither was his wife. Selfridge still refused to acknowledge them and Gordon Jr was still happy to hide them away. Tatiana Wiasemsky was now 18, Violette's son Blaise was 15 and her daughter Jacqueline 5. It was the last family holiday Violette and Jacques de Sibour would spend together. Their already fractured marriage broke apart soon after, leading to divorce. Beatrice fared no better in her marriage to Jacques's brother Louis. Two years later, they too divorced. At the end of the year, Harry's Christmas card showed a picture of his cherished 'celebrity window', the latest diamond-tipped signature being that of the Oscar-winning film director Frank Capra, who had visited the store while in London to promote his latest movie *You Can't Take It with You.*

In 1939, with his unerring eye for a brilliant idea, Selfridge launched a ground-breaking television department with a major in-store exhibition. Convinced of the power of television, for years he had enthused about the latest technology: 'Television is here – You can't shut your eyes to it!' ran his advertisements in the London and national press. The store offered the most comprehensive range ever put together in the new business of broadcasting, showing many models two months before they were exhibited at the New York World Fair, including those by Pye, Cossor, G. E. C. Ferranti, Marconiphone, Baird, His Master's Voice and Ekco. The seductive sets were priced from 23 guineas and, for those on a budget but who couldn't resist temptation, Selfridge's offered their own hire purchase terms.

As always with Selfridge's, it wasn't just about selling television sets but also about education and in-store entertainment. The store invested £20,000 in setting up a fully operational studio in the Palm Court which, in conjunction with the BBC, ran a live studio facility where visitors could see celebrities being filmed and, most appealing of all, where they could enter competitions to appear on screen themselves. Dancers, singers and comedians were encouraged to apply for a screen test, while eager mothers queued up to enter their daughters for children's dance contests. Fashion shows introduced by Gordon Jr were screened on fifty television receivers strategically placed throughout the store that broadcast at 11.00 a.m. each day. There were even make-up demonstrations to show how to eliminate shine before facing the camera. The Chief had thought of everything.

Selfridge's had earned a unique place in retail history in championing television ever since Baird's pioneering demonstration in 1925, but nothing could have prepared the public for the excitement of seeing themselves on screen. Thousands of visitors poured into the Palm Court, scrambling to be part of the excitement. Yet curiously the media coverage was lacklustre. Only *The Times* got the point of it all, but even then merely reported that 'the Exhibition was an interesting and, indeed, exciting occasion'. Sadly for Harry Selfridge, the excitement was short-lived. On the outbreak of war in September, the BBC ceased transmission. Manufacturers' skills were redirected towards weapons of war, and broadcasting wouldn't resume until June 1946.

Selfridge was among the many who knew war was inevitable. On his frequent trips to Germany where the store had long maintained a buying office, he witnessed at first hand Germany's ruthless persecution of the Jews. Sensitive towards their plight, and with many Jewish friends of his own as well as customers who used the Kosher food department and the Hebrew section of the book department, he wanted to do something to help. Throughout the spring of 1939, he devoted dozens of 'Callisthenes' columns to the topic of 'What Refugees Can Do for England', being particularly supportive of German Jews seeking a safe haven.

At Brighton Technical College, in a hall so crowded that loudspeakers had to be rigged up outside for the overflow, he gave a talk to students, explaining that 'much intelligent work is being done under the dictators Hitler and Mussolini and unless we of the democracies are going to do the same amount of work and use the same effort and intelligence, we are going to be beaten'. The young students were enthralled, the local *Argus* reporting that 'they cheered and applauded until it echoed around the hall'.

Selfridge received another remarkable ovation at the shareholders' meeting, despite the fact that he owed the store over £100,000 and the board's announcement that no dividend would be paid on ordinary shares. One colleague said he 'positively glowed with faith in the future', while a reporter remarked that 'he didn't look a day over sixty '– cheering news for a man who was now 83. Having finally been invited to Hollywood, Marcelle Rogez left London that year. Now Harry was, and would remain, alone.

On a business trip to America, Andrew Holmes was entertained by the new men in power at Marshall Field, by now also a business losing money. Asking about 'mile-a-minute Harry', Holmes was told: 'He was the greatest sales promoter and publicity man the store ever had. Quite the perfect showman.' To Mr Holmes, who didn't believe in showmanship, this merely confirmed his belief that 'Selfridge's greatest illusion is that he was a merchant, which possibly explains many of his mistakes.' On holiday early that fateful summer, Mr Holmes met the owner of an important carpet company, whose main topic of conversation was their long overdue account. Faced with what he described as 'a withering blast', Holmes went back to London and examined the books, discovering that many suppliers, used to waiting patiently for six months to be paid, were now expected to extend credit for over a year. A lot of them couldn't afford it. Worse, some were threatening legal action.

At some point that summer, Harry had a serious argument with his son, their uneasy relationship collapsing into acrimony. Playing politics, Gordon Jr said: 'Something has got to be done about my father.' In August, the Group Finance Director and latterly Company Secretary, Arthur Youngman, always devotedly loyal to the Chief, retired after thirty-one years in the job. His departure signalled a Board reshuffle and the appointment of a Holmes protégé, Arthur Deakin.

The store had spent the summer preparing for war. The Civil Defence Unit ordered 5,000 sandbags, tons of sand and timber, hundreds of rubber boots, respirators and steel helmets, waterproof overalls, gas masks and two and a half tons of bleach powder, to be used to extinguish fires. Staff underwent training under the direction of the indefatigable director Mr H. J. Clarke, who energetically put his 'emergency squad' through their paces on the roof and at the Preston Road sports ground. On 2 September the Wehrmacht marched into Poland. At 11.15 a.m. on 3 September the Prime Minister Neville

Chamberlain announced that the country was at war. Sandbags were piled around the Chief's private entrance at the rear of the store, and he was photographed going to work with a gas mask slung over his shoulder, smiling broadly for waiting photographers and saying it was 'business as usual'. Rapid adjustments were made to stock inventory. Vast quantities of blankets were ordered and Nellie Elt astutely bought in quantities of lipsticks and boxed soaps. Handbags 'designed to carry gas masks' were hastily put on sale and, for the lucky few, there was an exciting addition to the hosiery department – imported nylon stockings.

In a portent of things to come, the 'Callisthenes' column ceased publication on 2 September. For the past fifteen years, the column had been written by the journalist Eisdale MacGregor, but the last article, called 'A Final Word', was written by Selfridge himself:

> Their spirit of happy enthusiasm and of good cheer is hardly consistent with the sterner atmosphere of war. The articles have endeavoured to dignify that fine thing called business and surround it with strong and unbreakable bands of integrity. With this, then final word – final for the moment – we conclude this long, interesting and, we hope, character-building series.

In reality, the column's closure was due to a massive cost-cutting exercise being orchestrated by Mr Holmes, who was now poised to get rid of the most extravagant expense of all – Mr Selfridge. Gordon Jr vanished on an extended trip to America, staying away for over a month. Senior staff, curious about his absence, gossiped among themselves. When the blow came, most of Selfridge's inner circle had been expecting it for weeks – everyone, that is, except the Chief. Miss Mepham greeted Mr Holmes with professional politeness when he appeared at the door to the inner office on 18 October. She wasn't invited to take notes. At the meeting that followed, Holmes pointed out some salient facts. Selfridge owed the store in excess of £118,000. He owed the Inland Revenue in excess of £250,000 in back taxes. In addition, he had personal, undisclosed debts to the Midland Bank. All this was secured against his shareholdings in the company. He owned no freehold property, the store paid his costs at Brook House, and he had no company pension. Selfridge was given an ultimatum. Either he retire, relinquishing all form of executive control, or the company would demand immediate repayment of his debt. He was offered a pension of £6,000 a year free of tax on condition he gave his shares back to the business. He had no choice but to accept.

Selfridge sat silently as Andrew Holmes on behalf of the Prudential Insurance Company stripped him of his life's work, ending everything he had held dear by handing him the draft of a resignation letter which he was asked to approve on the spot. Always dignified, with that same remote quality that for decades his colleagues had yearned to penetrate, Harry Gordon Selfridge initialled his life away. Miss Mepham sat outside, knowing – as all good secretaries always do – exactly what was going on.

The Board issued an abrupt and clumsily worded announcement to staff and the press:

> The time has come when Mr Selfridge feels that he should relieve himself from the duties of detail [sic] management and he has therefore asked his colleagues to accept his resignation. Advancing years and their accompanying penalties have been bringing the wisdom of this step to Mr Selfridge for quite a long time … his resignation has been received with the greatest possible regret and at the same time, in view of his unique association with the company since its foundation [the Board] have invited him to accept the title of President of the Company.

Harry spent a day or so composing his own leaving letter, which was circulated to the staff on 21 October:

> The time has come when I must relinquish the management of this great and beautiful business … which I created and founded over

thirty years ago. My proverbial three score years and ten have long since been passed, and I have concluded, with much thought and great regret, to resign my several posts of Chairman and Managing Director and retire from the Boards of this Company and its subsidiary and associated companies … I have assumed the somewhat nominal title of President. This will not carry with it a controlling voice, but will put me in the position of an adviser when desirable … And now, my friends, I am taking a bit of a holiday. It is not that, but let us call it so. Another of my regrets is that if one of these raids occurs while I am away, I shall not be here to share it with you. During the last war I was in London continually and declined to allow the German bombs to interfere with my usual routine … wish me then, a good trip and a safe return to you all, and, as the man in the movies says – 'I'll be seeing you'. We can then again shake hands and talk about the yesterdays and the tomorrows.

And, as long as I live, my great love for this business and my deep feelings of friendship for the members of the staff will remain undimmed by time.

By the time the letter was circulated, he was gone. He couldn't bear to say goodbye. Two weeks later he boarded the SS *Washington* for his last trip to America.

The great building in Oxford Street was no longer the store of H. G. Selfridge. The name plates were swiftly put back up outside the building, and advertisements no longer showed the apostrophe in the title. Having pensioned off the father, Mr Holmes turned his attention to the son. If Gordon Jr had been under the impression there would be an enhanced role for him, he was wrong. There was no place in the business for the man whom *Time* relentlessly referred to as 'a playboy'. Mr Holmes restructured his job brief, obliging him to step down from his directorships of Whiteley's and the Gordon Selfridge Trust, leaving him as titular head of the provincial stores. Three months later, the provincial stores were sold to John Lewis of Oxford Street. Gordon Jr left the business, reportedly furious at the rapid dismantling of the empire. Within a matter of months he moved with his wife and children to America where he took a job at Sears Roebuck in Chicago.

Back in London, Selfridge found that not everyone had written him off, particularly the media. Newspaper proprietors gathered together to host a New Year's luncheon in his honour, where he sat with Ralph Blumenfeld, by now known as 'the father of Fleet Street', and Lord Ashfield, who spoke glowingly of his friend's 'transformation of Oxford Street', adding that perhaps he should after all have agreed to name Bond Street tube station 'Selfridges'. A powerful group of retailers applauded the post-lunch talk: Sir Montague Burton, Trevor Fenwick, Frederick Fenwick, Sir Woodman Burbidge of Harrods and L. H. Bentall. Everyone said Selfridge looked well. He wasn't. But he knew how to put on a show.

Surprising as it may seem, he still went into the store on most days, taking the lift once exclusively reserved for him but now designated for all directors and stubbornly sitting in his office, where he and Miss Mepham went through the ritual of 'let's pretend'. They pretended there were letters, memos, invitations or meetings. In reality there were none. He would still don his top hat and walk the store where staff, though pleased to see him, were also embarrassed. They didn't know what to say. What *could* they say? He was said to be 'making plans'. Why, no one could really fathom, but word went out that he had dreams of starting a new enterprise, and Mr Holmes struck again with a letter:

> It was clearly the intention of the Directors and especially in the minds of their advisers that for practical and psychological reasons, you would vacate the Managing Director's accommodation so as to give complete freedom to the new Management ... I am instructed by the Board to ask you to be good enough to arrange for such personal possessions as you would wish to be removed before the 26th April ... one other matter which the Directors view with some concern is that you are contemplating commencing independent business

activities … they do object and deprecate very seriously that such negotiations should be conducted from the store address.

In case Selfridge didn't get the point, he was given the use of a small office in Keysign House, a company property across the road, his pension was cut by a third and the services of Miss Mepham were withdrawn.

In May 1940, Selfridge was honoured by the dedication of a bronze plaque and illuminated scroll, to which the owners of forty-one stores subscribed and which was unveiled at a luncheon given in the store's Palm Court Restaurant. In thanking those present, Harry said: 'I realize my generation has pretty nearly lived out its life.' Conspicuous by his absence was Mr Holmes.

When the Blitz began, London braced itself. During one raid the store roof was hit by bombs that started a fierce fire. Most of the upper windows were shattered, including the Chief's much-loved signature window. When he went to inspect the damage, the old man broke down. It was the first time anyone had seen him cry. He continued to spend several hours a day sitting alone in his empty room on the opposite side of the street, writing letters to various acquaintances in authority, offering his services 'for the war effort' and hoping – in vain – that he might be given some useful work. Eventually he stopped coming.

In January 1941, just a few days before his eighty-fifth birthday, the Board stripped Harry Selfridge of his title of President and, with year-end net profits at an all-time low of only £21,093, slashed his pension yet again. Now living on a meagre £2,000 a year, Harry, Serge and Rosalie vacated Brook House and moved to a two-bedroom flat in Ross Court, Putney. In June that year, isolated and alone in Hollywood, Jenny Dolly committed suicide, hanging herself with the sash of her dressing-gown.

In August, Harry's cherished collection of rare French and English books was auctioned at Sotheby's. The family were struggling to make ends meet. While Serge spent his mornings drinking in the Green

Man, Rosalie could be found from time to time visiting a rather dubious antiques shop in the Lower Richmond Road, where she was forced to sell their valuables for hard cash. Her father spent his days reading correspondence, sifting through archives and playing the odd game of poker with the ever-cheerful Mr Robertson of the *Evening News*.

As Oxford Street was pounded by bombs, the store continued to be hit. The ground-floor windows were bricked up, the roof garden was left in ruins and the Palm Court Restaurant, the scene of so much excitement over the years, was decimated by fire and closed for ever. In 1942, the store's ex-star model Gloria once again made headlines when she was found dead in her Maida Vale flat, apparently having suffered a heart attack from an overdose of slimming pills.

Putting on a cheerful front, most of the family reunited at the King's Chapel in the Savoy in June 1943 to celebrate Tatiana Wiasemsky's marriage to Lieutenant Craig Wheaton-Smith. The wedding was followed by a small reception at Claridge's, the hotel where once Harry Selfridge had always had the best table. Later that summer, his 21-year-old grandson Blaise de Sibour, a pilot with the French Normandy Squadron flying sorties against the Germans, was shot down and killed in Russia. Violette de Sibour subsequently settled in America where she went to work for Elizabeth Arden. Conscious of his own mortality, Harry became reconciled with his son and grandchildren in America. He was increasingly frail and would sit by the fire in Ross Court, shuffling papers and burning his private letters while Rosalie looked on in despair.

On some days he would stand at his local bus stop on Putney High Street, his rheumy blue eyes searching the road for the arrival of a No. 22. Virtually deaf, his mind rambling, he hardly spoke. Harry Gordon Selfridge had retreated into his own private world, full of memories no one could share. Still wearing curiously old-fashioned formal, shabby-genteel clothes, his patent leather boots cracked and down-at-heel, his untidy white hair falling over a frayed shirt collar, his by now battered trilby pulled low, he moved stiffly, aided by a

Malacca cane. On the bus, he would carefully count out the pennies for his fare, buying a ticket to Hyde Park Corner, where he got off to wait for a No. 137 bus, quietly telling the conductor 'Selfridge's please.' Seemingly lost in memories of past glories, unrecognized by anybody, the old man shuffled the length of the majestic building before crossing the road to the corner of Duke Street. Stopping there, leaning heavily on his cane, he would look up to the roof of the store and along to the far right upper corner window, as though searching for something. Miss Mepham met him one day when he was suffering from a virulent attack of shingles and was in great pain. She fled back to her office, so distressed that she wept. Sometimes, when he was standing on the street, a hurrying pedestrian would bump into him. Once he fell heavily. On one pitiful occasion the police arrested him, suspecting he was a vagrant.

As he looked up at his great store in those desperate days of the war, Selfridge had no idea that deep below the ground, in the sub-basement he had had blasted out of the London clay, men from the US Army Signal Corps were on round-the-clock shifts protecting a top-secret telecommunications installation. Bell Telephone's X-system, codenamed Sigsaly and at the cutting edge of cryptography, was housed in what High Command felt was one of the most secure sites in London. Scrambled conversations between the men of war plotting and planning D-Day, indeed almost all communications on behalf of the British Government and the Allied forces, took place in that guarded room deep below Selfridges. How proud he would have been.

He would also have been proud to know that a perspiring subaltern returned to Company HQ after marching his platoon for many hot and weary miles on 'training' somewhere in England, to find his company commander and the CO sitting looking very pleased with themselves, holding a piece of paper. It turned out to be *The Times* crossword. 'Just finished it,' said the CO. 'We thought it had beaten us though, eh Major?' 'One blessed word,' replied the Major, 'but we rang up Selfridges Information Bureau and they knew.' Of course they did. Shortly thereafter, Mr Holmes closed the Information Bureau down.

Harry Gordon Selfridge died peacefully in his sleep at Ross Court on 8 May 1947. He was 91. Following his funeral, held at St Mark's Church, the local newspaper reported on the many floral tributes. Among them was a large wreath of red and white roses from Miss Rosie Dolly, the message simply saying 'from Rosie and Jenny', and a huge bouquet with a card saying, 'In memeory of a great citizen of the world who loved humanity' from the President, directors, vice-presidents and executives of Marshall Field and Co., Chicago, USA.

In his will, Harry left jewellery and what remained of his sculpture collection to his three daughters. He had once said: 'When I die, I want it said of me, "He dignified and ennobled commerce".' His family had no money for a headstone to honour the man who did just that – and it never occurred to Selfridges to pay for one. Instead, he lies in a humble grave near his beloved wife and mother in the quiet churchyard of St Mark's in Highcliffe, where leaves from the over-hanging trees gently fall around their tombs.

NOTES

I have been fortunate to be able to draw from the magnificent Selfridges Archives (which at the time when this book was originally written were held at the History of Advertising Trust – hereafter referred to as HAT – but have now returned to Selfridge's). The detailed documents, letters (both to and from H. G. Selfridge), ledgers, staff records and press cuttings collection (1907–75) have been an invaluable source for this book. I have also studied correspondence and documents made available to me by the House of Lords Library; Keele University; the University of Nottingham; the Baker Library at Harvard University; the Harry Ransom Humanities Research Center at the University of Texas, Austin; Princeton University; Stanford University; and the University of Chicago. I am grateful to Simon Wheaton-Smith, Harry Gordon Selfridge's great-grandson, who not only provided many family anecdotes but also made available his exceptional collection of treasured family memorabilia. The letters between Miss Elizabeth Arden and her London Managing Director, Teddy Haslam (1922–47 in author's possession), have been a most helpful source in respect of the personality and business practices of H. G. Selfridge and the store. I would also like to thank Gordon Honeycombe for permission to draw from his book *Selfridges: Seventy-Five Years: The Story of a Store*.

Early twentieth-century fashion detail was researched at the Condé Nast Library. On a personal note, I have found Elizabeth Ewing's books *Dress and Undress* and *The History of 20th Century Fashion* of inestimable help in researching the fashion of the period and must also recommend Fashion-era.com (text by Pauline Weston Thomas), which has been a fascinating and informed source. For those interested in the history of British retailing, I would recommend *Shops and Shopping* by Alison Adburgham as essential reading.

Chicago as a city during the late nineteenth and early twentieth centuries came alive to me both through Emmett Dedmon's superlative book *Fabulous Chicago* and Perry R. Duis's equally evocative essays collated in *'Challenging Chicago': Coping with Everyday Life, 1837–1920*. Authoritative documentation from experts in Chicago has included Trish Morse's wonderfully descriptive *'Midway Plaisance Walking Tour'*, which enabled me to trace Rose Buckingham's property development project. Further information was provided by the Hyde Park Historical Society, the Chicago Public Library and the Chicago History Museum.

. During the time he lived in London, in relation to his business dealings, Harry Gordon Selfridge was generally known as Gordon Selfridge. His family and close friends, however, always referred to him as Harry. For the main part, he signed his letters to friends both in England and America as Harry. I have chosen to refer to him by that name.

The notes that follow show the principal sources (other than those indicated above) on which I have drawn in order of appearance in the text. Books are listed by author and title only, but further details may be found in the Bibliography.

Accurate valuations on the correct value of the pound and dollar in the early part of the twentieth century to today are hard to pinpoint. I have followed official guidelines, which indicate that pre-First World War, £1 was worth £65 today. It subsequently dropped to £40 and settled at £25 post-war, until the Great Depression. Throughout this period, the exchange rate for the dollar was approximately $5 to £1. For further information, see Measuring Worth *www.measuringworth.com* and the Inflation Calculator *www.westegg.com/inflation*

Selfridges have kindly granted permission for use of many of the photographs reproduced in this book. Every effort has been made to trace copyright holders and to clear copyright permission. If notified, the publishers will be pleased to rectify any omissions in future editions. Any omissions of fact or errors are the author's own.

Introduction
Emile Zola, *Au Bonheur des Dames*; Alison Adburgham, *Shops and Shopping*; Reginald Pound, *Selfridge*; Lois Banner, *American Beauty*; Erika Rappaport, *Shopping for Pleasure*; Lloyd Wendt & Herman Kogan, *Give the Lady What She Wants*; Axel Madsen, *The Marshall Fields*; Lloyd Morris, *Incredible New York*; Michael B. Miller, *The Bon Marché*; Selfridges Archives.

Chapter 1: The Fortunes of War
Stephen N. Elias, *Alexander T. Stewart*; Lloyd Morris, *Incredible New York*; Lloyd Wendt & Herman Kogan, *Give the Lady What She Wants*; Robert W. Twyman, *Potter*

Palmer; Emmett Dedmon, *Fabulous Chicago*; Family Archives of Simon Wheaton Smith; The George Washington Masonic National Memorial; Robert W. Twyman, *The History of Marshall Field & Co.*; Selfridges Archive; John Tebbel, *The Marshall Fields*; Nancy F. Koehn, *Brand New*; Ishbel Ross, *Silhouette in Diamonds*.

Chapter 2: Giving the Ladies What They Want

Diana de Marley, *Worth*; Gail MacColl & Carol Wallace, *To Marry an English Lord*; Elizabeth Ewing, *The History of 20th Century Fashion*; Elizabeth Ewing, *Dress and Undress*; Madge Garland, *A History of Fashion*; Elizabeth Ewing, *The History of 20th Century Fashion*; Alistair Horne, *The Paris Commune, 1871*; Emmett Dedmon, *Fabulous Chicago*; Notes from Gordon Selfridge Jr, Selfridges Archive; Lloyd Wendt & Herman Kogan, *Give the Lady What She Wants*; Robert W. Twyman, *The History of Marshall Field & Co.*; Nigel Nicolson, *Mary Curzon*.

Chapter 3: The Customer is Always Right

Gordon Honeycomb, *Selfridges*; Reginald Pound, *Selfridge*; Robert Hendrickson, *The Grand Emporiums*; Axel Madsen, *The Marshall Fields*; About Inventors.com: Light-bulbs, Lighting and Lamps; Letter from D. H. Burnham & Co., Selfridges Archives; Emmett Dedmon, *Fabulous Chicago*; Brenda Warner Rotzoll, 'The Other Bertha Palmer', *Chicago Sun-Times*, 16 March 2003; Perry R. Duis, '*Challenging Chicago*'; Lois W. Banner, *American Beauty*; Nancy F. Koehn, *Brand New*; (on Rosalie Villas) Jean F. Block, *Hyde Park Houses* (text extracts courtesy of the Hyde Park Historical Society, Chicago; further information provided by Trish Morse, University of Chicago); Family Archives of Simon Wheaton Smith; Daughters of the American Revolution, Washington, DC; Author visit to Ely Cathedral; *Chicago Tribune*, 12 November 1890, p. 3.

Chapter 4: Full Speed Ahead

Emmett Dedmon, *Fabulous Chicago*; David F. Burg, *Chicago's White City of 1893*; James William Buel, *The Magic City*; Dennis Bell, 'The Man Who Invented the Wheel and Paid the Price', retrieved from the Internet; Rita Kramer, 'Cathedrals of Commerce', *City Journal*, New York, Spring 1966; Lois W. Banner, *American Beauty*; Lindy Woodhead, *War Paint*; Robert D. Tamilia, 'The Wonderful World of the Department Store', Ph.D., University of Quebec; Reforming Fashion, 1850–1914, costume.osu.edu/Reforming-Fashion; John Burke, *Duet in Diamonds*; Morell Parker, *Lillian Russell*; Peter Kurth, *Isadora*; Nigel Nicolson, *Mary Curzon*; Family Archives of Simon Wheaton Smith; Axel Madsen, *The Marshall Fields*; Vincent Vinikas, *Soft Soap, Hard Sell*; Duke University Advertising Research Project.

Chapter 5: Going It Alone

Family Archives of Simon Wheaton Smith; Chicago Public Library; Author interview with Nancy F. Koehn, Harvard Business School; Grace Lovat Fraser, *In the Days of My Youth*; Thomas Yanul, 'The Untold Story of Schlesinger & Mayer', retrieved from the Internet; *Encyclopedia of Chicago*, entry on Carson Pirie Scott & Co.; Nancy F. Koehn, *Brand New*; Reginald Pound, *Selfridge*; Selfridges Archives; Lloyd Wendt & Herman Kogan, *Give the Lady What She Wants*; Perry R. Duis, '*Challenging Chicago*'; *Saturday Evening Post*, Chicago, March 1935; Emmett Dedmon, *Fabulous Chicago*; (on gold mine) Family Archives of Simon Wheaton Smith; Selfridges Archive.

Chapter 6: Building the Dream

Selfridge Archive; Notes from Eric Dunstan, Selfridges Archive; (on Charles Yerkes) 'A Brush with History', National Portrait Gallery; John T. Slania, 'Loop Dreams', retrieved from the Internet; 'Receiver Named for Yerkes Estate', *New York Times*, 7 April 1909; Peter Watts, 'London's Underground History', *Time Out*, 17 April 2007; 'Mrs Harry G. Selfridge', *Chicago Daily News*, 8 June 1907; Emmett Dedmon, *Fabulous Chicago*; Reginald Pound, *Selfridge*; Gordon Honeycombe, *Selfridges*; (on Footscray House) *The Great Estates: Six Country Houses in the London Borough of Bexley* (Bexley Council, 2000), p. 52; J. B. Priestley, *The Edwardians*; Article on James Gilbert White, *Cornell Alumni News*, retrieved from the Internet; Selfridges Archive; J. B. Priestley, *The Edwardians*; (on Kreuger & Toll) Notes in Selfridges Archive; Letters from Waring & White to H. G. Selfridge, Selfridges Archive; Susan Mary Alsop, *Lady Sackville*; Kate Jackson, *George Newnes and the New Journalism in Britain*; Simon Jenkins, *Newspapers: The Power and the Money*; (on the store's opening) Selfridges Archive; The Library and Museum of Freemasonry, London (correspondence with Emily Greenstreet).

Chapter 7: Take-off

Selfridges Archive; Reginald Pound, *Selfridge*; Author conversation with Oliver Musker; John K. Winkler, *Five & Ten*; Grace Lovat Fraser, *In the Days of My Youth*; (on Violette) Notes from Eric Dunstan, Selfridges Archive; J. B. Priestley, *The Edwardians*; Elizabeth Ewing, *The History of 20th Century Fashion*; W. Somerset Maugham, *Of Human Bondage*; Alison Adburgham, *Shops and Shopping*; (on Bertha Palmer and Anna Pavlova) Museum of London; Judith R. Walkowitz, 'Cosmopolitanism and Erotic Dancing in Central London 1908–18', American Historical Review, Vol. 108, No. 2, April 2003; (on Blériot) Reginald Pound, *Selfridge*; Notes from Gordon Selfridge Jr, HAT; Gordon Honeycombe, *Selfridges*; *The Globe*, 26 July 1909; www.bleriot.org.

Chapter 8: Lighting up the Night

Project on 'The City', Harvard Design School Guide to Shopping; J. B. Priestley, *The Edwardians*; (on Pavlova), Staff notes, Selfridges Archive; Letters between Sir Edward Holden and H. G. Selfridge, Selfridges Archive; Reginald Pound, *Selfridge*; Lindy Woodhead, *War Paint*; W. J. MacQueen-Pope, *Gaiety*; International Perfume Museum, Grasse; Eugene Rimmel, Evanion Catalogue, British Library; The Letters of Ralph Blumenfeld, House of Lords Library; Letters between Ralph Blumenfeld and H. G. Selfridge, Selfridges Archive; Meredith Etherington-Smith & Jeremy Pilcher, *The 'It' Girls*; Richard Fisher, *Syrie Maugham*; Gerald McKnight, *The Scandal of Syrie Maugham*; Notes from Eric Dunstan, Selfridges Archive; Selfridges Archive; (on Sir Oliver Lodge) Staff notes, Selfridges Archive; Daughters of the American Revolution, Washington DC; A. H. Williams, *No Name at the Door*; Selfridges Archive; J. B. Priestley, *The Edwardians*.

Chapter 9: War Work, War Play

Reginald Pound, *Selfridge*; Elizabeth Ewing, *The History of 20th Century Fashion*; Selfridges Archive; A. H. Williams, *No Name at the Door*; Jeffrey Meyers, *Somerset Maugham*; The Letters of Ralph Blumenfeld, House of Lords Library; University of Chicago Library and Selfridges Archive; Family Archives of Simon Wheaton Smith; Gordon Honeycombe, *Selfridges*; James Gardiner, *Gaby Deslys*; Cecil Beaton, *The Glass of Fashion*; Irene Castle, *Castles in the Air*; Elisabeth Marbury, *My Crystal Ball*; Selfridges Archive; Reginald Pound, *Selfridge*; Susan Mary Alsop, *Lady Sackville*; The Woolworths Virtual Museum; John K. Winkler, *Five & Ten*; Denis Mackail, *The Story of J. M. B.*; *Letters of Arnold Bennett*, Vol. II, 1889–1915; W. Somerset Maugham, *Plays: One*, introduction by Anthony Curtis; Barbara Cartland, *We Danced All Night*; Selfridges Archive.

Chapter 10: Castles in the Air

Selfridges Archive; Condé Nast Library; (on Highcliffe) Background information provided by Ian Stevenson; 'Highcliffe Castle, Hampshire', *Country Life*, 1 May 1942; Edward H. Short and Arthur C. Rickett, *Ring Up the Curtain*, p. 274; Correspondence between Dr E. Dillon and H. G. Selfridge, Selfridges Archive; Papers of Dr Joseph Emile Dillon, Stamford University Library; (on Serge de Bolotoff) Family Archives of Simon Wheaton Smith; Selfridges Archive; *New York Herald* (Paris), 20 May 1906; *Legendary Aviators and Aircraft of World War One*; Author correspondence with Mr T. F. Boettger; E. Charles Vivian, *A History of Aeronautics*, retrieved from the Internet (further information provided by Brian Riddle, Royal Aeronautical Society); (on the Hope Sale) Department of Manuscripts and Special Collections,

Nottingham University, and information provided by Ian Jenkins, Curator of Greek and Roman Antiquities, British Museum; also Geoffrey B. Waywell, *The Lover and Hope Sculptures*, and Jonathan Scott, *The Pleasures of Antiquity*; Harry Gordon Selfridge, *The Romance of Commerce*; The Letters of Ralph Blumenfeld, House of Lords Library; Selfridges Archive; John Lane Papers, Harry Ransom Humanities Research Center, University of Texas, Austin; Family Archives of Simon Wheaton Smith; Reginald Pound, *Selfridge*; Documents (including *Barton Breezes*) provided by Ian Stevenson; *Bournemouth Daily Echo*, 16 May 1918.

Chapter 11: Vices and Virtues

Alan Jenkins, *The Twenties*; Kate 'Ma' Meyrick, *Secrets of the '43'*; Ronald Blythe, *The Age of Illusion*; Condé Nast Library; Stella Margetson, *The Long Party*; Notes from Gordon Selfridge Jr, Selfridges Archive; A. H. Williams, *No Name at the Door*; Elizabeth Ewing, *The History of 20th Century Fashion*; Selfridges Archives; Reginald Pound, *Selfridge*; Condé Nast Library; Stella Margetson, *The Long Party*; Barbara Cartland, *We Danced All Night*; Andrew Barrow, *Gossip*; Information provided by Ian Jenkins, Curator of Greek and Roman Antiquities, British Museum; Selfridges Archive; *Daily Express*, 31 May 1920; Reginald Pound, *Selfridge*; Ralph Blumenfeld, *Diaries*; Philip Tilden, *True Remembrances*; *Bournemouth Daily Echo*, 25 May 1920; Information provided by Ian Stevenson; Violette de Sibour, *Flying Gypsies*; Staff notes, Selfridges Archive; Correspondence of H. G. Selfridge, Selfridges Archive; Arnold Bennett, *Journals*, Vol. II, p. 159; Trinity College Library, Cambridge University; Reginald Pound, *Selfridge*; Charles Savoie, 'The Mysterious, Super-élite Pilgrim Society', May 2005, retrieved from the Internet; Anne Pimlott Baker, *The Pilgrims of Great Britain*; Notes from Eric Dunstan, Selfridges Archive; James Gardiner, *Gaby Deslys*; Norman Hartnell, *Silver and Gold*; Joan Kahr, *Edgar Brandt*; Mary Blume, *Côte d'Azur*; Charles Graves, *None But the Rich*; Kate 'Ma' Meyrick, *Secrets of the '43'*; Selfridges Archive; Family Archives of Simon Wheaton Smith; Notes from Eric Dunstan, Selfridges Archive.

Chapter 12: Making Waves

Alan Jenkins, *The Twenties*; Ronald Blythe, *The Age of Illusion*; Staff notes, Selfridges Archive; Information provided by Ian Stevenson; Information provided by Merton Council; *Kelly's Directory*, 1925; *Bournemouth Daily Echo*, 26 February 1924; *Time Magazine*, 23 September 1929; Selfridges Archive; Reginald Pound, *Selfridge*; Family Archives of Simon Wheaton Smith; A. H. Williams, *No Name at the Door*; Ronald Blythe, *The Age of Illusion*; Reginald Pound, *Selfridge*; Kate 'Ma' Meyrick, *Secrets of the '43'*; Gary Chapman, *The Delectable Dollies*; *The Picturegoer*, April 1921, courtesy of Exeter University; Elsa Maxwell, *I Married the World*; Janet Aitken Kidd, *The Beaverbrook Girl*; Mary Blume, *Côte d'Azur*; 'Inventing the French Riviera: The Early Days of Radio Normandy', www.ibcstudio.co.uk; The Diaries of Ralph Blumenfeld; Gordon Honeycombe, *Selfridges*.

Chapter 13: *Tout Va*

Selfridges Archive; Staff notes, Selfridges Archive; Letter from Elizabeth Arden to Teddy Haslam, April 1926; Reginald Pound, *Selfridge*; Family Archives of Simon Wheaton Smith; (on Suzanne Lenglen) www.tennisfame.org; Mary Blume, *Côte d'Azur*; Harry Yoxall, *A Fashion of Life*; Caroline Seebohm, *The Man Who Was Vogue*; Condé Nast Library; Gordon Honeycombe, *Selfridges*; Richard Buckle (ed.), *Self Portrait with Friends: The Selected Diaries of Cecil Beaton, 1926–1974*; 'The Riviera Season', *Vogue*, 22 February 1928, illustrations by Cecil Beaton; Charles Graves, *None but the Rich*; Axel Madsen, *Coco Chanel*; Gary Chapman, *The Delectable Dollies*; Alan Jenkins, *The Rich Rich*; *Time Magazine*, 11 and 25 April 1927; Maurice Corina, *Fine Silks and Oak Counters*; Selfridges Archives; Ronald Blythe, *The Age of Illusion*; Stella Margetson, *The Long Party*; Andrew Barrow, *Gossip*; Selfridges Archive; Elsa Maxwell, *I Married the World*; Gloria Vanderbilt & Lady Thelma Furness, *Double Exposure*; (on gaming) Author interview with Professor Gerda Reith; (on Maude Loti) *International Herald Tribune*, 1925; Charles Graves, *None but the Rich*; Gary Chapman, *The Delectable Dollies*; Mistinguett, *Mistinguett by Mistinguett*; A. H. Williams, *No Name at the Door*; Reginald Pound, *Selfridge*; Kate 'Ma' Meyrick, *Secrets of the '43'*; 'The Season at Le Touquet', *Vogue*, illustrations by Cecil Beaton; Staff notes, Selfridges Archive; *Time Magazine*, 1 August 1927; Gordon Honeycombe, *Selfridges*.

Chapter 14: Flights of Fancy

Philip Tilden, *True Remembrances*; Letter to Mr Skinner, Selfridges Archive; Reginald Pound, *Selfridge*; A. H. Williams, *No Name at the Door*; *Memoirs of the Rt. Hon. The Earl of Woolton*; Staff notes, Selfridges Archive; Charles Graves, *None but the Rich*; Gary Chapman, *The Delectable Dollies*; Roy Moseley & Victor Saville, *Evergreen*; Ronald Blythe, *The Age of Illusion*; Stella Margetson, *The Long Party*; Alan Jenkins, *The Twenties*; Selfridges Archive; *Time Magazine*, 12 March 1928; Arnold Bennett, *Letters to His Nephew*, p. 268; *Business Magazine*, January 1930; *Time Magazine*, 24 March 1930; Gordon Honeycombe, *Selfridges*; *Time Magazine*, 24 September 1928; Violette de Sibour, *Flying Gypsies*; Author correspondence with Mary Gardener; *The Scotsman*, 5 November 1930; 'Callisthenes', 'An Aeroplane Which We Sold', *The Times*, 29 November 1930; Gary Chapman, *The Delectable*

Dollies; 'Gloria's Memoirs', *News of the World*, 31 May 1932; *Time Magazine*, 21 July 1930; (on Ivar Kreuger) Dale L. Flesher, *National Forum*, Autumn 1997, retrieved from the Internet; Letter from H. G. Selfridge to Ralph Blumenfeld, Archives; *Time Magazine*, 25 August 1930; Reginald Pound, *Arnold Bennett*; Daphne Thynne, *The Duchess of Jermyn Street*; Selfridges Archive; *Milwaukee Journal*, 7 September 1932; *Time Magazine*, 14 March 1932 and 17 July 1933; Selfridges Archive.

Chapter 15: Over and Out

Milwaukee Journal, October 1935; *Daily Tribune Chicago*, 22 October 1935 (cuttings provided by the Wisconsin History Society); *Time Magazine*, 4 November 1935; A. H. Williams, *No Name at the Door*; Election Party Guest Lists, Selfridges Archive; (on Sibyl Thorndike) A. H. Williams, *No Name at the Door*; Condé Nast Library; Underwear advertising, Selfridges Archives; *The Passing Show*, 28 September 1935; Gordon Honeycombe, *Selfridges*; Reginald Pound, *Selfridge*; (on Wallis Simpson) Ronald Blythe, *The Age of Illusion*; (on the sale of the SS *Conqueror*) National Maritime Museum & correspondence, Selfridges Archive; Staff notes, Selfridges Archive; (on Gordon Jr's flight to Spain) *Time Magazine*, 17 August 1936; H. G. Selfridge letters to Ralph Blumenfeld, Archive; (on Father Christmas) *Business & Finance Magazine*, 20 December 1936; (on 'Callisthenes' in USA) *Time Magazine*, 18 October 1937; Coronation Décor Catalogue, Selfridges Archive; H. G. Selfridge letters to Ralph Blumenfeld, Archive; Reginald Pound, *Selfridge*; (on gambling) A. H. Williams, *No Name at the Door*; 'Television Is Here: You Can't Shut Your Eyes to It', Selfridges Archive; (on Holmes) Gordon Honeycombe, *Selfridges*; Staff notes, Selfridges Archive; (on Gordon Jr.) Reginald Pound, *Selfridge*; Staff notes, Selfridges Archive; (on war stocks) Notes from Nellie Elt, Selfridges Archive; Letters from board of directors, Selfridges Archive; (on sailing to America) *Time Magazine*, 13 November 1939; (on post-retirement luncheon) *Store*, February 1940; (on restructuring the business) *Time Magazine*, 3 February 1941; (on life in retirement) Family Archives of Simon Wheaton Smith; Notes from Mr Robertson, Selfridges Archive; Sotheby & Co. catalogue, 11 August 1941 ('sale of valuable French and English Books, Property of a Gentleman', under which he had written H. Gordon Selfridge) provided by Maggs Bros.; Information on 'Sigsaly', Selfridges Archive; Obituary, *The Times*, 9 May 1947; (on funeral) *Bournemouth Echo*, 13 May 1947; Last Will & Testament of H. G. Selfridge.

BIBLIOGRAPHY

All books were published in London unless otherwise stated.

Adburgham, Alison, *Liberty's: A Biography of a Shop* (Allen & Unwin, 1975)
—— *Shops and Shopping, 1880–1914* (Allen & Unwin, 1964)
—— *Victorian Shopping* (David & Charles, Newton Abbot, 1972)
Allan, Tony, *Americans in Paris* (Bison Books, Chicago, 1977)
Alsop, Susan Mary, *Lady Sackville: A Biography* (Weidenfeld & Nicolson, 1978)
Appel, Joseph, *The Business Biography of John Wanamaker* (Macmillan, New York, 1930)
Arlen, Michael, *The Green Hat* (Collins, 1924)
Artley, Alexandra (ed.), *The Golden Age of Shop Design, 1850–1939* (Whitney Library of Design, New York, 1976)
Baker, Anne Pimlott, *The Pilgrims of Great Britain: A Centennial History* (Profile Books, 2002)
Banner, Lois W., *American Beauty* (University of Chicago Press, Chicago, 1983)
Barrow, Andrew, *Gossip* (Pan, 1978)
Beaton, Cecil, *The Glass of Fashion* (Weidenfeld & Nicolson, 1954)
—— *Self-Portrait with Friends: The Selected Diaries of Cecil Beaton, 1926–74*, ed. Richard Buckle (Weidenfeld & Nicolson, 1979)
Benjamin, Thelma, *London Shops and Shopping* (H. Joseph, 1934)
Bennett, Arnold, *Journals* (Stratford Press, 1933), Vols. II and III, 1922–8
——*Letters of Arnold Bennett*, Vol. II, 1889–1915, ed. James Hepburn (Oxford University Press, Oxford, 1968)
——*Letters to his Nephew*, ed. Richard Bennett (William Heinemann, 1935)

Bennett, Richard, *A Picture of the Twenties* (Vista Books, 1971)

Black, Jean F., *Hyde Park Houses: An Informal History, 1856–1910* (University of Chicago Press, Chicago, 1978)

Blume, Mary, *Côte d'Azur: Inventing the French Riviera* (Thames & Hudson, 1992)

Blumenfeld, R. D., *Diaries, 1887–1914* (Heinemann, 1930)

Blythe, Ronald, *The Age of Illusion: England in the Twenties and Thirties* (Hamish Hamilton, 1963)

Bowlby, Rachel, *Just Looking: Consumer Culture in Dreiser, Gissing and Zola* (Methuen, 1985)

Bret, David, *The Mistinguett Legend* (St Martin's Press, New York, 1990)

—— *Tallulah Bankhead: A Scandalous Life* (Robson Books, New York, 1997)

Browne, J. Crawford, *The Early Days of the Department Store* (Scribner's, New York, 1921)

Buel, James William, *The Magic City* (Arno Press, New York, reprinted 1974)

Burg, David F., *Chicago's White City of 1893* (University Press of Kentucky, Lexington, 1976)

Burke, John, *Duet in Diamonds: The Flamboyant Saga of Lillian Russell and Diamond Jim Brady in America's Gilded Age* (Putnam, New York, 1972)

Calder, Robert, *Willie: The Life of Maugham* (Heinemann, 1989)

Callery, Sean, *Harrods: The Story of Society's Favourite Store* (Ebury Press, 1991)

Cantor, Eddie, and Freedman, David, *Ziegfeld: The Great Glorifier* (Alfred H. King, New York, 1934)

Carter, Ernestine, *20th Century Fashion: A Scrapbook, 1910 to Today* (Eyre Methuen, 1975)

Cartland, Barbara, *We Danced All Night* (Hutchinson, 1970)

Castle, Irene, *Castles in the Air* (Da Capo Press, 1958)

Chalmers, W. S., *The Life of Beatty* (Hodder & Stoughton, 1951)

Chapman, Gary, *The Delectable Dollies* (Sutton, 2006)

Chase, Edna Woolman, *Always in Vogue* (Victor Gollancz, 1954)

Collas, Phillippe and Villedary, Eric, *Edith Wharton's French Riviera* (Flammarion, Paris, 2002)

Cooper, Lady Diana, *The Rainbow Comes and Goes* (Riverside Press, Cambridge, 1958)

Corina, Maurice, *Fine Silks and Oak Counters: Debenhams* (Hutchinson, 1978)

Cowles, Virginia, *The Astors* (Alfred A. Knopf, New York, 1979)

Cruikshank, R.J., *Roaring Century* (Hamish Hamilton, 1946)

Curtis, Anthony, *Somerset Maugham* (Weidenfeld & Nicolson, 1977)

Dale, Tim, *Harrods: The Store and the Legend* (Pan, 1981)

Davis, Dorothy, *A History of Shopping* (RKP, London & Toronto, 1966)

Dedmon, Emmett, *Fabulous Chicago* (Random House, New York, 1953)

Ditchett, S. H., *Marshall Field & Company: The Life Story of a Great Concern* (Scribner's, New York, 1922)

Duis, Perry R., *'Challenging Chicago': Coping with Everyday Life, 1837–1920* (University of Illinois Press, Chicago, 1998)

Elias, Stephen, *Alexander T. Stewart: The Forgotten Merchant Prince* (Praeger, Westport, Conn., 1992)

Etherington Smith, Meredith, and Pilcher, Jeremy, *The 'It' Girls* (Harcourt, Brace, Jovanovich, San Diego, 1986)

Ewing, Elizabeth, *The History of 20th Century Fashion* (Batsford, 1974)

——*Dress and Undress: A History of Women's Underwear* (Batsford, 1978)

Ferry, John, *A History of the Department Store* (Macmillan, 1960)

Fisher, Richard, *Syrie Maugham* (Duckworth, 1978)

Fraser, Grace Lovat, *In the Days of My Youth* (Cassell, 1970)

Gallati, Mario, *Mario of the Caprice* (Hutchinson, 1960)

Gardiner, James, *Gaby Deslys* (Sidgwick & Jackson, 1986)

Garland, Madge, *A History of Fashion* (Orbis, 1970)

Goldring, D., *The Nineteen Twenties* (Weidenfeld & Nicolson, 1945)

Graham, J. A. Maxtone, *Eccentric Gamblers* (Mowbrays, 1975)

Graves, Charles, *None but the Rich: The Story of the Greek Syndicate* (Cassell, 1963)

Gray, Stuart, *Edwardian Shops and Stores in London: A Biographical Dictionary* (Duckworth, 1985)

Green, Martin, *Children of the Sun: A Narrative of Decadence in England after 1908* (Basic Books, New York, 1976)

Gregory, Alexis, *The Golden Age of Travel* (Cassell, 1991)

Halliday, Stephen, *Underground to Everywhere* (Sutton, 2001)

Hartnell, Norman, *Silver and Gold* (Evans Bros., 1955)

Hendrickson, Robert, *The Grand Emporiums: The Illustrated History of America's Great Department Stores* (Stein & Day, New York, 1933)

Herndon, Booten, *Bergdorf's on the Plaza* (Knopf, New York, 1956)

Hess, Max, Jr, *Every Dollar Counts: The Story of the American Department Store* (Fairchild, New York, 1952)

Honeycombe, Gordon, *Selfridges: Seventy-Five Years: The Story of the Store* (Park Lane Press, 1984)

Horne, Alistair, *The Terrible Year: the Paris Commune, 1871* (Macmillan, 1971)

Jackson, Kate, *George Newnes and the New Journalism in Britain, 1880–1910: Culture and Profit* (Ashgate, Aldershot, 2001)

Bibliography

Jefferys, James, *Retail Trading in Britain, 1850–1950* (Cambridge University Press, Cambridge, 1954)

Jenkins, Alan, *The Rich Rich: The Story of the Big Spenders* (Weidenfeld & Nicolson, 1977)

——*The Twenties* (Heinemann, 1974)

Jenkins, Simon, *Newspapers: The Power and the Money* (Faber, 1979)

Kahr, Joan, *Edgar Brandt: Master of Art Deco Ironwork* (Harry N. Abrams, New York, 1999), foreword by François Brandt

Kidd, Janet Aitken, *The Beaverbrook Girl* (Collins, 1987)

Kinross, Lord, *The Windsor Years* (Viking, 1967)

Koehn, Nancy F., *Brand New: How Entrepreneurs Earned Consumers' Trust from Wedgwood to Dell* (Harvard Business School Press, Harvard, 2001)

Kurth, Peter, *Isadora: A Sensational Life* (Little, Brown & Co., Boston, 2001)

Leslie, Anita, *Edwardians in Love* (Hutchinson, 1972)

Lieven, Prince Peter, *The Birth of the Ballets Russes* (Allen & Unwin, 1935)

MacColl, Gail, and Wallace, Carol, *To Marry an English Lord* (Workman, New York, 1989)

Mackail, Denis, *The Story of J. M. B., Sir James Barrie* (Peter Davies, 1941)

McKnight, Gerald, *The Scandal of Syrie Maugham* (W. H. Allen, 1980)

MacQueen-Pope, Walter James, *Gaiety: Theatre of Enchantment* (W. H. Allen, 1949)

Madsen, Axel, *Coco Chanel* (Bloomsbury, 1990)

—— *The Marshall Fields* (Wiley, New York, 2002)

Manley, P. S., *Clarence Hatry* (Abacus, 1976)

Marbury, Elisabeth, *My Crystal Ball* (Hurst & Blackett, 1924)

Marcus, Stanley, *Minding the Store* (Little Brown, New York, 1974)

Margetson, Stella, *The Long Party: High Society in the 1920s* (Gordon Cremonsi, 1974)

Marly, Diana de, *Worth: Father of Haute Couture* (Elm Tree Books, 1980)

Masters, Anthony, *Rosa Lewis* (Weidenfeld & Nicolson, 1977)

Maugham, W. Somerset, *Of Human Bondage* (Heinemann, 1934)

——*Plays: One* (Methuen Drama, 1997)

Maxwell, Elsa, *R.S.V.P.* (Heinemann, 1952)

——*I Married the World* (William Heinemann, 1955)

Meyers, Jeffrey, *Somerset Maugham: A Life* (Vintage, 2005)

Meyrick, Kate, *Secrets of the '43'* (Parkgate Press, 1933)

Miller, Michael B., *The Bon Marché: Bourgeois Culture and the Department Store, 1869–1920* (Allen & Unwin, 1981)

Mistinguett, *Mistinguett by Mistinguett* (Elek Books, 1954)

Morris, Lloyd, *Incredible New York: High Life and Low Life* (Bonanza Books, New York, 1950)

Mosely, Roy, *Evergreen: Victor Saville in His Own Words* (Scholarly Book Services Inc, New York, 2002)

Newby, Eric, *Something Wholesale* (Picador, 1985)

Nichols, Beverley, *The Sweet and Twenties* (Weidenfeld & Nicolson, 1958)

Nicolson, Nigel, *Mary Curzon* (Weidenfeld & Nicolson, 1977)

——*Portrait of a Marriage* (Weidenfeld & Nicolson, 1973)

Obolensky, Serge, *One Man and His Time: The Memoirs of Serge Obolensky* (Hutchinson, 1960)

Parker, Morell, *Lillian Russell: The Era of Plush* (Random House, New York, 1940)

Peiss, Kathy, *Hope in a Jar: The Making of America's Beauty Culture* (Henry Holt, New York, 1998)

Porter, Roy, *London: A Social History* (Hamish Hamilton, 1994)

Pound, Reginald, *Arnold Bennett* (Heinemann, 1952)

—— *Selfridge* (Heinemann, 1960)

Priestley, J. B., *The Edwardians* (Heinemann, 1970)

Raphael, Frederic, *Somerset Maugham and His World* (Thames & Hudson, 1978)

Rappaport, Erika Diane, *Shopping for Pleasure: Women in the Making of London's West End* (University of Princeton Press, Princeton, 2000)

Roberts, Cecil, *The Bright Twenties, 1920–1929* (Hodder, 1970)

Ross, Ishbel, *Silhouette in Diamonds: The Life of Mrs Potter Palmer* (Harper & Brothers, New York, 1960)

Roux-Charles, Edmonde, *Chanel* (Collins, 1989)

Schiaparelli, Elsa, *Shocking Life* (Dent, 1954)

Scott, Jonathan, *The Pleasures of Antiquity: British Collectors of Greece and Rome* (Paul Mellon Centre, USA, 2003)

Seebohm, Caroline, *The Man who was Vogue: The Life and Times of Condé Nast* (Weidenfeld & Nicolson, 1982)

Selfridge, H. G., *The Romance of Commerce* (John Lane, 1917)

Short, Edward H. and Rickett, Arthur C., *Ring Up the Curtain* (Herbert Jenkins, 1938)

Sibour, Violette de, *Flying Gypsies* (G. P. Putnam, New York, 1930)

Siry, Joseph, *Carson, Pirie Scott: Louis Sullivan and the Chicago Department Store* (University of Chicago Press, Chicago, 1988)

Souhami, Diana, *Mrs Keppel and Her Daughter* (Flamingo, 1977)

Stansky, Peter, *Sassoon: The Worlds of Philip and Sybil* (Yale University Press, New Haven, 2003)

Tebbel, John, *The Marshall Fields* (Dutton, New York, 1947)

Thomson, George, *Lord Castlerosse* (Weidenfeld & Nicolson, 1973)

Thynne, Daphne, *The Duchess of Jermyn Street* (Eyre & Spottiswoode, 1964)

Tilden, Philip, *True Remembrances: The Memoir of an Architect* (Country Life, 1954)

Twombly, Robert, *Louis Sullivan: His Life and Work* (Viking Penguin, 1986)

Twyman, Robert W., *The History of Marshall Field & Co.* (University of Pennsylvania Press, Philadelphia, 1954)

—— *Potter Palmer: Merchandising Innovator of the West* (University of Pennsylvania Press, Philadelphia, 1951)

Vanderbilt, Gloria, and Furness, Thelma, *Double Exposure* (Hamilton, 1961)

Veblen, Thorstein, *The Theory of the Leisure Class* (Macmillan, 1899)

Vickers, Hugo, *Cecil Beaton* (Phoenix Press, 1985)

Vinikas, Vincent, *Soft Soap, Hard Sell: American Hygiene in an Age of Advertisement* (Iowa State University Press, Ames, 1992)

Waywell, Geoffrey B., *The Lever and Hope Sculptures* (Gebr. Mann Verlag, Berlin, 1986)

Wendt, Lloyd, and Kogan, Herman, *Give the Lady What She Wants: The Story of Marshall Field* (Rand McNally, Chicago, 1952)

Westminster, Loelia, *Grace and Favour* (Reynal, New York, 1961)

White, Palmer, *Poiret* (Studio Vista, 1973)

Williams, Alfred H., *No Name at the Door: A Memoir of Gordon Selfridge* (W. H. Allen, 1956)

Wilson, A. N., *The Victorians* (Hutchinson, 2001)

Wilson, Edmund, *The Twenties* (Macmillan, 1975)

Wilson, Sandy, *The Roaring Twenties* (Eyre Methuen, 1976)

Winkler, John K., *Five & Ten: The Fabulous Life of F. W. Woolworth* (Robert McBridge, New York, 1941)

Woodhead, Lindy, *War Paint: Helena Rubinstein and Elizabeth Arden, Their Lives, Their Times, Their Rivalry* (Virago, 2003)

Woolton, Frederick James, *The Memoirs of the Rt Hon the Earl of Woolton* (Cassell, 1959)

Yoxall, Harry, *A Fashion of Life* (Taplinger, New York, 1967)

Zola, Emile, *The Ladies' Paradise (Au Bonheur des Dames)* (1883)

ACKNOWLEDGEMENTS

Harry Gordon Selfridge left the store in 1939, and died aged 91 in 1947, so the chance of my meeting anyone who knew him in his prime, or worked with him from the early days, was never feasible. Biographers, however, depend on luck as well as their own judgement, and I was lucky with the treasures I found in the magnificent Selfridges archives (at the time when this book was originally written, maintained by the History of Advertising Trust, but now returned to a permanent home in the store itself).

The archive collection contains not just the old press cuttings books – with virtually every clipping personally noted by HGS himself – but also lists and notebooks, his private ledger, letters, photographs, personal ephemera and store catalogues, price lists, promotional material and advertisements. Over the years, friends, family and retirees have donated all manner of additions with the result that it is one of the finest examples of British retailing history in existence today.

In the early 1900s HGS invested in a gold mine, at one point being told by the engineers that they had struck a seam. Sadly, it was worthless, but I struck my own seam of pure gold when Sue Filmer (of HAT) passed me a folder full of notes gathered by the store management in 1951 when they had the idea of publishing an official biography of Harry Gordon Selfridge. At that time, Selfridges was owned by Lewis's of Liverpool, who agreed to finance the project. The book went through a series of three prospective authors and at least two publishers and agents before the finished work, *Selfridge* by Reginald Pound, was finally published in 1960. The project was co-ordinated by the redoubtable Miss Mepham, who had been the gatekeeper to HGS's inner sanctum. She was the one woman still alive who had intimate knowledge of what his son later described as 'the several sides of my father'. She stayed at the store until 1957 and thanks to her diligence virtually all the senior retirees still alive between 1951 and 1957 were interviewed in depth to gather stories about HGS. Very few of them lived to see the finished book, but their contribution lives on.

Charles Clore's company, Sears Holdings Ltd, acquired Selfridges in 1965. It is precisely because of take-overs and mergers that archives are often lost, deliberately destroyed or simply thrown away. Not so under Charles Clore and his deputy chairman Leonard Sainer, who put in place a budget, an archive room and a devoted archivist, Victor Yates, who presided over the memorabilia with efficient enthusiasm. Without this initiative this book could not have been written. To those past guardians of the archives, amongst them Mr Victor Yates who was at Selfridges, Barry Cox, Margaret Rose, Chloe Veale, Sue Filmer and David Thomas (the latter all at HAT), go my grateful thanks.

In 1956, A. H. Williams, who had worked for Harry Gordon Selfridge for twenty-eight years, wrote an affectionate book called *No Name at the Door*. Sears also commissioned the broadcaster and author Gordon Honeycombe to write *Selfridges*, celebrating seventy-five years of the store in 1984. Both books have been invaluable and informative sources.

No documents, however detailed, can substitute for seeing things for oneself. For that reason I would like to thank Sindee Hastings at Highcliffe Castle in Hampshire, which following shocking decline is now owned by Christchurch Borough Council and is currently undergoing extensive, sympathetic restoration. Sindee and I donned hard hats to tour the cellars and old kitchens in 2005, enabling me to understand castle life at the time the Selfridge family lived there. For those interested in Highcliffe's fascinating history, I urge you to visit www.highcliffecastle. co.uk which gives excellent notes and a list of books published about the castle. I owe thanks to Sindee for introducing me to the local historian Ian Stevenson. He has worked tirelessly to provide me with facts about the castle and Christchurch during the early 1920s. He has also sent copies of press cuttings and verified many details. Thanks also to the Reverend Garry Taylor of the charming St Mark's Church at Highcliffe, Beverley Morris of the Hampshire Records Office and S. C. Munsey at the Hampshire Local Studies Collection.

Although Selfridge's tenure is recognized by a blue plaque, Lansdowne House today bears little resemblance to how it was when he lived there. Spliced and sliced by various developers over the decades, it is now a private members club, with much of the building completely changed. There is however a hint of the glorious grandeur of Harry's era, with a drawing room on the ground floor where guests take afternoon tea hardly changed from the days when Lois Selfridge and her son would have done the same thing. The Yarborough Mansion in Arlington Street has also long since vanished. But you begin to understand something of the lifestyle of Selfridge and his neighbours the Duke and Duchess of Rutland by walking past the Ritz Hotel and the hotel's recently acquired (and magnificently restored) adjacent property Wimborne House, and on down the street towards the Caprice restaurant, where I enjoyed several lively lunches with contributors to this book. Selfridge was a devotee of both the Caprice and the Ivy, and Mario Gallati's memoirs proved an invaluable source.

In Chicago, I was helped immeasurably by Trish Morse, Lorna Donley and Teresa Yoder at the Harold Washington Library Center and Rob Medina of the Chicago History Museum.

Elsewhere in America I was assisted by: Laura Linard of the Baker Library at Harvard; Mandy Shear, Faculty and Research at Harvard Business School; Geraldine Strey of the Wisconsin Historical Society; John Dorner of the Illinois Lodge of Research Library; Mark Tabbert of the George Washington Masonic National Memorial; Rachel Hertz at the Harry Ransom Humanities Research Center, University of Texas, Austin; Stephen Showers and Marybeth Roy of Otis; Darcie M. Posz of the Daughters of the American Revolution; Mattie Taormina and Polly Armstrong at Stanford University Library; and Lauren Robinson-Brown at Princeton University. The author Pauline Metcalfe, who was writing her own biography of Syrie Maugham at the time that I was writing about Syrie's one-time lover H. G. Selfridge, sent cheering emails offering information, as did her editor Mitch Owens. Patricia Erigero, a specialist on the history of race-horses, advised on the Selfridge stable of steeplechasers, and Arnie Reisman and Ann Carol Grossman gave support, advice on books to read and suggestions on people to talk to. I am particularly grateful to Professor Nancy F. Koehn of Harvard Business School who not only made time to be interviewed but also couriered copies of her HBS paper on Marshall Field to help me meet a deadline.

Gary Chapman, author of *The Delectable Dollies*, has been both enthusiastic and helpful in giving freely of information, as have the authors Anne Sebba in respect of her book on Jennie Jerome and James Gardiner who wrote devotedly about Gaby Deslys.

In my quest for links between Harry Gordon Selfridge and his friend Arnold Bennett, I would like to thank Helen Burton at Keele University and most particularly John Shapcott of the Arnold Bennett Society who was kindness itself in supplying all manner of detail. Janice Francoise at Southwark Library provided information about Kingswood House; and Sarah Gould at Merton Libraries and Heritage Services went to endless trouble to check details about the Wiasemskys' tenure at Wimbledon Park House. The noted genealogist Timothy Boettger provided his expertise on Russian titles, and Ian Jenkins, Curator of Greek and Roman Antiquities at the British Museum, educated me on both the Hope Sculpture Collections and the splendid collections once kept at Lansdowne House. Denise Summerton at the University of Nottingham provided information on the Hope Sale. Dr Gerda Reith of Glasgow University took time to explain the intricacies of the gambler's mentality. From Australia, Mary Garden provided information about Mr Garden's epic flight to Australia in the plane he bought at Selfridge's. At Condé Nast in London I would like to thank Nicolas Coleridge, Harriet Wilson and her team, and Brett Croft, who runs the Condé Nast Library, for undertaking so much copying and putting up with my erratic schedule. I must also thank Annie Pinder of the House of Lords Record Office, Jane Rosen of the Imperial War Museum, the Bill Douglas Centre for the History of the Cinema and Popular Culture at the University of Exeter and the staff at the London Library. Since the hardback edition was published, several readers have taken the time to write with their own memories and additional information – including noting in some instances discrepancies and errors on my part – and in particular I would like to thank Clive Vaisey, Daphne Hall, William Cavendish, Malcolm Neal and Lucy Baruch.

A special thank you to Suzy Menkes, Rodney Fitch, Peter Wallis, Vittorio Radice and Scott Malkin, all of whom took time to answer questions about retailing today in the context of the department store and H. G. Selfridge.

I am most grateful to HRH The Prince of Wales for permission to quote from his 1990 speech 'Accent on Architecture', given at the American Institute of Architects gala dinner, and to Amanda Foster, Press Officer to the Prince of Wales and the Duchess of Cornwall.

Harry Gordon Selfridge's great-grandson Simon Wheaton Smith was generous with his time, memories of his mother and grandparents, and his precious family archives. I would also like to thank Gordon Selfridge Jr's daughter, Jennifer MacLeod.

Friends and contacts who have sent information, given advice and encouragement, and even on occasion done my shopping during the many months I was glued to my computer include: Alison Cathie, Oliver Musker, Simon Rendall, Giles Chapman, David Burgess-Wise, Alisdair Sutherland, Samantha Conti, Robert Harding of Maggs Bros, Melissa Wyndham, Charlotte Milln, Tim Leon-Dufour, Margaret Muldoon, John Rendall and Susan Farmer.

To my husband, who has put up with a lot over the past three years, special thanks for his discerning eye in selecting photographs. He read chapters from the very beginning, as did my son Max. Both laughed in the right places and gave wise advice. Ollie (who himself once worked at Selfridges) preferred to wait for the finished book but has cheered me at every turn. My sister Nikki, her daughter Julie and her grandson Jake, who was born while I was writing this book, have all played their part in keeping the home fires burning.

This book wouldn't have happened without the encouragement of Eugenie

Furniss and Lucinda Prain (who were, at the time when the book was originally written, both with William Morris). Lucinda is now at Casarotto Ramsay,
where she managed the deal with ITV to bring the book to television. My literary
agent, Eugenie Furniss, has also since struck out on her own, and is now running
FurnissLawton, from where she is encouraging the development of this book into
territories far and wide. I owe them both huge thanks for their support and enthusiasm. Thanks also to Claudia Webb at WME, who is keenly following the progress
of the title to what we all hope will be its wider audience. At my publishers, Profile
Books, Andrew Franklin deserves a special mention for resolving the book's title
and keeping a watchful eye over the entire project. At Profile, my editor was Gail
Pirkis, whose wisdom, patience and graceful original editing kept me on track.
Thanks also to Penny Daniel and Nicola Taplin at Profile, who managed the book
through to its final stages, and to the most knowledgeable, eagle-eyed indexer any
biographer could ask for: Douglas Matthews. My grateful thanks also to Anna-
Marie Fitzgerald for spearheading the publicity with such enthusiasm and finally
to my current editor, Rebecca Gray, for helping to update this special edition and
prepare it for re-publication.

Since the book was first published, readers have sent me notes about small
errors that slipped in. Often I received letters offering additional, fascinating information and support. To all of you, I am grateful. No author, however hard we try,
can hope to get all the technical detail correct in a story as sweeping as the development of British retail history.

Thanks to your helpful advice, we have made several corrections to names,
places and dates. Any errors remaining are the author's own.

Finally I must turn to Selfridges, where the Creative Director, Alannah Weston,
must have been astonished to get a letter from out of the blue, telling her that I was
writing a book about the founder and that I hoped they would 'help me out with
some information'. She took it well. Nothing has been too much trouble for the staff
at the store who have been kindness itself and have allowed me to explore every
nook and cranny of the place, even identifying where Harry Selfridge's 'private
lift' – for his exclusive use – was positioned. They have answered innumerable
questions, their lawyers have given copyright approval for archive materials and
photographs to be used and the press office has checked details for me. To Mr
and Mrs Galen Weston, Alannah Weston, Paul Kelly, Anne Pitcher, Michael Keep,
Bruno Barba, Sue Minns and Caroline Parker go my heartfelt thanks. I hope you
enjoy reading this new edition of the book as much as you will undoubtedly enjoy
watching the television drama series adapted from it.

London, 2012

*

The author and publishers wish to thank the following for permission to reproduce images: Plates 1, 3, 19, family archives of Simon Wheaton-Smith; 2, 4, 5, 6, 7, 8, 9, 10, 11, 12, 14, 16, 17, 20, 21, 22, 23, 24, 27, 28, the Selfridges Archive; 25, Otis Elevators; 13, *Chicago Daily News* Negatives Collection, Chicago History Museum; 15, private collection of James Gardiner; 18, private collection of Ian Stevenson; 26, Getty Images.

INDEX